# DEFEATED DEMONS
## FREEDOM FROM CONSCIOUSNESS PARASITES IN PSYCHOPATHIC SOCIETY

## THOMAS SHERIDAN

*Dedicated to the Survivors of Psychopathic Abuse:*

*An acorn has to rise above the dirt
to become a mighty oak.
Always know this.*

# DEFEATED DEMONS
## FREEDOM FROM CONSCIOUSNESS PARASITES
## IN PSYCHOPATHIC SOCIETY

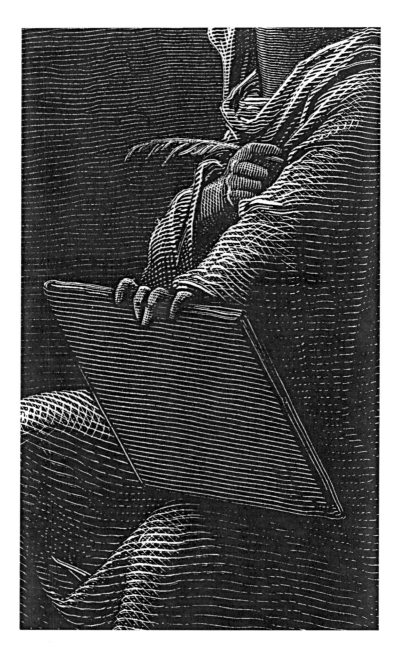

# EVERYTHING I KNOW ABOUT LIFE, LOVE & FREEDOM I LEARNED FROM PSYCHOPATHS

*If you dance with the devil then you haven't got a clue*
*for you think you'll change the devil but the devil changes you.*

The analytical psychologist Carl Jung had two primary terms he preferred to express the archetypes of the unconscious mind: *anima* and *animus*. According to him, the *anima* finds expression as a feminine inner personality in the unconscious of the human male. In the female unconscious it is expressed as the male *animus*.

Jung co-opted the term *anima* for his own uses, but there exists an older definition of the word. In Latin, *anima* describes the animating principle: *the soul*. In the classical sense, the opposite of *anima* is *persona*, and it is the custom-designed, meticulously crafted and professionally presented *persona* that a psychopath depends upon as a substitute for a soul and to pass as human amongst humanity.

You may be interested to hear that the Romans used the word *persona* to describe a mask used in a play; this is what we fell in love with: a monster in a mask.

Account after account bears witness to the emotional intensity that is the hallmark of the beginning stages of a relationship with a psychopath. Without exception, the target is convinced they have at last found their soulmate. They are virtually picked up and carried along on a tsunami of flattery and attention, utterly suffused with the joy of discovering the one human on the planet hungry to know absolutely everything about them. The most seductive aspect of these head-spinning early days is how perfectly matched you are in dreams, desires, personal tastes, values and philosophies; it's as though you were *designed* for one another…

Regrettably, you have been—just not by Cupid.

The psychopath will leave effusive and flattering comments on your social network page after you friend them. They will text you numerous times a day and call you on the phone just to hear your voice before they sleep. They continually quiz you about your sexual fantasies, then enthusiastically promise to fulfil them all on the day you physically meet. Steadily and by degrees, they build a comprehensive profile of you in order to have a clear blueprint for constructing a flawless, mirror-perfect soulmate *persona*—and then they claim you. They claim your heart, your energy, your creativity, happiness, peace, sanity, strength and—in some cases—all or most of your worldly goods. Then, they begin to destroy you. Eternally hungry, eternally empty, eternally stalking the one thing that makes you human and the one thing they will always lack, they want to consume your *anima* like a double bacon cheeseburger with a large order of fries, then discard what is left of you like an empty fast food container.

Regarding governments, corporations and religions, we inhabit a psychopathic world dominated by this unholy trinity. National governments want our obedience, loyalty and industry. Corporations want our adherence, brand loyalty and money. Religions want our obedience, loyalty, unpaid industry, money and—*hey!*— why not throw in your eternal soul while you're at it? Above all, governments, religions and corporations want us to be good, subservient little workers, worshipers and consumers. If you want to do drugs you must do government-approved and corporation-produced drugs. If you want to have sex, you must have it according to government-registered and religion-approved marriage contracts, and then spend a lot of money on cake, clothes, champagne, flowers, a flawless diamond or two, a venue and a band. Oh, and a honeymoon. And a photographer. Maybe a limo. If you want to kill someone, you can always join the army. If you want to gamble, you can work on Wall Street and if you want to rape, pillage and cause maximum destruction in minimum time, you can work for Monsanto, the Military/Industrial Complex, Big Pharma, politics or as a corporate lawyer for any of the above.

The unholy trinity wants to know absolutely everything about you, then they want to consume you, then they want to discard you before you become a drain on the system, but not before you've offered up a generation of your offspring for their lunch. And if you deviate from the agenda, if you truly want to be free, they will put a roof over your head at any number of fine new penal institutions. For example, the United States Corporation has locked up more people than any other nation on earth—a half million more than China, which has a population five times greater than the US. Looking at it another way, the US has 25% of the world's prison population, but only 5% of the world's people. Why is this happening? Are Americans really that naughty? Not particularly, *it's just business.* In fact, it's the perfect partnership of government and corporate interests merged into a single, elegant and completely unified psychopathic agenda.

Imagine being an employer and not having to worry about your workforce ever going on strike. Imagine never having to pay unemployment insurance, or vacation time, or worker's compensation. Imagine your employees are on full-time, twenty-four hours a day if you say so. They never show up late. They are never absent from work due to an ill child or a death in the family. Imagine that if they ever complain about earning twenty-five cents an hour you can throw them into solitary confinement.

This is not a fantasy; this is current events, and if you have enough money and enough clout in the halls of government, you too can build your own prison and utilise all the money-making benefits of a cheap and relatively trouble-free workforce.

The private prison industry is the fastest growing business sector in America. Its investors are on Wall Street and it has its own trade exhibitions, conventions, websites, and online catalogues.

It also has direct-advertising campaigns, architecture companies, construction companies, plumbing supply companies, food supply companies, armed security, and containment cells in a nice selection of fashionable colours.

One of the things that has continued to stump the average citizen is that murderers and rapists are eligible for parole and manage to hit the streets in just a fraction of the time served by nonviolent offenders. It all begins to make sense, though, when you approach the issue from the point of view of a psychopath—oops, *employer*... Who would you rather have on your factory assembly line: some guy who ripped out someone's grandmother's eyeballs and then set her cat on fire? Or gentle Joe the marijuana grower?

It's simple once you approach it from a psychopathic standpoint; the private contracting of prisoners for work fosters incentives to lock more and more people up; in other words, *more laws.* What's more, stockholders who make money off prisoners' work continually lobby for longer sentences—and more laws—in order to expand and extend their workforce.

What exactly does this workforce produce? 93% of all domestic paint sold to Americans is manufactured by American prison labour, as well as 36% of home appliances, 21% of all office furniture and—this may be my favourite—100% of all military helmets, ammunition belts and bullet-proof vests. And yet... the United States *prohibits the importation of any goods made through forced labour in foreign countries.*

So, there you have it; ninety-seven percent of federal inmates in the United States have been convicted of nonviolent crimes and federal prison is where they are going to stay, because once you have a cheap, reliable, relatively non-aggressive employee you may as well hang on to him *for the rest of his life.*

What is happening in psychopathic society serves to illustrate precisely how much your personal psychopath will ever value you; namely, for as long as you are still of some use to the psychopath and as long as you make no claim on them in return.

Between the psychopath whose only interest is the chase, capture, claiming and consumption of your *anima* and the larger agenda of psychopathic governments, corporations and religions to monitor, control and inform every decision you ever make in life, you must be feeling pretty surrounded by now. I wouldn't blame you if you felt overwhelmed with despair. But remember, psychopaths dine on your despair just as readily as they gobble up your initial romantic exhilaration—it's all the same to them. Your *anima* is sustenance and they don't care what emotion flavours the meal. They will stick a straw straight into your energy and suck it all down right before they toss what's left of you aside like an empty juice box.

So what can we do to fight the psychopath? Actually, nothing. You can't fight a psychopath and win. Fighting, resisting, hating, debating and seeking revenge—all are forms of energy directed at them. A couple of slices of bread, a little mustard and they can make a meal off that energy and indulge in a satisfying belch afterwards.

So what are we to do? We must:

*learn to look within for everything we need. If there is anything we perceive as missing in ourselves, the last place we should ever look for it is within in another person.*

That sounds pretty extreme, I know. Maybe even cynical. Maybe even bleak. If so, allow me to take you there gradually. You may still not agree with me by the end, but all I can do is my best to point the way.

In general, humans are convinced they must live within a clearly defined and strongly maintained hierarchy like government, tribal law, gang affiliation, family rules or religious traditions. Other groups are continually sowing the seeds of rebellion in favour of their style of hierarchy and sometimes they prevail, and so on, and so on, all throughout human history. Nothing ever really changes; there is always a hierarchy and there are always people in various states of satisfaction or dissatisfaction with it. This is the way that societies have always been organised, and the entities we know as psychopaths have developed and adapted to exploit this need for their own agenda.

I was in a discussion the other day about the definition of a 'police state.' What we came up with was in good times the police state is *covert* and in bad times the police state is *overt* but whether in good times or bad, it's still just *business as usual* on the part of government, corporations and religions.

In good times, people tend to believe that a government or corporation or religion actually cares about them. This is the sort of blindness we've all experienced in the relationship with our own personal psychopath and the sort of blindness that makes it difficult for the patriotic, the religious and the romantic to admit falling victim to. It's easier to get away from a psychopathic individual—eventually—than it is to escape from a hierarchy whose policies inform nearly every aspect of our waking lives, though both impact us to a devastating degree for the same reason: the twin terrors we always hold of *standing alone* and of *what other people must be thinking about me.*

Almost without exception, when psychopaths admit why they are drawn to a specific target the number one reason they cite is a perceived unfulfilled emotional need to which they respond by researching and designing a specific *persona* to suit that target's desires.

Where hierarchies like government and religion are concerned we are brainwashed to accept and even revel in the position of 'child' or 'dependent.' The hand of government/religion/parental authority gives and the hand takes away. The government looks out for our corporeal security, and religion our spiritual security, and the majority of humanity has a comfortable working relationship with those concepts. The individual psychopath also brainwashes us into total dependence, just before they abandon us forever.

Whether an individual or an organisation, the only way a psychopath can be assured they actually exist is *by observing how others react to the things they do.* Humans are the mirrors they look into to check their hair and makeup; the thrill of one mirror wears off, they move on to the next. The 1986 film *Manhunter* illustrates this beautifully when the serial killer lines up the bodies of his victims and covers their eyes with bits of broken mirror.

Psychopaths are empty inside. They are the ultimate actors, and the void inside the shells of their bodies must be filled with a script and fed by the response of others. Once the applause and adulation from their target no longer does it for them, they seek the thrill of causing pain. When that pales, they move on.

Psychopaths love whipping the emotions of others into a frenzy because it not only reassures them they exist, but also that they are *powerful*—that they have a perceptible effect upon the world. Governments could control the population much more efficiently than they do if the psychopaths in charge were not hooked on observing and gloating over and deriving nourishment from the effects of their control over others. Hence the media circus, shock jocks, glorification of combative sports, celebrity culture and schizophrenic standards in entertainment whereby depictions of gruesome murders are allowed and an image of a mother lovingly nursing a newborn baby is disallowed lest a nipple stray into view. We are continually bombarded with these images and they make us feel emotions. Human life force, human energy and human emotion is meat and drink and life's blood to psychopaths, particularly when they know they are the catalyst.

The biggest fear a human can ever have is the realisation that they are alone. We all die alone. We all suffer pain alone. No one can do either for us. Neither can anyone know exactly what we see with our eyes or hear with our ears or dream when we sleep, no matter how we strive to communicate those things through poetry, painting or music. No one knows exactly what you feel, and how you feel it, but you. Because you have been trained to think that seeing the beauty of your soul is vanity and that you need someone else in your life who can mirror that beauty for you is what the psychopath sniffs out and seeks to exploit. *"Here I am,"* they say, *"I understand you. I know you. We are connected. You never have to be alone again. I love you. I need you. We are soulmates."*

This search for a soulmate translates into the desire to alleviate the feeling of being utterly alone in the experience of your life. That the 'soulmate' you thought you had found made a nightmarish transformation into a psychopath has left you feeling even more alone than before the relationship, but herein lies a gift: perhaps meeting, falling for and being discarded by a psychopath is the final test for souls who have passed through every other fire and stand on the verge of spiritual maturity.

The primal fear of being alone is the only thing standing between you and experiencing the sovereignty of your own soul. You can come out the other side of this test and *enjoy* relationships based upon mutual respect and adventure and love rather than the *I need you I crave you I can't live without you* assault pushed by psychopathic major media in the form of romantic novels, films and love songs. Most of all, you will realise the concept of *need* is never a facet of a healthy relationship beyond the age of puberty.

Your *anima* is the most precious thing that has ever existed in the history of the universe; psychopaths certainly crave souls and will stop at nothing to claim them. The most important step you can ever take is to begin to realise the worth, the depth, the breadth and the beauty of your soul without needing anyone else on earth to mirror its worth for you.

When you finally overcome the fear of being alone there will be no way a psychopath can hurt you ever again. You won't even register as a blip on their radar.

This is where the pain can end. This is when the fun can begin.

Welcome to your wonderful life.

*Holly Ollivander*
*St David's Day 2012*

# The Psychopath's Prayer

Hallowed be my name. Protect me this day from detection and background checks. May my rat-like smirk be hidden and my pupils not dilate, allowing me to woo my targets with pity plays, sob stories about cancer and tales of childhood abuse. Grant me wild mood swings which happen in an instant. Help me find new social issues I can align with in order to look good. As I saunter through the Valley of the Shadow of Fabrication carrying unread Carl Sagan books to show how intellectual I am, may search engines be my guide. May the rod and staff of righteous indignation prove my superiority over all.

I shall believe what I think others would like me to believe until I discard all those losers the instant they require something from me in return. I shall get married to avoid paying rent, have children just to see what it is like, then act like a caring parent until I lose interest in them when people give them attention that should be mine. I will invent beautiful admirers to flirt with me on social networks and have sex with something, anything, everything, to show others how desirable I am. Leadeth me not unto successful past targets who act like I don't exist, for no one deserves to be happy without me. Deliver me from red flags, for mine is the kingdom of power over the gullible, forever.

Amen.

When the psychopath swears that they cannot live without you they are being somewhat genuine in terms of their needs and desires of the moment. You are their soulmate—for now. Psychopaths do not value your personality or your humanity and the only thing they find special or unique about you is the specifics of the payoff to be gained by manipulating you. You may be entertainment or a place to stay or their benefactor when you leave all your worldly goods to them in your will, all these are in addition to their ultimate thrill:

**picking the lock on your insecurities
in order to exploit them.**

"Everything about me is tailor-made to perpetuate a certain persona that will allow me to get through life with as little aggravation and as much admiration as possible."

*- Dispatches from Psychopaths*

# An Equilibrium
# of Singular Nothingness

It was the weekend just prior to the Fourth of July, 2011. I was sending out emails to my various American friends wishing them a happy celebration of their national holiday. When I checked my email in-box, I noticed a message bearing the title 'I AM A PSYCHOPATH WE SHOULD TALK.' As I get at least one of these kinds of emails every couple of weeks, I was not taken aback by the candid introduction and opened it, half expecting it to be another joke by a teenager having a laugh or some deluded individual who owns the DVD version of *American Psycho* and thinks he is Patrick Bateman. As soon as I began reading the email I realised there was something different about this one. By the syntax and sense of grandeur within the opening paragraph, all generously lavished with the obligatory word salad to impress the reader, I could tell this was indeed the genuine article.

A genuine psychopath in the UK was contacting me to say he had read my book and watched my videos and wanted to congratulate me on my insight. He then proceeded to give me a front row seat in the theatre of his own inner world, and his toxic true self fairly leapt off the stage. I was given a glimpse behind the façade which psychopaths present to the rest of society and was once more reassured beyond any doubt that they are a life form which mimic the human aspect but are instead something very, very alien, indeed.

He said his name was Tony and he was thirty-eight. After a whirlwind romance in which he had converted to a CofE Protestant, he had recently married a woman who came from a 'well-connected' Church of England family. Before meeting his current wife he was a passionately outspoken atheist. He explained how he was sending this email from someone else's apartment while he was waiting for one of his other enablers to 'come home from work and fuck him.' Tony had been married less than a week and had six other women and two men on the side. His unfortunate wife, meanwhile, was basking in post-nuptial bliss, having absolutely no idea what she had just married or the horror that would inevitably befall her at some point in the future. A chat message alert then came up on the screen with his email address and I began talking to him on a one-to-one basis.

I had previously discovered that the most accurate and insightful way to interview a psychopath is to ask them impromptu questions on the fly, disallowing them their usual technique of using prepared and well-rehearsed responses. Not making eye contact with them is crucial as well since they are unable to read (or more importantly, quarry emotional energy from) the interviewer's expressions and responses. Instant Messaging is an ideal media in which to confront these predators and gain a more telling window into their true nature.

After the nauseating formalities of introduction, he boasted about having sex with another man the morning before his wedding. He told his heartbroken gay lover (whom he met at a Humanist meeting in London in 2008) that he was his true love but that he 'had to get married' for his family's sake. Tony then explained how 'fucking stupid' most people are and will believe anything you tell them as long as you liberally apply the magic words, 'I Love You'. He then said, "The best ones are the ones who didn't get any love as kids; parents were a bit cold and so on. People from these families will do anything you want if you tell them you love them. They are like addicts or something. They never had, you know, parental affection and love as kids. It's a bit weird, alright, but you can spot these types a mile away."

When I asked him what was going through his mind when he

was putting the wedding ring on his new wife's finger inside a large cathedral in the south of England, and in front of several hundred wedding guests, he replied, "Nothing at the service, but I did feel something when I was with that whore during the honeymoon in Cuba; I felt like a king or something. Knowing that there is nothing in this life which holds me back. It is the best feeling in the world."

In 2008, I began writing what would eventually become the book *Puzzling People: the Labyrinth of the Psychopath*. This was an earnest attempt to try and alert other members of the human family that we were under attack from something hidden in plain sight within our own species, an entity very different from us indeed, a predatory parasite that was not just another product of poor families, unfortunate social conditions, structural brain damage or some other 'diagnosis' from the increasingly contradictory and bizarre world of psychiatry but a thing apart from humanity.

At the same time, I wanted to help people understand that this mutation exists for a reason. Simply put, they are the reason and means for humanity to evolve to the next stage of existence; hence why I stress that no hate campaign or violent oppression of the non-murderous psychopath should be undertaken. The only weapons of defense we require are knowledge of the predator and NO CONTACT EVER AGAIN. Nature will take care of the rest.

I laid out my arguments as best I could in straightforward language—that the psychopath is a mutation akin to a human-shaped spiritual tapeworm, which is wreaking havoc among the lives of billions of people on this planet and a disease more deadly than any pandemic, a predator more dangerous than the most insatiable carnivore, and a cultivator of human misery more wrathful and sadistic than any monotheistic god—imaginary or otherwise.

*Puzzling People* was my own attempt to shine a light into the abyss and to alert people not to venture too near the edge, yet even up until the publication of the book the term 'psychopath' conjured up images of frenzied serial killers and Hollywood cartoon-like slashers. In the early days of our working together my publisher queried why I would not use 'narcissist' or 'sociopath' since these terms were used far more freely than 'psychopath' to describe the pathology. I made my case that the term 'psychopath' needed to be reclaimed from the sensational (and often mythological) imagery it conjures up in the minds of the majority and be brought back into the daily terminology of people in their everyday lives. Besides, psychopaths hate the term 'psychopath.'

Five years ago, information of the socialised psychopath was still relatively obscure and somewhat difficult to source. Even though there was a wealth of knowledge out there, the nitty-gritty of the well-validated and tested scientific research describing the pathology was mainly filed away in the world of academia. Among the general population, it was still an obscure and almost surreal term; certainly not an aspect that most would have considered to have ever impacted upon their lives. Yet the tragedy existed that roughly four percent of the population in the West, to some degree, were making life unbearable for the other ninety-six percent.

As this book is being readied for publication in the first weeks of 2012, something truly seismic within the collective human consciousness is occurring. Enter the term 'psychopath' into Google Trends and see the explosion of interest in the subject during the last few years alone. The sudden upswing in the graph started around 2008 and speaks volumes as to just how much our society is waking up.

Despite a marketing budget of zero, I was determined to do anything I could think of to promote the book since I was driven to get the message out to the world. I sent the first press release out on March 3, 2011; within six months, I was given a full hour on prime-time television, broadcast live all over Europe. The book had reached number one in its category on Amazon UK. I had contributed articles to numerous publications and websites, and spoken on scores of radio interviews. *Puzzling People* is currently among the most popular titles in the genre globally, and I found myself travelling overseas to do speaking engagements and workshops. My modest manifesto had tapped into something—a resonance, an unspoken meme that many people were finally ready to hear. And gratifyingly, they wanted to hear more.

## SPEAKING TO YOURSELF
## IS THE FIRST SIGN OF SANITY

There are two kinds of truth. There is what we term scientific or empirical truth, validated by testing and repeating tests according to strict laboratory conditions yielding a result which confirms or disproves a hypothesis and which in turn becomes accepted fact. There is also another kind of truth, based upon our own intuitive understanding; a noetic experience which flowers within our being aside and apart from any evidence charted by Newtonian formulae.

When we experience this *Participation Mystique*, we require no clinical or peer review studies to know that what we have just learned is beyond question because it resonates in a visceral way. Like finding the first two matching jigsaw puzzle pieces, we know we are on our way to completing the entire picture even if we cannot yet prove the image exists empirically . This is what is happening today when people hear the message regarding socialised psychopaths and how they operate in our personal lives, including how they even control the world in the political and corporate realms.

The average person reads through the list of psychopathic traits and machinations and begins to open long sealed-off vaults and dark chambers within the depths of their own consciousness. Suppressed memories of abuse, neglect, exploitation, degradation and emotional and sexual torture come flooding out from behind the cobwebbed curtains of their personal psychological history. Suddenly, a major mystery in their lives finally begins to make sense; they have the first two or three pieces of the puzzle. The psychopaths who were previously excused or explained away are revealed as the liars, manipulators, users and abusers that they are, the ravagers of hopes, dreams and emotions in the guise of workplace bullies, con-artists, ex-partners, parents and authority figures.

Psychopaths were confident that their true nature as a predatory mutation would never be uncovered. They depended upon the shame and embarrassment their targets felt to keep them hidden, but knowledge is spreading; humans are beginning to talk, to compare notes, to get angry. Internet forums serve as a liberating wildfire, clearing the tangled undergrowth and lighting the way to ultimate freedom while at the same time cutting off the psychopaths' feeding ground, including the ones at the top of the corporate and governmental food chains. The eye at the top of the pyramid is revealed to be the cold, dead stare of *homo psychopathicus*, and this is becoming clearer to more and more humans with each passing day.

The time has now come. The cat is out of the psychopath's drowning bag and it is never going back in. However, staying stuck at feelings of hatred or vengefulness towards the psychopath will only serve to blunt the most powerful weapons humans possess against the adversary:

KNOWLEDGE, INTUITION AND CREATIVITY.

The psychopath can only mimic intuition and creativity, never command, and this gives humans a decided advantage. The age of the psychopath feeding with impunity upon the energy of your labour, your soul, your psychology and your humanity is finally nearing an end. All indications show the last breeding population of feral psychopaths are in the final frenzy of their own unstoppable self-annihilation. All it took was the small percentage of the ninety-six percent of empathic human souls to start sharing knowledge and lessening fear.

The Psychopath Emperor has no clothes. Its persona-encrusted skin suit was stolen from someone else and the thing to bear in mind is that whether aristocrat or peasant, the psychopath never had any clothes of its own to begin with. Being the eternal parasite, it mimics the traits and mannerisms of others. It fed on our souls, our life energy, the sparkle in our eyes and the spring in our step and the song in our heart in order to fill the empty void within its being, sometimes just to alleviate its boredom and blankness.

This book is primarily concerned with our victory and rejuvenation. For this reason, I will no longer refer to people who have been abused by psychopaths as victims—I have instead chosen to use the term targets. In other words, the word victim carries the emotional resonance of someone who has been damaged permanently; a target can always be aimed at, but can be either hit or missed. When the psychopath has taken aim at your body, mind and soul—or your workplace, religious institution or nation—you were fooled at the time into thinking you were a victim. Once you have cultivated the three weapons—Knowledge, Intuition and Creativity—you will always have the tools to move the bull's eye out of their sight for good.

This book will also deal with child psychopaths, handicapped psychopaths and New Age cult leader psychopaths, as well as detailed behavioural profiles of the most common specific persona types now being utilised by psychopaths to gain trust and locate enablers/targets. As their supply is being cut off, psychopaths are scrambling to invent more complex and devious personas. I will also go into the latest scientific research dealing with relevant neuroscience and behavioural understanding, the increasing overtly proto-psychopathic social order, psychopathic agendas in mainstream mass media, and the attempted destruction of the *anima* aspect of human collective consciousness. I will also focus on target survivors' testimonies, case studies, historical and mythological aspects, and recovery tools.

The time has now come to move beyond the age of psychopathic abuse and on towards a more holistic understanding of human psychology and emotions, what it really means to be a target of a psychopath and what the implications are for us all in terms of personal growth and consciousness elevation. If psychopaths are hard-wired to be predators, then by extrapolation, are some targets also hard-wired to be targets? If so, how do we break the cycle? There is meaning in all of this and it is a bountiful harvest of opportunity and potential just waiting for us to claim.

One of the few criticisms of my previous book was that is was 'too emotional' in its approach to recognising, dealing with and recovering from a psychopathic encounter and that it would have benefitted by being more objectively clinical. I took the approach I did in order to warn readers just how dangerous all psychopaths are. This was reflected in my cut-to-the-chase approach. If I found myself in a foxhole during combat and an enemy grenade was lobbed in among my comrades, I would not alert them to the danger by embarking on a footnote-rich opus concerning the trajectory of the grenade, an in-depth analysis of the chemical compounds used in its construction or comparative studies on ballistics of other explosive devices. I would shout, "GRENADE!"

Having grown up in the high-rise slums of northside Dublin in the 1970's and 80's, I can tell you that sometimes the common touch is the one that saves your backside.

## CONSCIOUSNESS PARASITES

Similar to the organic parasite, a consciousness parasite has always managed to find hosts within the Psychopathic Control Grid; their ultimate aim being to control the destiny of their enablers to serve their own ends. The consciousness parasite can be embedded in or be an expression of a dysfunctional relationship, a family unit, a street gang, an organisation, the prevailing culture, and the workplace with its enabler-dependent littering of psychopaths and proto-psychopaths. Consciousness parasites wait for a target to arrive on their own self-created dung heap and then take control of the target's consciousness. It is time for us to get off their dung heap and take back our own consciousness. It is time for all of us to break the cycle—at home, in the workplace, and within our collective societies. Identify and cease enabling the psychopaths and proto-psychopaths within our personal lives— and then take the same approach to the Psychopathic Control Grid in order to get the society we need and deserve.

When gauging personal or societal survival or annihilation there can be no philosophically-minded grey area. It is a very different world today than the one we knew even a decade ago. The stakes have gone up. With the completion of this book, I can step back from the battlefield and see that the previously overlooked, discounted or arcane enemy is most certainly now in retreat. The consciousness parasites no longer enjoy an unlocked door to our psyche. We are witnessing the early stages of a global Psychopath Awareness Movement. Babylon is breaking.

## "WINSTON, HOW MANY FINGERS AM I HOLDING UP?"

The days when people targeted by psychopaths were declared as 'unstable', 'hysterical' and 'over-reacting' to the treatment they endured is coming to an end. They can no longer be silenced by being told "it was just a relationship that didn't work out—get over it!" They are refusing to be gaslighted by psychiatrists who—like the Inner Party member O'Brien from George Orwell's *1984*—inform the targets that they are the ones who need to be made sane—for a one thousand dollar consultation fee and some brain-dissolving chemicals, of course. Ordinary people who have been put though this experience have had enough. They are speaking out, writing books and creating blogs.

Targets who have had a consciousness parasite ravage their psyche have been subjected to a kind of soul rape. Months and years later there is an aura of pain that comes off their words and actions and even when they seem dynamic and successful once more, a sensitive observer can still pick up a frequency that something terrible was done to that person. It is often found most clearly in their eyes—the windows to a plundered soul.

In my own well-traveled, very eclectic and diverse life/career story, I have encountered around a dozen people whom I would consider to be—beyond a doubt—pure psychopaths. That is out of the thousands I have known personally. Our chances of encountering, and worse still, being targeted by a psychopath in a close-up personal or business setting is fairly slim, but if you do have this unfortunate experience, you will never forget it.

I can also state, with absolute certainty, that the closer one gets to the top of the socio-economic pyramid the more one is certain to encounter them. In the same way a lizard finds a rock to bask in the sun, the psychopath's Reptilian Complex is constantly moving closer to the blinding light emanating from the all-seeing eye at the top. The psychopath generally rises to the top, mainly because their true nature has been hidden from the rest of us for far too long.

### WOMEN ARE STILL THE PRIMARY TARGETS

The greatest clustering of potential and former targets of psychopaths in any socio-economic grouping is, by far, middle to upper-middle class women—predominantly women who work in professional fields such as finance, government, advertising, media, health care and marketing. It never ceases to amaze me how many attractive, intelligent, economically/socially successful and previously very confident women from these fields contact me wanting to know just what the hell was done to them, why they are in such a bad way now, and why the effects of their psychological and emotional exploitation remains so deeply entrenched within their psyche.

Men are also put through this same experience by female psychopaths. However, this still being primarily a man's world, the tragic irony is that the more successful a woman is in a man's world, the more she is likely to be targeted by a psychopath. This has to stop. We are dealing with nothing less than a pathological glass ceiling of sorts to keep any kind of human decency (via the feminine consciousness) from entering business and politics. The 'Old Boy Network' should really be re-branded 'The Old Psychopath Network.' All you have to do is look at the world and you can see it is a product of powerful male wastrels and parasites undermining the incredible achievements and potential of humanity at large.

## THE SAME PREDATOR
## IN DIFFERENT SKIN SUITS

Never assume that you fully understand how psychopaths operate. They are akin to snakes shedding their skin for a new version of themselves which they have carefully planned and implemented. Likewise, never assume that particular aspects of their pathology are representative of the actions they are presently undertaking. Psychopaths implement cunning, perfectly-crafted assaults on the psychology of their targets. Even when psychopaths beat someone up (they are all cowards who pick fights with targets they know won't hit back harder) it is often a mind-control tactic for someone else's benefit. A psychopathic husband will slap his wife around—more to get the children to 'play ball' rather than to teach her a lesson.

Psychopaths function in a very different manner to the rest of us and we cannot apply normal human rationale for violence and revenge when dealing with them. Their angle of attack is not always the individuals and institutions who get hit directly. It can come in the form of a passionate kiss, lavish gifts, flattery or a business deal just as much as a kick in the teeth or witnessing them bursting into a rage. Even when they just embarrass the targets in public, they are up to something much more. In all cases, the target is being 'coached' towards an agenda which often the target will not come to understand until the devaluation and discard stage. This is perhaps the most traumatic experience one can have in this life, but from another angle it can also be seen as a great gift, and once we learn to use it to scale up our understanding of the world, it will be a gift like no other we have ever received.

Even though the spectrum of psychopathology ranges from lazy parasite to genocidal despot, we must never forget that even when the psychopath's life ambition is no more than to sit at home all day in his mother's house playing video games, they are still potentially just as dangerous as any Ted Bundy. When all is said and done, all psychopaths are driven by the same selfish, reptilian drive to thrive through their cold need to hold power over others. There is no 'moral fail-safe switch' in them. None of them.

All it takes is a breakdown in social order, a war or a totalitarian regime to unleash the 'inner Ted Bundy' in all of them. Consider how the social unrest in the USA during the 1960's gave all kinds of psychopaths, from John List to the Manson Family, an opportunity to take their pathology up a notch. The John List story in particular is a classic saga of a previously mundane psychopath using a personal and social crisis to 'move on' by casually murdering his entire family with no more emotional depth than if he had just cut up his credit card. Even inside the most placid appearance any psychopath is a potential Bundy waiting to get out, one way or another.

Events such as the Holocaust would not have been possible without the low-level psychopaths doing the dirty work. Most of the guards and staff at the death camps were local psychopaths who finally found a job which suited them. Couple this with the psychopaths among the Jewish and Roma communities who helped march members of their own ethnic and cultural groups into the machine gun pits without a care in the world.

The mass murders ordered by Trotsky in the early years of the Soviet Union against anyone they could arrest for little or no reason were undertaken by the local wastrel psychopaths who were recruited for this very purpose. Being a psychopath himself, Trotsky knew these low-level psychopaths would be eager to murder hundreds of innocent people in killing rooms since they were also offered the opportunity to steal the personal belongings and loot the houses of the dead afterwards. The same thing happened during the Chinese Cultural Revolution. This is why psychopaths, regardless of the level of their pathology, are the most dangerous organism on this planet. I am not being hysterical at all here. History gives us the full truth.

## OUR COMMON BURDEN—OUR SALVATION

This is the entire thrust of my books, lectures and media appearances on this subject: to help people understand that there is a conduit between people's personal experiences with psychopaths and the ones who are in power. Ultimately, it is all the same experience manifesting and ravaging across the entire pathological spectrum.

The Psychopathic Control Grid can begin with on-line dating and end in a mass grave—all experiences with psychopaths, from the micro- to the macrocosm are identical expressions of their drive to gain dominion over others, no matter the cost. The only variable is the frequency, or degrees of the pathology. The intensity of the psychopathic targeting, along with their need for domination is not determined by any morality fail-safe switch inside them. Their pathological ambitions are limited only by the punitive economic and cultural parameters of the society that hosts them. Most psychopaths settle for enablers; however, *they all want an empire*. If there were no laws, then psychopaths would not be found in varying degrees. They would embrace anarchy and social breakdown as a pathological free-for-all, which may explain their apparent rarity within hierarchical indigenous societies where they have a tendency to meet with 'unfortunate accidents' on hunting trips. While in a Western context they are free to hide, move and reinvent themselves as soon as they are seen for what they are.

Native wisdom is once again warning us of the 'soulless ones', the consciousness parasites, the emissaries of Babylon in our bedrooms, boardrooms, in our bodies and in our souls. This book will serve to guide readers through this transitional period into the post-feral psychopathic world which beckons all humans to step forward and claim.

"Typically, if I am a regular at a restaurant, I tip well to maintain good relations with the staff. If it's a one-off place, I will tip well if I intend to make a move on the waitress."

*- Dispatches from Psychopaths*

## CHAPTER ONE

# THE ERA OF THE ELUSIVE PREDATOR IS ENDING

The term extinction refers to the ending of a species or sub-species due to events both natural and environmental and is specifically accepted to mean the death of the last individual specimen of the species. The capacity to recover their numbers towards a sustainable population has been lost long before the last of the breed has expired.

Speciation occurs when a new species develops and expands their numbers due to the discovery and successful exploitation of a new ecological niche. When this species faces extinction due to being unable to survive, the downward trajectory towards oblivion is rapid and unavoidable. This is the history of the psychopath's rise to dominance over the rest of the human population and the fate that is now rapidly unfolding for them. Thanks to growing public awareness, the *homo psychopathicus* ecological niche has been steadily eroding. Knowledge is power and combined with intuition and creativity, humans will prevail.

The predatory psychopathic sub-species of humanoid has fed upon the life energy of normal empathic human beings for thousands of years. The energy which psychopaths once so freely harvested is most often manifested in an emotional rape, and this palpable sense of damage and insult is the hallmark of a psychopath's passage through an individual human's life.

Clandestine energy harvesting comes in many forms: attaining material wealth, cultivating fears, playing on insecurities, manipulation and mind games, along with sexual and psychological exploitation of others, all the way up to the extreme psychopathic power plays of the IMF technocrats, 'political animals' and other corporate and aristocratic machinations. More often than not, this energy is stolen from others without them realising it until the predator becomes bored and moves on to feed elsewhere. The psychopath may have arrived in the guise of a prince or a pauper—the end result for the individuals and groups they targeted was nonetheless the same: psychological rape. This is how it has been for as long as human civilisation has been around—from the days when the Babylon consciousness parasite took stewardship of the human condition.

At the time when crops were first being harvested from the Mesopotamian fields—controlling the diet and destiny of humans—the same demon-worshipping, psychopathic priest class of Babylon planted seeds in the minds of others. That seed was to prevent us from noticing that one group of humans was attacking the rest of us, invading our minds and then moulding us like clay statues for the benefit of the psychopaths in the palaces, temples and marketplaces. Back then, they used complex religious and symbolic rituals. Today, they use TV and newspaper journalism—advertising, pornography, artistic, cultural and social trends, the fashion industry and pharmaceuticals. The end result of this process was always the same—keep us ignorant and keep us shopping.

Indigenous peoples have always known about the psychopaths amongst their populations. They were and remain fully aware of the 'soulless ones' who embed themselves within their community and feed off the energies and labours of the tribe. This is why the colonial powers slaughtered indigenous peoples in their hundreds of millions as civilisation moved across the globe. The psychopathic elites of the conquering empire and corporation had deceived and manipulated their own society for generations, successfully suppressing the knowledge of the collective native wisdom of humanity and they certainly didn't want it awakening once more by exposure to indigenous cultures.

In 61 AD, Suetonius Paulinus, after enormous logistical effort, managed to get his army across the Menai Strait in Wales and massacre the last of the Druids to make sure that what little remained of an intact native Celtic-Briton culture and wisdom tradition would be obliterated forever. This is just one example of how terrified the Psychopathic Control Grid is of 'native wisdom' and what drove them to continue their manifest destiny across the Atlantic centuries later to look for more enemies of their control grid. They did not want any form of uncontrolled (and uncontrollable) human native wisdom filtering back to the plebs at home. Hence why these groups, even when they attained remarkable levels of technical and social complexities, were still portrayed as 'uneducated savages' or 'lesser races'.

In exactly the same way, a psychopath in a relationship will tell a beautiful woman she is ugly and stupid in order to destroy her sense of self. Likewise, the retainers of the psychopathic emissaries of Babylon in the guise of Conquistadors and those Victorian men of 'science and reason' gazed upon the colossal architectural legacies of the Mayans, Egyptians, Incas and Aztecs and declared them to be a product of primitive monkey men. By the time they implemented their genocidal solutions upon the native population of the Americas, they had become bored and lazy and went about simply infecting people with disease-filled blankets presented as gifts, starved them to death on reservations or simply shot and stabbed them wholesale to get them out of the way. Just business.

Instead of complicated rituals and pageants used by previous generations of psychopaths to blind and bind the population to their unknowing fate as fodder, they simply began murdering them in their millions for no other reason than they finally had the cost-effective technological means to bring this about. Their new business model was efficient and streamlined and the 'reasoned and rational' scientific modern approach generally embraced by the target populations as 'progress.' Ingenious social, religious and ritual mind control to further the psychopathic agenda smoothed the way and, as we shall see, this eventually morphed into the burgeoning fields of public relations, marketing, advertising, newspaper journalism, feature films and television.

From General Jacob H. Smith's orders to kill everyone over the age of ten in the Philippine–American War, to the Nazis using IBM computers and software to more effectively help wipe out European Jewry and Roma populations, on to Irish playwright George Bernard Shaw of the Fabian Society praising the 'humane murders' of Lenin's and Stalin's purges in the early decades of the Soviet Union, not only does it still go on, but it has been stepped up to an almost unthinkable degree in the past two decades, except… they can't be as blatant about it as they were back then. These days, they get journalists and professional 'debunkers' to use subterfuge, shilling, misdirection, diversionary tactics, outright ridicule, half-truths and solid lies in order to suppress anyone who starts thinking for themselves but even this approach is not yielding the results the Psychopathic Control Grid needs to maintain a hold on the human mind as effectively as it once did.

Only a sort of primal, psychopathic, reptilian fear can drive individuals and organisations to go to such extreme lengths in order to control others. Psychopaths need to impose conformity upon their enablers and targets to allow them to control the agenda whether one-on-one or in an increasingly homogenised and globalised world. The psychopath knows no other means of survival because it cannot compete on a level playing field with the rest of humanity and they know that the business of harvesting energy is significantly easier when the target is distracted by popular entertainment or gaslighted by manufactured conflict on the mainstream 'news' and as a result completely oblivious to what is really going on.

When humanity had developed the means to rise to the top of the food chain in most situations one thing we failed to notice was that there was still one predator that remained and was still attacking and feeding off us from within our own species: the psychopath. With the rise of personal communication and note-comparing via Internet forums, this rat is now backed firmly into a corner, but from the psychopathic viewpoint it's all taking root from the most unexpected place; their prey is fighting back. People who have been targeted and damaged in personal relationships with these entities are now the ones who are becoming the shock troops of the global insurgency against the psychopathic agenda. They have slain the dragon in their own lives and are emerging from the labyrinth with an expanded awareness of the vast reach of psychopathic culture infecting modern human society, and profoundly aware that the problem needs to be dealt with once and for all.

What James Joyce referred to as the monomyth—which springs forth from the soul of ordinary humans (native wisdom)—is now providing the means to allow us to come to terms with the existence of the psychopathic predator and isolate it from the rest of the species. Not only for the sake of our personal and collective survival, but also to bring humanity towards the next evolutionary leap. As Carl Jung, Joseph Campbell and others have pointed out, this hero's journey of going into the labyrinth in order to slay the demon or dragon fulfils all our collective mythologies. If one is receptive to it, it becomes incorporated into our own life and beyond. This archetype of the heroic and very personal journey involves abandoning your fears and then returning to the real world to change the culture at large.

## PSYCHOPATHIC BABYLON IS BREAKING

There has been a noticeable shift in recent times whereby an increasing number of people are indeed politically and socially 'waking up'—please forgive the tired and over-used phrase. Granted, most of the population are still snoozing, and they seem perfectly content to channel hop between vampire-porn TV shows, celebrity gossip and royal weddings for the rest of their biological existence upon this planet, but just enough of the human race is switching off the TV, ignoring all the other mass media bombardment and looking for a more meaningful interpretation of reality. The tipping point has arrived.

They know there is something not right with their lives and the world around them. A lot of this has to do with the fact that thanks to people fighting for their rights and demanding more from their psychopathic masters, the quality of life in the West has increased to the level where more and more humans have moved beyond the basic need for survival. Now they can begin looking towards a more philosophical, spiritual and creative meaning to their own personal story.

At some stage, no matter how good-natured, innocent, or New Age-intoxicated on 'good vibes' they are, the effects of psychopathology will impact upon them and they will have to deal with it. Be it an abusive relationship, a guru/preacher who ripped them off and left them ruined, or a government who taxes them into borderline poverty after handing their nation over to the IMF, the demon in the shadows will have to be confronted in some manner and accepted as fact.

The game is now ending and the once abundant energy supply for psychopaths is rapidly drying up. Their hunting ground is no longer fertile with compassionate humans ignorant of the parasite among them. The ordinary psychopath in the community is being identified more and more in the wake of a steadily growing mass understanding that there is indeed something stalking the human population and attacking from within.

A genuine emerging consensus is now gaining hold. The parasitic psychopath, which has infected every strata of society is finally on the run. They are the real social, economic, political and environmental disaster endangering life for all on this planet, not the touted 'deadly pollutant' carbon dioxide. The collective veil of ignorance is lifting, and the predator is finally being isolated and quarantined from the rest of society, one individual psychopath at a time.

## THE BACKLASH HAS BEGUN

The Psychopathic Control Grid is presently so terrified of humans waking up to the confidence game they have always run that after decades of ignoring the issue they are sending out their propagandists in journalism, the medical profession and science to attack humans with their usual arsenal of sound bites, ridicule, paid-off experts and other flim-flam men on the corporate and government payroll.

We are being patronised and continually re-indoctrinated in the guise of 'alternative' journalists, Nobel Prize nominations and tenure-seeking academics who are all attempting to take ownership of the issue of psychopathology away from the 'useless eaters' and back into the hands of the ruling class. Obviously, a layman's knowledge of psychopaths, how they function and how to spot them, is far too dangerous for the average citizen to be aware of.

So the agenda now is to ridicule people like myself (although to be fair, I have got it comparatively easy as they tend to reserve their harshest criticism for women authors) who are not 'experts', as well as to focus the agenda back on the stereotypical 'jailbird' or murderous psychopath, and away from the far more insidious socialised psychopath seeking out targets from Facebook to Capitol Hill and all strata of 'respectable society' in between.

George Orwell's former employer—that bastion of propaganda and social engineering, the BBC—ran a farcical story in November 2011 about the doctor who believes he can cure psychopaths without explaining how other than suggesting they should be reformed in childhood. In much the same way feeding grizzly bear cubs tofu and broccoli will stop them from eating backpackers when they grow up, presumably. This was just one example of the damage control being utilised by the powers-that-be to shut off growing awareness of the issue of socialised psychopaths. Apparently, Leon Trotsky and Dr. Josef Mengele are now to be considered poor unwell people who need our love and support. You couldn't make this up.

The typical expert interviewed in these reports will talk about their work on criminal psychopaths in jails and then issue some platitudes along the lines of their hope to see the day when science and the legal system understand that these individuals have a disorder and that this disorder is treatable. Without a single shred of evidence that psychopaths can be treated. Complete, groundless nonsense. Such academic buffoonery gives rise to the increasingly circulated notion that psychopaths 'want to be cured'.

Just recall the post-arrest smug grin of the mass murdering psychopath Anders Behring Breivik—whom after having already killed ten people with a car bomb outside government buildings in the Norwegian capital Oslo then went on to shoot dead sixty-nine teenagers at point blank range on the island of Utøya. Not only did Breivik show no remorse for his actions but he revelled in the media attention given to him. It was what he wanted. He was no longer a nobody psychopath obsessed with guns and prostitutes; he was the person the entire world was finally looking at.

Breivik also demonstrated many of the core classic secondary (Relative) traits associated with the modern male psychopath: from pretending to be a police officer (or some other public official), to refusing to plead guilty—even with overwhelming evidence against him—including horrific helicopter news images of him murdering teenagers begging for their lives in the shallow waters around the island.

A psychopath is never wrong and never apologises because— in their minds—they have done nothing wrong EVER. His classic word salad and endless contradictory manifesto entitled *2083: A European Declaration of Independence* was emailed to more than one thousand addresses, in which he compared himself to a knight. His Facebook page showed him smugly grinning in his Freemasonic garb, displaying the usual psychopathic need to feel important and influential while at the same time over-compensating for the reality of his social mediocrity.

This is classic psychopathic behaviour—even with the non-violent ones. It is only when they commit crimes of this magnitude that we are given an unrestricted view into how they all are. Both the violent and the overwhelmingly non-violent (in the physical sense) psychopaths are alike. From a female psychopath walking out on her heartbroken husband and young children for a new 'soulmate' she just met on Facebook, to a CEO paying himself a multi-million dollar bonus package for destroying a company— all will behave in precisely the same manner: an unapologetic and smug demeanour where the psychopath portrays themselves as either the hero or the victim of their own appalling and remorseless actions.

Psychopaths very much adore being psychopaths. This is why psychopathic killers rarely commit suicide before middle age; they crave the media attention and spotlight of a high profile court case before they die. This is also why female psychopaths demand big weddings and male psychopaths demand high-profile celebrations of their milestones. Tony Blair is currently going around the world with a huge smirk on his face as a consultant to other mass-murdering war criminals on how to win Nobel Prizes.

Psychopaths adore their pathology even when it is potentially destroying them; it thrills them just being in the heat of the action. They are not suffering—everyone else is. And this is what drives their godlike hubris to the very last days of their lives. Consider Peter the Great: as a boy he played with 'real life toy soldiers' who were killed during mock battles, and towards the end of his life— literally on his deathbed—introduced a complex taxation system where the main burden was imposed upon and payable by serfs and paupers in order to keep them at starvation level. There is no retirement age for a psychopath—they just keep being a psychopath to the bitter end.

Another nugget of misinformation pedaled by the psychiatric industry is that psychopaths are a product of low self-esteem and poor social upbringing. This one statement alone demonstrates how modern psychiatry is now more disturbed than the individuals they claim to be treating. The likes of George Bush was hardly a product of a disadvantaged upbringing in some inner-city ghetto by a single parent. Such frankly obnoxious pop-psychiatry drivel drives home how psychopathology is still very much class-ridden. As a friend of mine recently stated, "The ruling classes would like to keep their current system going whereby the criminal psychopaths that are poor are sent to jail and the ones with education and money wind up in upper level management jobs."

Most mainstream journalists will never tackle the issue of socialised psychopathology in an honest and direct way because the owners of the media organisations which employ them wouldn't allow it. I'm convinced mainstream media's next tactic will be to declare that pointing out someone who clearly demonstrates psychopathic behaviour is inciting a hate crime. Just hold on—it is coming.

Ultimately, this is all a sign that the psychopaths in control are getting worried and are frantically trying to end this dialogue once and for all. Too late now. What is seen cannot be unseen and what is heard cannot be unheard.

## THE SELF-REALISED PREDATOR

Contrary to propaganda by the pathologically-driven, genetics-obsessed elitist faction that psychopathy is 'all in the genes', there remains as yet no hard, conclusive evidence that psychopathology is the result of genetic predisposition. There is no objective proof that if you are the children of psychopaths, then you and your siblings are more likely to inherit some arcane 'psychopath gene'.

Likewise, there is currently no hardcore scientific data to back up the claim that if you have children with a psychopath, then you unknowingly partook in a form of genetic lottery by bringing them into this world. This myth, peddled by prescription-happy psychiatrists—not to mention some rather sinister individuals within pop science—is creating enormous anxiety among ordinary people. For many who came to the horrific realisation that they either gave birth to, or fathered a child or children with a psychopath, this 'in the blood' approach can be very disturbing. They are being given the message that the most likely outcome is that their child is destined to be a psychopath, too.

This is the same elitist mentality which gave birth to Eugenics, a scientific theory which came to prominence during the 1920's. Eugenicists believed that all poverty, promiscuity and alcoholism were traits that were inherited—only amongst the poor, naturally. In the same way, they now want us to believe that all psychopathology is inherited from the bottom of the gene pool up.

To eliminate those social problems and improve society's gene pool, proponents of the Eugenics theory argued that those who exhibited undesirable traits should be sterilised by force. Some of

America's most powerful public and business figures of that time were ardent, if not hysterical Eugenicists, including Dr. Clarence Gamble of the Procter and Gamble fortune and James Hanes of the company now known for its underwear and T-shirts. Hanes was one of the founders the Human Betterment League, which promoted the cause of Eugenics for the health of the planet and survival of the human race. The success of the Human Betterment League so impressed the Nazis that, later on, it became essentially their blueprint for the Holocaust.

The word 'Eugenics' was first coined in 1883 by English scientist Francis Galton, who was a cousin of Charles Darwin. He used the term to promote the ideal of perfecting the human race by getting rid of its 'undesirables' while multiplying its 'desirables'. Fifty years or so later, it took root in the USA, beginning initially as a method to control welfare spending on poor white women and men. Just as it is today, corporations and the super wealthy back then wanted all the welfare spending lavished upon them. Over time, several states in the American Deep South began targeting more poor women and more blacks than whites. A third of the sterilisations in North Carolina were performed on girls under the age of 18. Some were as young as nine years old. This same mentality is what is driving the current fetish with the 'psychopath gene'.

If—and I stress if—the day ever comes when conclusive proof of such a thing as a psychopathic gene was found, is there anyone reading this book deluded enough to assume that elite psychopaths would allow themselves to be tested for the betterment of all? The bottom-feeding psychopaths would be sterilised (and it would be a great excuse to take care of poor non-psychopaths, too), while the elite psychopaths would still continue to enjoy business as usual. Like all psychopaths do, they would project their own insanity onto the rest of society and away from themselves. All poor people would eventually be declared 'potential psychopaths' in just the same way the multi-millionaires and aristocrats of today currently look down from their private jets on the 'carbon criminals' below them.

A similar agenda by the ruling classes has resurfaced in recent years concerning the issue of psychopathology and genetics. At the time of the Eugenics Movement, it was considered inconceivable that affluent and educated people could be degenerates and subsequently unworthy of life. Today, the descendants of the same psychopathic and proto-psychopathic elites are attempting to apply these rules with psychopathology. Given the chance, they will be sterilising low level 'potential psychopaths' while ignoring the far more destructive high-rolling real psychopaths in the corporate boardrooms and government buildings. The desire to find a mythical psychopathic gene will be used to justify this.

Consider this: mainstream scientific foundations are well-funded by major corporations—the pharmaceutical and chemical giants being the main ones—and have and still do put enormous pressure on working scientists by either dangling the purse strings or threatening to take the carrot away. In the worst case scenario, money isn't even an issue as scientists daily go in fear of their lives if they fail to toe the company line; from 2001 to 2005 nearly one hundred scientists either turned up dead under very questionable circumstances or vanished from the face of the earth completely. In the six years since, a further 112 mysterious deaths and disappearances have been reported worldwide. Get on a search engine and enter the term, "Dead Scientists." Be prepared to be appalled.

Scientists must fudge data in favour of governmental, pharmaceutical, military and psychiatric agendas to suit commercial and globalisation mandates (Climategate, 2009 Swine Flu 'pandemic', GMOs, the DNA patent process, etc.). Psychopaths are at the top of the scientific pyramid, too, and have their own agendas which very often match those of the government and aristocratic psychopaths who guided them into their current positions to begin with.

## MOMMY OR DADDY DEAREST?

On the other hand, there is plenty of research which shows the reverse to be true: that psychopaths just seemingly arrive out of nowhere as a kind of predatory savant in amongst a family of perfectly compassionate and normal individuals. The opposite also happens—where psychopaths give birth to normal, compassionate and loving people. Not surprising when one considers that the primary factor in all this (and everything else) is human consciousness.

Legendary neuroscientist Wilder Graves Penfield, the 'greatest living Canadian,' devoted his brilliant lifelong career to understanding the functioning of the mind. Likewise, Sir John Carew Eccles, the Australian neurophysiologist who won the 1963 Nobel Prize for his work on the synapse, arrived at a simultaneous conclusion with Penfield that our conscious minds are not inside our bodies. So why then are we looking for psychopathic minds inside the DNA? Can we please stop indulging this absurd notion that consciousness is in the electrical activity of the brain and that it is passed on from generation to generation within the genetic code of our DNA?

We must never lose sight of the fact that psychopaths are very different from humans (unless they come from very affluent families or have powerful political connections, of course) and go through their lives continually flirting with their own destruction and never learning from their mistakes. Even the ones who are the most successful and appealing and have cultivated their social mask to perfection are still ticking time bombs in the sense that even the most brilliantly manipulative and socially dynamic psychopath is not fully in control of their own impulsiveness—they are always walking a tight rope.

Another fatal flaw is the psychopath's obsession with idealisation and perfection. They are determined to attain the best of everything at any cost. This idealisation permeates the psychopathic mass media with its image of perfection and eternal beauty and is thus projected onto society, encouraging and rewarding proto-psychopathic behaviour in the masses. The manner in which the Psychopathic Control Grid has imposed popular notions regarding beauty and perfection has also directly influenced past immigration and Eugenic legislation in several Western nations at throughout history.

In recent times this issue has also touched upon bio-ethics and technology. As long as society is driven by the psychopathic obsession with the idealisation of perfection, then people will continue to make decisions about others based upon superficial concepts of a person's image, their level of fame, career success or social status rather than their personality. Such a society suits the psychopaths as they continue to hide in plain sight and prey upon others more effectively by projecting the image of perfection or taking the role of final arbiter of perfection in others. The rest of us are paying a terrible social and personal price for this superficiality. Consider Mary Shelley's 1818 novel *Frankenstein;* in order to demonstrate his godlike ideology of power and control, an aristocratic scientist attempts to create perfection and instead produces a physical monstrosity.

In the novel, Shelley shows us how the scientist's creation unleashed the monstrous shadow of his own imperfections. Frankenstein was unable to acknowledge the undeniable truth that his scientific zeal was profoundly spiritually and morally flawed. This can be similar to the experience of parents who give birth to children and then later realise their partner or spouse is a psychopath. In the period of grief following the end of the relationship they can project a paranoid resentment at their child before there is a realisation that the child is not some default spawn of the devil after all.

The neurology of the psychopath is not a genetic hand-me-down from a psychopathic forebear. We make the brain we need in life. So ignore the 'DNA or Nothing' school of thought when it comes to their scientific 'proof' of a genetic predisposition for psychopathology. Always assume that your children are born pure and beautiful and not polluted by the seed or egg of the predator. Your own intuition, as well as increasing numbers of non-partisan scientists and researchers are beginning to confirm what you knew in your heart all along.

## BAD FAMILIES AND STRANGE SCIENCE

There are two kinds of individuals who are enchanted by the 'psychopath gene' propaganda. On the one hand, the Darwinian secular religion faction, which believes that all scientific research should be undertaken (even cosmology) to validate the Victorian aristocrat's notions of who is and who is not fit to live on the same planet with them; in other words, long-dead, imperialist inbreds who mated with their first cousins and produced future inmates secretly sequestered away in various mental hospitals throughout the British Isles. This is because their elite paymasters intensely—and for sinister motives—desire that their Survival of the Fittest dogma remains infallible at all costs. They either hide away any findings which are contrary to the theory or send out propagandists to explain how Punctuated Equilibrium (where vast numbers of new species just magically appear out of nowhere) is the be-all and end-all of evolutionary biology.

Now and again the Psychopathic Control Grid presents us with red flags of their own. In a talk marking the 150th anniversary of the publication of *On the Origin of Species*, Dr John Baross, a researcher at the NASA Astrobiology Institute, stated with a straight face, "I really feel that Darwinian evolution is a defining feature of all life and that Darwinian evolution will be the driving force of life anywhere in the universe." Interestingly, in the same year, the Vatican's chief astronomer and papal science adviser Gabriel Funes explained in the newsletter of the Vatican Observatory that the God of the Judeo-Christian bible also created aliens. No doubt if asked, the American Psychiatric Association (APA) would most probably tell us that aliens invading Earth and eating us is a direct result of repressed sexual trauma in accordance with the Gospel According to Sigmund Freud.

Step back from all of this and look at how dogmatic and crackpot the ruling elite and their propagandists are. One of my personal favourite red flags from the mainstream scientific community in recent times is NASA's Planetary Science Division report entitled, *Would Contact with Extraterrestrials Benefit or Harm Humanity?* Incredibly, these brilliant scientific minds—drunk on their infallible peer reviews and hunger for research grants—stated that aliens would destroy humanity to punish us for our carbon footprint. This serves to remind us that the so-called mainstream scientific community can be as delusional and corrupt today as the Vatican during the days of Galileo, and we should not take *anything* they tell us at face value. Chances are some wealthy psychopaths behind the scenes are controlling the agenda.

On the other side of this 'psychopath gene' obsession, we have victims of psychopathic relationships; most often distraught and heartbroken women who in order to deal with the aftermath trauma of a relationship with a psychopath often unfairly (but somewhat understandably so) declare the psychopath's entire bloodline to be 'all psychopaths!' Some of these women have created websites, written books and given birth to a cottage industry, all on the back of their often misguided and misdirected revenge fantasies. Where at times it seems that everyone except them is a psychopath, sociopath or a 'narc', (narcissist) in most cases the family of the psychopath is simply trying to be loyal to their kin and have in many cases been manipulated and lied to by the psychopath with smear campaigns against his/her ex. This does not make them psychopaths but rather, enablers.

In the middle of all this 'psychopath gene' hysteria are the unfortunate men and women who happened to have had children with individuals they later found out were psychopaths. Is it not enough that these people are not only suffering through the emotional and psychological trauma of being victimised by a psychopath, but their misery and pain is then further compounded by a fear that the child they hold in their arms may also grow up to be a psychopath one day, too. The 1997 Andrew Niccol film *Gattica* perfectly illustrates how this increasingly neurotic obsession with genetics can lead to a society tormented with disillusionment and self-hatred. The desire for human perfection can—in the individual sense— give rise to medical conditions such as Obsessive Compulsive Disorder (OCD) or anorexia, or an over-use of plastic surgery by some people to the extent of making Frankenstein's monsters of themselves. Do we really want to add a whole new social neurosis based on who may or may not have a psychopathic gene?

Perhaps this is one of the evolutionary lessons given to us by the presence of psychopaths on our planet: their existence may teach us to look for the soul/humanity of the individual before we consider whether they need a nose job or lose weight or get their teeth straightened and whitened. That a child born into either a wealthy or poor family deserves an equal chance to prove themselves later on in life and not be pre-judged, sorted, sequestered and dismissed according to in-vogue nature/nurture theories. We have to find meaning in the experience of the psychopaths who come into our lives and who currently rule our planet. We also need to look at ourselves and ask if and why we may present ourselves as a tempting target to any passing psychopath.

Contrary to what you may be thinking after having read the above paragraphs, I myself have great respect for science, traditional psychology and the skills and techniques of medical professionals—particularly nursing. We need to cherish and safeguard these institutions from further manipulation and tampering by aristocratic, corporate and governmental demands in the guise of 'altruistic' interference in research and findings. For the most part the influence of organised religion in these professions has steadily declined over the centuries, but the task before us now is to seize them from the money men and the bureaucrats and give it back to the scientists who should be nurtured in their vocations and unbridled quest for knowledge without the all seeing eye towards corporate profit.

Mass media cannot be automatically trusted to provide you with proper information relating to scientific discoveries (or anything else, for that matter). From the broadsheets to the tabloids, from the BBC to FOX News, we are bombarded with propaganda and appalling standards of journalism—and it is only getting worse.

Modern journalism has a tendency to regurgitate any statement a scientist makes without even questioning the research; there is simply no skepticism applied these days. The mass media considers and treats it all as infallible for one simple reason: both the media and the scientists are owned by major corporations with profit motives to guard and nurture. When a story broke in 2009 announcing a Dislike of Brussels sprouts gene found in the human DNA, journalists reported this without blinking. Story after story purported that we are apparently genetically pre-dispositioned to either love or loathe Brussels sprouts—just like you may or may not have a 'psychopath gene'. Proof of the existence of either is pure speculation at this point, but for some reason it suits the corporate agenda of the moment to make us all believe this is true..

When a scientist speculates in terms such as *could be* or *may well suggest* or *we suspect*, once broadcast or published, these noncommittal terms magically transform into scientific fact without the legal rigamarole attached to making the declaration absolute; the simple fact that it was featured in a 60 second television news story is enough to make it transform into holy writ in the minds of the majority. There is indeed a gene controlling taste sensitivity that scientists have named TAS2R38. This gene produces a protein that interlocks with the chemical PTC (phenylthiocarbamide) and gives the taste sensation of bitterness. PTC is also similar to chemicals found in brassicas such as Brussels sprouts and cabbages. Therefore, just as they have done with the mythical psychopathic gene, some scientists have suggested that the ability to taste or not taste PTC might explain why some people dislike Brussels sprouts.

Through the sleight of hand known as writing catchy copy this sort of manipulation leads to most television viewers accepting without question that if the BBC says there is a psychopath gene, well, it must be true. It was on TV. The next day, their co-workers are talking about this new scientific 'fact'. Neither the sprouts or the psychopath gene reports have definitively proven anything, yet to be heard to question it a person risks being ridiculed by the majority.

We must safeguard knowledge from any further elitist psychopathic misuse and mass media exploitation and we do this by not unconditionally accepting what we are being told as undisputed fact by the mainstream media (and alternative media). We must become our own researchers. Knowledge and discovery is an on-going journey, not a destination. Do not follow the example of modern newspaper journalists by simply accepting university, corporate and government press office statements as unbiased fact. Think for yourself. Question, research and embrace the wonder of discovery and learning, for it is something no psychopath is capable of doing. Smugly strutting around town with a copy of Dr. Stephen Hawking's *The Grand Design* does not an intellectual make. Likewise, the same goes for my books—do your own research. I can point the general direction, but the realisations you will treasure most are the ones you put together. Mass media is the worst place to go to when seeking out unbiased knowledge and information. It is a labyrinth of half-truths, hidden realities, selective disclosures, outright distortions and above all, profit motives. Just like when you are in a personal relationship with a psychopath, after a certain point you have to dig for the real story behind the illusion.

To drive this point home, look no further than UK newspaper journalist James Hipwell who was jailed in 2006 for writing positive stories about companies in which he owned shares. Hipwell was given a six-month prison sentence for making close to £41,000. He mentioned his stocks in a financial section of the *Daily Mirror* and then quickly sold them as their value increased. With what appears to be a delighted smirk, Hipwell testified at an ethics inquiry in 2011 that phone hacking was a 'standard tool' for all journalists.

With this insight into the world of journalism, consider the numbers of 'respected' journalists who sit down with globalist policy makers to decide what stories should and should not be reported so as to not upset the large corporations, governments and the foundations who bankroll them all. Bottom line: mass media is not your friend. It never has been. It never will be.

The more reductionist science tries to promote the exclusively psychopathic genetic personality, the more results come back to further undermine the desire to prove what was never true to begin with. Now consider the following mysteries of the mind that, despite incredible advances in the fields of neuroscience, complex brain chemistry and overall understanding of the functions of the brain, science still cannot fully determine:

- How the brain stores and retrieves memories
- What emotions are, precisely
- What dream states are and how they relate to mental health
- How the mind conceptualises the future
- Why the brain seems to function in a different time state than the world around it
- What the actual baseline activity of the brain is
- What intelligence is and how it relates to imagination and perception
- How the specialised partitions of the brain interact with one another

There is also the matter of function versus structure of the brain—function being the purpose of the mind and this, by extension, leading onward to psychology and the study of mental faculties. Structure on the other hand relates to form and shape of the physical brain itself, which in psychopaths is basically identical to non-psychopaths except for how it processes information and hormonal responses. The obvious answer to all of these anomalies is that consciousness is the determining factor in all of us—including psychopaths.

Most certainly, the brain can be damaged; blunt trauma injury, birth deformity or substance abuse included. Likewise, the psychology of an individual can be distorted by stress and emotional abuse, creating or cultivating neuroses such as the proto-psychopathic condition within an otherwise normal human being acting out psychopathic tendencies—the military training process could be held up as an example in many cases. However, with the true psychopath—the Intra-Species Predator as Dr Robert Hare of the University of British Columbia termed them—I have no doubt in my own mind that the underlying predatory consciousness of the true psychopath is the primary factor at work. Their brain and neurological eccentricities are the end products of a non-organic to organic process chain which began with their underlying predatory consciousness. To imply otherwise is akin to claiming that Lady GaGa herself resides inside your iPod when you are listening to her

music, or that the Kardashian family actually resides inside your
television.

*Anne's Story*

"After thirteen years of no contact, out of the blue I received a text message from John. I'd first met him as a sev-
enteen-year-old and had experienced 'love at first sight'.
Such was the intensity and magnetism experienced in that
moment I felt we had known each other before except that
moment had nothing to do with being past-life lovers—it
was subconscious pattern recognition from childhood conditioning received from my psychopathic stepfather. The
situational context was completely different, but time had
only stood still when I first saw John because what I had
thought was a deep, spiritual romantic connection was actually the fixed stare of a predator. What manifested after
that event was nothing more than a very short-lived casual
fling (his term).

John tapped straight into my empathic nature with sob
stories that could rival any Shakespearean tragedy of family sabotage, betrayal and victimhood; a brother who stole
all the money from his 'Free Trade' business (which turned
out to be a racket) sending him into bankruptcy (that he
didn't declare), the mother who despised him so much she
had him sectioned due to his cocaine addiction which had
been in response to his traumatic childhood.

He was the scapegoat of the family, the victim of an
abusive father. He called himself a survivor and I related
to that; we shared similar backgrounds, enduring life with
psychopathic fathers. It didn't occur to me that John was
using his previous knowledge of my childhood to deceive
me. By the end of the night he made his declaration of
love.

What started out as a long-distance relationship quickly
turned into a fast-track to Hell. Everything I asked for—
time, space, peace to complete my degree—was denied. I
was suffocated by his demands for my undivided attention.
He quickly worked out that as an empath and under-grad
psychologist I always had time to listen to his issues, and

he'd feign intentions of resolving his problems knowing full well I'd support his 'recovery'. He turned up at my newly rented apartment unannounced and proceeded to move in under the guise of starting full-time employment with his first love, horse racing. He kept telling me that I needed protecting, which I found insulting given my nomadic and independent lifestyle.

As soon as I agreed he could stay for a few weeks and lent him money to get himself back on his feet, he wasted no time in unveiling his true self.

The sabotage began. The constant energetic draining, the sniping and put-downs that I should chuck my degree in and get a proper job, discovering my revision notes in the rubbish bins outside and missing textbooks. A treasured gift my best friend had given me prior to his death went missing as well and artwork by my family was found damaged, all of which had moved around the world with me for years and never had so much as a scratch on them.

One night in the back of a taxi he told me we should get married. After picking my jaw up off the floor I reminded him that I had no intentions of ever marrying, but he spoke over me, stating we should get married over and over like a mantra. By now I was disturbed, especially afterwards when I caught him walking off with a very drunk female friend by the hand. When confronted he tried to deny what I had seen with my own eyes.

The day I had intended to walk away from the relationship was also the day I discovered my pregnancy. We'd only been together a few months. I went into denial. I wanted to be wrong. I wanted him to prove me wrong. I hung in there believing I was honouring our unborn child's right to two loving parents. However, as my pregnancy progressed and after the completion of my degree, John's behaviour became increasingly callous and manipulative. He wanted us to relocate to the other side of the UK but instant red flags warned me I would be isolated. I refused and instead moved into my mother's house to prepare for our baby's arrival.

My energy levels were affected whenever I was in John's

presence, even when he was in love bombing mode. I'd feel drained, irritable, depressed, reality took on a surreal aura. During a bad argument, when I asked him why he demanded empathy when he was incapable of giving it in return, his response was to laugh and ask me what empathy was. When I explained it to him he calmly told me that he 'wasn't wired up like normal people'. He then blamed this on his receiving Electro Convulsive Therapy (ECT) during a 'stay at hospital'.

John never clarified the exact reason for being sectioned. He was ambiguous about his diagnoses; he couldn't make his mind up whether he'd had schizophrenia, cocaine addiction or depression. My suspicions that he'd lied about ECT were now being confirmed, so I asked him what therapy he had undergone and if he had consented to the procedure; he claimed upon his arrival he had literally been pinned down, injected with sedatives, knocked out and came around to having his brain fried. He knew I was interested in 'questioning authority' and he also knew I'd studied psychology. He must have thought he was spinning a convincing conspiracy-style yarn.

I had a difficult labour and after two days I finally gave birth to our son. The midwives left the room, and John sat holding the baby in the most disturbingly possessive way looking at me with hate and began to berate me, telling me he thought I couldn't have children. The midwife came back ready to stitch me up and overheard him then promptly threw him out. The next day, exhausted, I came home to his apologies and promises to be a good father,. By the end of the day he had verbally attacked me again while breast feeding, causing our baby to suffer colic from the stress, and cortisol levels in the milk. It was when he called me an unfit mother that flashbacks hit me; my step-father had said those exact words to my mother after the birth of my sister. I kicked John out and didn't hear from him for three weeks.

He'd taken my car and furniture; both were needed as baby and I were moving into a new home, but instead of dropping off my belongings he came into the house and in a patronising tone informed me that if I didn't let him stay at the new house he wouldn't repay me the money I'd lent him and we'd be homeless. I was being blackmailed. Sick with sleep deprivation and turmoil, I gave into it. I made it clear to John we were not 'together' and he didn't care. Respite came while he was away on work trips to different race courses throughout the UK, but upon his return he'd flip between trying to win me back with pity, and when that didn't work he'd go into love bomb mode. When that didn't work he'd give me the silent treatment.

John was not interested in our son. When he did hold him it was in the same possessive manner as I'd witnessed in the delivery room, but there was no bond. I sensed John perceived our child only as a meal ticket, a roof over his head.

Cognitive dissonance was amplified by exhaustion but when I did manage to sleep for an hour or so, my intuition converted to precognitive dreams. I would literally dream the truth behind John's deceptions and what he was really up to. One experience that stood out was a warning dream of him walking around a car park in a trance, as though he were the walking dead. No matter how much I tried to get his attention, he didn't hear my cries or my desperately tugging at his arms to acknowledge me, his eyes fixed into a dead stare, walking aimlessly around in circles. In hindsight, I believe my intuition had picked up that he was psychopathic and tried to warn me.

The intuition literally led me to discover his 'other phone' used for cheating purposes, stacks of betting slips and blue pens hidden in the shed along with bank statements which showed me exactly what he had spent my money on and remnants of the drugs he'd been taking.

I had evidence against him and demanded he take responsibility by going to his doctor and getting some help; he went along with it 'to keep me sweet' and attended one Cognitive Behavioural Therapy session. He refused to attend any more because of the nationality of the doctor. It came to a head when one night he returned to the house unexpectedly and I felt that my son and I were in danger. I

tried to rationalise the fear away, but found myself bringing pots, pans and rolling pins into my room for protection.
I picked up my sleeping baby, quietly put him in the car
and drove to my mother's house and stayed there for two
weeks.

The only way I could break out of the hypnotic despair
and feelings of being submerged in limbo was to invoke
my anger; not violent anger but justified anger, to burn out
any lingering desire or conditioning that kept John and I
locked in the destructive cycle.

That inner fire was the energy that brought strength to
my voice when I commanded him out of my home. I heard
myself threatening to call the police as he had no legal right
to be in my house; the anger reset my perception, weaken-
ing cognitive dissonance and strengthening my resolve to
end the nightmare. With this came acceptance that I had
loved an illusion, but the ability to trust myself was damaged because I'd potentially put my son in danger by resisting the reality of our situation, so self-discipline was
called for.

I put myself through an emotional boot camp disman-
tling cognitive dissonance; I treated everything that came
out of John's mouth as a lie. He was guilty until proven innocent. This broke his spell over my emotions. I embraced
single parenthood and promised to do whatever it took to
protect my son from harm. I cut off unhealthy friendships
and became The Hermit, only interacting with immediate
family. Healing came in the form of walking miles and
miles with my mother and son each day in nature regardless of the weather. If it rained, I would cry with the rain, if
it was windy I would visualise the winds blowing out the
imprint of pain from my heart and mind. This elemental
exercise revived me.

After he left, I walked into my house and the atmosphere
no longer dragged with despair. It felt free from the pol-
lution of fear. That feeling lasted for a few days until the
stalking began. John would call my home phone at exactly
the moment I'd arrive back with my son; he was watching
us. To begin with I answered him, but it became clear he

was looking for another angle to worm his way back in. Sob stories of renting rooms from drug dealers and being caught in police raids didn't ring true; I had finally become immune to his repetitive empty promises and lies. He became enraged by this but I stuck to my guns, defined my boundaries and conditions. I arranged for his visitations to be conducted at a supervised contact centre or at my mother's house but he was no longer welcome in my home.

In response to this, John ignored the visitation options and threatened legal action. He was excellent at playing the victim and so he went to town portraying me as this unreasonable, spiteful ex who had made him homeless and was blocking him from having contact with his son. I argued that he'd have to disclose the full extent of his mental health records given his admission of 'not being wired up like normal people'. I was naturally terrified for the safety and well-being of my child. When he had the opportunity to be a father, he instead demonstrated boredom, irritation, jealousy and resentment; he was thoughtless and dangerous towards our son's needs on both a practical and emotional level. It became clear John wanted to control me by using our child as a weapon.

Predictably, John refused all my conditions, denied the allegations and told me he'd see me in court. The judge gave John supervised access at a contact centre for one hour a week. He walked out of court with a smirk after his solicitor failed to mention to the judge this had been my original condition for his having visitation rights. I knew it was only a matter of time before he would try to gain unsupervised access and I was terrified, knowing that John had no real intention of looking after our son and I began to fear the worst. How far was John prepared to go to get back at me? I experienced the return of severe panic attacks which hadn't burdened me since I was seventeen years old, I honestly thought I would die from the stress but my son and mother kept me going.

There was a case when John 'gaslighted' himself in mediation; he had told so many lies he couldn't get his stories straight. In an attempt to have my mother be perceived as an unsuitable point of contact for visitation, John recalled a time when he had 'disclosed' his father had sexually abused him. This extension on his childhood abuse story had been created as a sob story to excuse his vile behaviour towards me. It had been an obvious lie and my mother called him out on it. John then quickly denied his father had abused him and changed his story to 'nearly being raped by a boy on his paper round' and then accused my mother of slander towards his father. It was absolute madness.

Because we attended court every six weeks we were offered mediation by CAFCASS—a UK government agency which looks after the interests of children involved in family proceedings. John, in his infinite arrogance, believed that because he was protected by a confidentiality clause in mediation he could torment me in front of the mediator and get away with it. He cockily stated, 'I'm winning'. I remember looking at the mediator and saying, 'he thinks it's all a game'.

John retold half this story, placing emphasis on my mother not believing his own father had sexually abused him; when the mediator asked, 'and did your father sexually abuse you?' John immediately replied, 'no'; he then tried to retract the story and began to babble about his memory not being great. The mediator looked at John in disbelief as he continued to malfunction. It turned out the mediator gave out recommendations to the judge based on what she had observed; she supported my line of reasoning, supervised contact to be continued and full disclosure of medical records to be handed to the judge.

In between the court cases, I went to work, researching contact centers and Family Law. When John claimed poverty, I paid for half the supervision bill—I spent a serious amount of time putting together evidence to file to the court, counteracting his lies with factual evidence. I felt like a legal secretary, researcher, PI, clinical psychologist and single mother rolled into one. John wasn't getting what he wanted from the court, so played the poverty card even though he was in a very well-paid job and refused to attend the contact centre.

My solicitor warned me to start thinking outside of the box because of the risk of my being in contempt of the contact order, punishable by imprisonment or a hefty fine. I was cornered, having no other option but to allow John to come to my home for visitation. I was furious, but also knew this could be an opportunity for him to either prove my fears wrong by honouring his role as a father, or the opportunity would be the metaphorical rope he'd hang himself on.

Less than an hour after trying to coerce me into a fight, harassing me and endangering our toddler, he hung himself on his own behaviour. John had shut our son in his car with the keys in the ignition. I rescued my son, then while I comforted him in my arms, John attempted to hit me in the face. He was stopped only by the presence of neighbours. He was enraged with me because I had made him leave my home a year and a half before. It finally came home to roost that he had only wanted 'a family' for the house we provided and the image of respectability. We had been a convenience to him and nothing more. The police were notified and John stated he'd been 'set up'.

We went back and forth to the courts over a nine month period; each time I stood my ground with reference to John's mental health. All the judges re-ordered him to hand in his medical records. He over-rode this by giving them a badly photocopied A4 piece of paper with a header stating 'medical insurance' that he'd attained from his work place. By way of demonstrating my own transparency, I offered up my own medical records which came bound in a professional format, comparing my authentic medical records with his A4 piece of paper. It became obvious John was hiding something.

His lies were catching up with him. He could no longer deny the existence of having had a mental health assessment, because right at the bottom of the medical insurance page was a recent scribbled note from his doctor urging the council to re-house John urgently because of his mental health. John had used his mental health background to get a newly-built council house, but there still was no mention of the exact psychological issue.

The contact centre supervisor had also sent her assessment of John's sessions with our son to the court and it mirrored my own concerns. The supervisor noted John's lack of interaction and care with our child; she had prevented many near-accidents from occurring and noted his preoccupation in slandering me. His mask had slipped; he had gone from charm mode with the supervisor to becoming arrogant.

The judge re-ordered John to hand into the court his authentic medical records and ordered a date for us both to be cross-examined on the stand for two hours each to determine the truth of the situation. John was also ordered to attend parental classes and both of us to attend a SPIP (Separated Parents Information Programme) class. I knew then John's confidence was waning and had a hunch that he was not going to jump through the hoops which the judge had ordered on him. I was right, as he refused to return to the contact centre—but by doing this he was again cornering me for being in contempt of contact order.

I can only describe what happened next as intuitive intervention; my dreams instructed me what to do next. I dreamt of three sheep dogs. I clearly heard the word 'strategy' being said in the background. I woke up and knew what to do. I paid the contact centre for a full month of supervision with another report for court purposes—I knew John wouldn't go and this would demonstrate his lack of interest in our son and also by doing this I was no longer in contempt of the contact order. I was right; and he refused to go back to the contact centre, but what sickened me about this was during his final visitation our son had finally called John 'daddy' for the first time. John had waited for our child to recognise him as his father before cutting off from him.

John still hadn't handed in his medical records and I needed to know why. John had cut off all contact with his family, though I knew his mother was the only person who knew the truth about him. I had no contact details, but I vaguely remembered his sister's name, so I put her first and maiden name into Facebook, along with their home town and unbelievably she came up at the top of the search list.

A few days later his mother informed me that the last time he'd contacted her John had refused to discuss our son and had instead threatened his brother with a hit man. It transpired that he had never been abused by his father and that he had been a problematic child. As he'd been a premature baby, she had wondered if his low birth weight had anything to do with his neural development. She also clarified that she hadn't sectioned him, but had arranged an appointment for him to attend a psychological assessment because she feared he had serious pathological problems. He attended one interview and never returned.

These epiphanies were finally destroying the fear John held over me and then the final breakthrough came: my solicitor, fed up with John's pleas of poverty, arranged for us all to attend court to get permission from the judge to use legal aid for the purpose of getting his medical records. John didn't turn up. The judge gave John one last opportunity to attend court and when he didn't turn up the second time, the contact order was ripped up and I was finally given full residential custody.

The judge acknowledged my concerns and agreed that it did appear that John had psychological issues. The relief was overwhelming; my son and I were free from John's legal control over us. I remained cautious for months after the case, waiting for the zombie to come back to life. It was actually this week (mid-December, 2011), nearly four months after the court case while writing this, that my solicitor rang; he had news of John's departure from this country. Having secured himself a job in Dubai, John wanted to pass on his email address to keep him up to date on our son.

The next day, a big Christmas card came through my mother's door with a letter to me enclosed. It was from John; in the letter he still refuses to take responsibility for the lies and devastation he caused; he repeats the same empty promises from three years ago. It's amazing looking at this letter reflecting the mindset of someone with no

conscience, no remorse and no emotion. The only reply I
have for him is, no contact ever again.

Anne's testimony gives us an insight into why so many targets of
psychopaths come to believe that the entire family structure from
which their ex derived may be a nest or spawning ground of psychopaths. Anne did her own research into John's family background and
discovered that not only was he lying about being sexually abused
by his own father but that the rest of his family were well aware
that something was profoundly dysfunctional about him. John is
the classic pathological savant-style psychopath who can manifest
within a mostly otherwise non-disordered family unit.

Often, the psychopath will try to keep the target away from his
or her family in order to hide the actual truth concerning fabricated childhood abuse stories and other smear campaigns which all
psychopaths spread. There is always a pity-cultivating sob story of
an alcoholic mother or cold father presented during the early love-
bombing and pity-mongering stages. Sometimes there are tiny
scraps of truth to these fables. Often they are one hundred percent
fabricated. Always they are hand-tailored to manipulate the target.

## PUZZLING PEOPLE CREATE PREDATORY BRAINS

The psychopath's neurological eccentricities are a by-product of
their own consciousness in that their brain structure, physiology
and neuro-electrical and neuro-chemical states are a reflection of
what they themselves are as individuals—along with that which
they desire from life. We all develop the brain we need. Our brain
creates new neural pathways all the time in order to learn new skills
and/or develop new means of processing information as it is presented to us. This duality of consciousness—both positive and
negative—is just another expression of the overall duality of the
cosmos. Psychopaths are here to feed upon the empathic. It is part
of a complex evolutionary process. Even so, they are the dregs of
consciousness, clearly demonstrated by their lack of compassion or
understanding towards others beyond the need to use and exploit

them and by their inability to tell the difference between mimicry and true creativity.

The human brain—including the development of new synapses, the protein sequences in certain genes and the electrical activity within the cerebral partitions—is a product of self-realised neurological plasticity created by the underlying consciousness. You create the brain you need based on the nature of consciousness you possess. It is not exclusively a product of mom or pop.

My message to people—both male and female—who have children with psychopaths: do not become traumatised by the fear of genetics unleashing a nasty surprise, unless you begin to notice ongoing psychopathic behaviour in your child which shows no sign of waning, though remember: the chances of this happening are very small. Even if the child does begin to demonstrate the pathology of the psychopathic parent there is still a good chance that this is a learned behaviour and in such cases these children can be helped with love and understanding. Hence why courts should immediately give sole custody to the non-disordered parent with a lifetime restraining order on the psychopathic parent once they have been fairly and professionally diagnosed as such.

We can't play Russian Roulette with the children of psychopaths. These children run the risk of being either emotionally or psychologically damaged, used as pawns in court cases, economically exploited by the psychopath for the rest of their lives, raped, pimped-out and/or cultivated into being proto-psychopaths. No clinically diagnosed psychopath should be allowed any form of legal access to their children—PERIOD.

Our consciousness is non-local to our bodies and probably existed before we were even born, in some form or another. It was either empathic or psychopathic at the point it manifested you, me and the rest of us. As it went through biological development, it tailor-made the brain it needed. Ask yourself: why would a psychopath create a brain and neural network designed for empathy and compassion, when all it requires is a brain customised for the business of psychopathic predatory intent?

The genetic aspects of how proteins are created in DNA structures have now been shown to not always be due to random mutations and thus can be triggered by our thoughts. This goes a long
way to understanding why people get diseases after having been
abused by psychopaths—and also how the predatory consciousness develops a predatory mind with a highly-specialised predatory brain structure.

## HORSES FOR COURSES

'Horses for courses' is a shorthand phrase for development of
a racehorse to compete on a specific terrain and is an appropriate
metaphor to describe the specific choices and adaptations in the
psychopathic brain for dealing with any situation in which they can
tailor an individual approach to prey upon others.

Mainstream science—and especially psychiatry—has been feeding the public many unproven assertions about the mysteries of the
human mind over the past century. Science, by its own design, re-
lies upon empirical evidence to prove theories and since human
consciousness can be neither weighed, measured or quantified according to classic laboratory standards, scientists tend to hide behind all the letters after their names, throw out any wild claim and
hope they are believed.

I watched a BBC documentary recently in which a scientist was
put under an MRI and asked a series of questions. What the MRI
results demonstrated was that the scientist's brain knew the answer
a full six seconds before he was asked the question. The experiment
demonstrated that his mind had travelled forward in time, heard
the question there and his brain began to generate the answer before the researcher even asked it. The scientist was so disturbed by
the test that he literally had to sit down on the steps outside the
research facility in order to deal with the shock of travelling six seconds forward in time and then back again.

One sometimes gets the impression that mainstream reductionist science would prefer that human consciousness did not exist
to begin with. It's messy, you see, in a world dominated by charts,

graphs, measurements and predictable Newtonian equations. For this reason, the Transhumanist movement is actively seeking to destroy it. The human consciousness is too daunting and paradoxical to their methodologies and assumptions. Reductionist science is a beautiful system for evaluating, quantifying and understanding the material universe and human consciousness is beyond the pale of the material universe. Reductionist science simply refuses to acknowledge aspects of human consciousness which lie beyond the neural network nuts-and-bolts of the brain itself.

I come from the viewpoint of Natural Philosophy, and I accept that the world of the non-material—our imagination, dreams, artistic visions and intuition—exist as an expression of this observer behind the mind, and that this is no less important than the material world into which these five sense experiences happen to manifest. Modern notions of science and scientists date only to the nineteenth century. Prior to this, 'science' simply meant knowledge and the label of 'scientist', as such, did not exist. If this approach was good enough for Aristotle, Newton, Blake, Swedenborg, Jung and Da Vinci, then it is good enough for me. I value all of the mainstream research and study into how psychopathology comes about in a mechanistic sense, but I am equally aware of reductionist science's shortcomings in this matter.

Contemporary science has locked itself into a narrow bandwidth of 'acceptable' understanding and as a result a reductionist fundamentalism has taken root. To a degree this is understandable as some branches of religious fanaticism are endangering precious scientific knowledge in favour of a deity who created a world in six 24-hour work sessions. The study of the psychopath is a multi-faceted discipline, as the effects of being abused by a psychopath is as much a 'spiritual' trauma as a physiological, economic, emotional and psychological trauma. If you find this hard to believe then you have never been the victim of a psychopath.

When undertaking research into the mysteries of the mind, science tends to become almost exclusively bogged down in the land of genetic predisposition to the point where they can make absurdly arrogant statements along the lines that Darwinism is also a fact on other planets. Something is seriously wrong here. Is science too eager to put forth ideas such as our personality traits being completely derived from our DNA, and from this assumption proceed to 'prove' this without due consideration to the full nature of human consciousness? Is this really science, or is this a form of Genetic Napoleonic Code whereby our DNA makes us automatically guilty and we then have to prove our innocence? Such notions are a godsend to psychopaths in the court system and a potential goldmine for lawyers and court-appointed psychiatrists.

## REFUGE OF THE INCURABLES

Genuine psychopaths cannot be reformed, cured or even be made to understand the impact their pathology has upon others. They simply don't care, and see no reason why they should. No tampering with their brains in any laboratory has been shown to make empathic people out of psychopaths.

However—and this is something else we need to understand if we are to grasp just how potentially dangerous our many psychopathic leaders are—it has been demonstrated that everything from certain drugs to magnetic fields placed near the limbic regions of a normal person's brain somehow switches off their empathy. You can't make an empath out of a psychopath, but you can most certainly make a proto-psychopath out of an empathic individual.

This realisation becomes significant in relation to the plight of normal children with a parent who may be a full-blown psychopath. Otherwise normal children can tragically emulate their parent's psychopathic predatory lifestyle via a form of pathological imprinting. As mentioned previously, this unfortunate situation can often be reversed and these children can be eased back into normal society. The other loving, healthy parent can reform the negative traits in these children; these would be the negative and destructive anti-social habits picked up by being in the psychopath's company. Again, I am not talking about real psychopaths here, but children who had a psychopath role model.

My intention is certainly not to give out the message that this can be extended to full-blown, cradle-to-grave pure psychopaths, or to suggest they can be cured with extra love and understanding. To even attempt trying it is a death sentence for the target.

## CELLULAR PLASTICITY

There is no aspect of our physiology which does not have a neurological cause and effect. Biological consequences caused by thoughts generated in the brain are now becoming an accepted paradigm in modern neuroscience. Recent studies at The Center for Neurology and Genetics at Harvard Medical School have shown that our thoughts can literally turn our genes on and off.

The Neurology Department at Massachusetts General Hospital discovered that with every thought we reshape the neural network in our brain. This has also been shown to cause changes in gene activity. We build the structure of our brain and affect its functioning with each and every thought we have. I cannot stress enough that our brain will not waste valuable resources on creating a brain which the underlying consciousness has no use for. Again, if your thoughts are predatory, non-empathic, non-creative and lack deeper insights into the subtle contextual meaning of things, emotions and ideas, your brain and physiology will reflect this.

The pre-frontal cortex of your brain will show little or no activity in this region under an MRI scan. Likewise, your mirror neuron functions will be repressed and consequently you will eventually give people the creeps with your unnerving stare, unsettling energy, flip-flop personality and persona switching. All mental activity requires remodelling of synapses, including the manufacture of proteins for new genetic activity. This can be a good or a bad thing, depending on the intention behind the underlying thought processes.

## EPIGENETICS AND THE BAD SEED

Epigenetics is the study of changes in gene expression or cellular phenotypes caused by mechanisms other than changes in the underlying DNA sequence, including modifications to the genome that do not involve a change in the nucleotide sequence. In 2011, it was demonstrated that the methylation of mRNA has a critical role in human energy homeostasis (maintaining internal stability to stimuli that would tend to disturb its normal function), and this has finally been given credibility in the emerging science of Epigenetics. This field will in time be considered an important factor in explaining why psychopaths just seem to arrive in families out of nowhere and how they go on to develop a very different neurology than the rest of their families. Even more importantly, Epigenetics may also one day lead to understanding why people who have been abused by psychopaths are damaged to the point where many will remark that they 'have no idea who they even are any longer'. A common statement I hear from these people is, "I looked at myself in the mirror one day, and I did not recognise the person looking back at me."

A recent case study came to light concerning a very rare condition known as Rapid-Onset Obesity with Hypothalamic Dysfunction, Hypoventilation and Autonomic Dysregulation, or ROHHAD for short. This involved identical twins at the Children's Memorial Hospital in Chicago. Until this case—one of the twins had RO-HHAD while the other did not—it was a given fact that ROHHAD was 100% genetic in hereditary terms . The only conclusion to be garnished from this case suggests that Epigenetics, or the way our cells read our genes, may play a greater role than the actual genes themselves.

In short: identical twins have the same DNA sequence, but read their genes differently. Epigenetic changes turn certain genes on or off. Astounding stuff in terms of this undermining the 'all in the genes' mantra. However, obtaining funding for this research has been very difficult for researchers to procure. Why so difficult? Because the concept of Epigenetics completely undermines the obsession with locating every aspect of our humanity inside our DNA. Big Pharma and psychiatry have all their eggs in the DNA-only basket, and will not allow this lucrative gravy train of expensive medication treatments to be taken from them so readily.

## PROTECTING YOUR OWN DNA

It is worth reiterating this point: that if Epigenetics bring up concerns that if psychopaths can alter their own gene sequence, can they also alter their target's DNA as well, by just being around them? What about Epigenetics being a factor in targets being subjected to the psychopath's saliva, semen and vaginal fluids? A targeted individual in a relationship with a psychopath, or having been brutally and coldly discarded out of the blue by one, will be constantly bombarded with gaslighting and projection and this, likewise, must also modify the genetic activity in the target's brain.

The psychopaths are doing this on purpose, fully aware of the consequences. Since childhood, psychopaths have noticed that sudden, sadistic treatment disturbs and confuses other people. This is also when the psychopaths find they get a 'rush' from manipulating people and situations, not to mention the satisfaction gleaned from the destruction of the target's health, mental processes and self-confidence. The adult psychopath will have these sadistic skills customised to the level of a fine art, hence why getting away from psychopaths and staying away forever is even more vital for the health and safety of the target than had been previously asserted.

Brain states in both psychopathic and empathic people are a consequence of the underlying consciousness processing particular thoughts, so guard your consciousness at all costs. Psychopaths—from the ones in the street to the ones in advertising, in big business, and especially in government—are always trying to get in there and remodel your brain according to their agenda.

"My connection with people runs as deep as what they are able to do for me. When my friends are inconvenient, they are no longer my friends."

*- Dispatches from Psychopaths*

CHAPTER TWO
# THE DRAGON'S TAIL

In the correspondence I receive from people who have had the misfortune of encountering psychopaths 'up close and personal', comments regarding the eyes are commonly reported, although a riveting gaze is not common to all psychopaths which is why I did not include it among my Five Absolute Traits listed in *Puzzling People.*

Targets make references like 'his predatory lizard stare'—a piercing, intense and paradoxically 'dead' stare would be unleashed during periods of heightened emotions, or when the psychopath was on the verge of 'a win' and/or undergoing 'the rush'. This is indicative of the energy-harvesting that all psychopaths ultimately seek as a result of their predatory mind games and overall schemes. I also must point out that there are many non-psychopathic people who have intense staring eyes, but they are not psychopaths. 'Dead eyes' or a 'dead stare' can also be the result of a stroke or substance abuse in normal people. One aspect that sets the psychopathic stare apart is the looking into the target's eyes constantly during the initial targeting stage. When coupled with the psychopath's love-bombing and devious and manipulative use of language, it qualifies as hypnosis.

In some psychopaths, this stare has been noted as always being there in one form or another. These psychopaths sometimes camouflage their dead or soulless eyes by wearing sunglasses more than is required by weather conditions, or they will use narcotics usage or heavy chain-smoking as a cover story. Others invent tales of having had a stroke, or having been in an accident which resulted in damage to their optic nerves. In other psychopaths, 'the stare' would only manifest at times of anger, jealousy or thinking they had sneakily pulled off 'a win'. Often, this would be accompanied by a rapid smirk—think of The Joker's grin from the *Batman* stories—even when the psychopath was claiming to be saddened by the turn of events which they purposely created, manipulated and exploited for their own aims to begin with.

The pupils of the human eye most commonly dilate when we see something we desire. Often, sexual attraction brings this state on. But so does coveting a prized material object or other desired possession. An animal's eyes, on the other hand, get large and round when they are evaluating a target and about to leap in for the kill. This is the most common description of the classic 'psychopath stare' constantly reported by former targets. As one woman told me about her ex-psychopathic boss. "What was staring back at me wasn't human, not even close!"

I have witnessed this psychopathic feral stare close up; it is not something one forgets in a hurry. The stare can also frantically sweep from side to side in a wild-eyed response to certain exterior stimuli which the psychopath is evaluating. In the study *Pupil Dilation During Visual Target Detection* in the August 2010 *Journal of Vision*, it was outlined how predatory pupil dilation in response to target detection happens deep in the brain stem in a region called the reptilian complex—or the R-Complex. This is among the most ancient parts of the human brain and is the location of basic instincts and avoidances.

The psychopathic stare is also an excellent example of the 'Horses for courses' analogy I gave earlier. They have a predator's consciousness and this in turn, via complex cellular plasticity, generates for them the brain they need in life. They simply get right down to business. Once we are aware of why and how this happens, we—along with recognising the other traits and behaviours—then become aware that we are in fact dealing with a full-blown psychopath. A proto-psychopath would not have such traits as the 'reptilian stare'.

Upon the realisation of what we have been dealing with all along, as we gaze into the ruthless energy-harvesting eyes staring back at us, we then begin to implement the NO CONTACT EVER AGAIN strategy to deal with them. Psychopaths are so hardwired towards your exploitation and destruction that you have no choice but to build a wall for all eternity between you and them.

With its evolutionary throwback assemblage of neuro-transmitters, various heavy metals and glyco-fibers, the The R-Complex is also, interestingly enough, the colour blue (blue bloods?) from being tinted with high doses of melanin. This early part of the evolutionary human brain controls how we perceive and respond to danger along with genetic survival and the 'kill or be killed' instinct. When the brain becomes aware of such a threat or sexual opportunity, the amygdala (which can be thought of as the gear box of the brain) and limbic system transmit specific signals (though it is still not completely understood from where these impulses manifest) to the R-Complex. This floods the brain with the stress hormone norepinephrine for implementing high states of vigilance.

This leads the hyperactive R-Complex found in psychopaths to provide a wide open highway for the reptilian signals to kick into full psychopathic mode. This is when we get to see the real smirking predator and not the bespoke custom-tailored persona that the psychopath has invented to work their specific target.

This is why psychopaths lack any kind of introspection or pause for thought, which is assumed to be processed in the gap between the two halves between the brain's right and left hemispheres. The septum pellucidum, located in the mid-line of the brain, is associated with septo-optic dysplasia. This may result in problems with vision, coordination, and intelligence. Loss of or damage to the septum pellucidum has been used as proof that pathology is a result of brain damage, yet no conclusive proof has shown it to be the cause of psychopathy as studies involving psychopaths' brains have also shown perfectly intact and functional septum pellucidum.

The psychopath gains 'a rush' or a sense of excitement when going from nought to ninety in full predatory mode, with the R-Complex acting like a turbo-charged, norepinephrine-injection engine. It's just all business with these types. They know exactly what they are doing and you'll eventually find out one way or another what they really were all along. It most certainly wasn't what they promised you at the start.

Equally important in the case of psychopathy are the effects on the septum oxytocin receptors. Research has shown that suppressed neural development in this region leads to promiscuous sexuality in mammals. When the hyperactive reptilian part of the psychopath's brain receives a threat signal, the repressed septum is not able to minimise this and this in turn leads to the 'reptilian stare' commonly seen in psychopaths.

Due to the psychopath's under-developed septum pellucidum, synesthesia is common. Synesthesia is a condition in which one sense (for example, hearing) is simultaneously perceived as though it were one or more additional senses such as sight. Another form of synesthesia joins objects such as letters, shapes, numbers or people's names with a sensory perception such as smell, colour or flavour. For example, a person with synesthesia may see certain colours when listening to a certain song on the radio. However, it should be noted that most people who have synesthesia are not psychopaths.

Other anomalies which have been observed in psychopaths' brains that are worth inclusion in this section but as yet have not been conclusively validated, are:

An interrupted uncinate fasciculus—which is between the limbic system and the frontal lobes. The uncinate fasciculus feeds conduits directly into the reward circuits of the brain, the psychopath becomes addicted to praise, sexual orgasm, drugs and being the centre of attention.

A hyperactive striatum constantly craving dopamine, suggesting hypersensitivity to reward circuits of the brain. An addiction to constant pleasure and pathologically seeking it out. Most commonly manifested in the constant need to manipulate and control others by having targets fall in love with them or gain their total devotion, just to see if the psychopath can 'pull it off' before de-valuing and discarding them for another target.

## PSYCHOPATHS AND SPEECH

One of the main reasons I am highly optimistic that we will once and for all come to terms with the danger posed by psychopathology upon society is the fact that psychopaths are so very similar in how their pathology manifests. Regardless of ethnicity, social status or level of education, psychopaths have a similar underlying nature and a collection of predictable behavioural traits common to all.

One of these traits is how they process and use language. Anyone who has been in a close relationship with a psychopath will attest to their unusual, almost scripted use of language and how they seem to implement the same script over and over again, as well as the manner in which they can contradict themselves within the same sentence. They tend to pause during questioning in order to invent yet another cover story and place special emphasis upon deliver-ing a 'word salad' to bewilder and disorientate the listener. When in a debate or argument, they deflect by putting the other person in a position of having to defend their humanity, intellect or ethics before the subject at hand can even be discussed—which it never is, as the psychopath ignores the person who is fruitlessly trying to communicate with them.

Psychopaths also tend to perform idiosyncratic vocal manner-isms, such as humming, whistling, making and/or speaking in strange, obnoxious or 'cartoon style' voices to a far greater degree than a non-psychopath would. It is often one of the things many targets recall from their past relationship with a psychopath. This has also been noted for some time among researchers and criminal psychologists. There are most certainly distinctive characteristics in how psychopaths use speech and this has now been scientifically determined for the first time using computers.

One has to wonder why it took so long for this research to be un-dertaken; it would seem that it should have been carried out long before now considering the vast repository of recorded interviews, interrogations and court statements made by psychopaths over the decades. As is the case with so much of the research into psychopathology, the basic groundwork into simply identifying these predators tends to take second place to complex clinical studies, genetic and neurological research.

In October 2011, a new study was published which finally gave validation to how psychopaths use language in a way very different to the rest of the population. Fourteen psychopaths were identified during interviews with fifty-two convicted murderers by Jeffrey Hancock, the lead researcher and an associate professor in Communications at Cornell University. Please bear in mind that although this research—like nearly all such studies—was undertaken on convicted criminal psychopaths, the findings are equally applicable to your psychopathic ex-spouse or the psychopath bully at work. You will, if you think back, find the results of Hancock and his research team also resonate deeply with your own experiences in a relationship with a psychopath.

The researchers asked the subjects to describe their crimes in detail; specialised software programs were then used to analyse their use of words and phrasing. It was discovered that the psychopaths spoke in terms of cause-and-effect when describing their crimes, focusing their rationale on basic needs, such as food, drink and money.

This is interesting for me, as it validates the basic premise laid out in my previous book, that psychopaths are 'all business'—no matter what the business is—from marriage to murder to hostile corporate takeover. The endgame, in terms of the psychopaths' needs and desires, is the only consideration. The personal, psychological, and emotional impact on targets are never an issue with the psychopath. Likewise, concepts such as ethics and compassion are looked upon by psychopaths as obstacles to their objectives.

## LEXICON OF THE DAMNED

The use of speaking in the past tense is an excellent indicator of psychological detachment (see: transitional psychopaths/persona switching), and it was found that psychopaths used it more than the present tense when compared with the non-psychopaths being interviewed in the same survey, as if another version of them was responsible and not the one being interviewed. It's as though a previous persona had committed the crimes and the present version of them are simply not accountable for their past actions. There is no current admission of guilt. They will say, 'I am not a rapist. I was a rapist when I raped that girl, but I am not a rapist now, because I am not currently raping her…'

Psychopaths appear to have a very different concept of time than other people, as though they live exclusively within the here and now and are entirely dependent upon monitoring a watch or a clock in order for them to be able to place themselves definitively into chronology. I have noticed that all psychopaths are very watch-bound. They constantly monitor time, yet seem to demonstrate a lack of understanding of what time is in terms of how the rest of us experience it.

Psychopaths can return after destroying your life and expect to just pick up again from the moment they left off as if nothing happened in between, even though many years may have passed. They also have an obsession with ritual and recalling certain dates of their past 'wins'.

The human brain has been shown to function in a different space-time than the reality around it. One theory that may explain this is that the brain and nervous system must do this or else we would not be able to grasp the reality we are in. It needs time (literally) to process the information from our five senses, as time does not exist as a universal law or constant. For whatever reason, psychopaths have difficulty locking into this and need constant checking of the time of day. This is also why they can vanish for hours on end and seem to have no concept of just how much time has passed.

The research also uncovered a greater use of disfluencies among psychopathic speech. This being the 'ehs', 'uhs' and 'ums' that interrupt a conversation. Disfluencies indicate that the speaker needs some time to think about what they are saying. With psychopaths, the 'ehs' and 'ums' are really about buying time to put a mask of social sanity on top of their underlying pathology. It is perhaps one of the first predatory skills they develop as children.

It was also discovered that psychopaths' language contained more subordinating conjunctions—'because' and 'so that'—associated with cause-and-effect statements. This indicates once again that there is nothing random about the intentions of carrying out their actions as the logical consequence of pre-planning and deceit.

It was also revealed that psychopaths used double the number of words relating to basic survival requirements and self-preservation, including eating, drinking and accessing financial opportunities and resources. Further, it was shown that when discussing concepts such as family, relationships, spirituality and creativity, psychopaths only considered such matters in terms of their own self-preservation, such as the wealth and net worth of parents, siblings and so on. I myself recall when being in the company of a psychopath who found out one of his parents was terminally ill made a specific note of what a catch the surviving parent would be for an opportunistic suitor. This was all they made reference to—the profound loss of a parent or of one of his parents losing their long-term marital partner wasn't even considered.

## THE PSYCHOPATH'S CHEMICAL WARFARE

The psychopath reads their subjects like a book in the early days, and subsequently the target is unknowingly 'groomed' according to the specific requirements of the target's personality/needs—in much the same way a paedophile will win the trust and admiration of the child they wish to eventually rape. As soon as the psychopath has compiled this required dossier on the current target and their wants, needs, desires, shortcomings, failings, along with their negative and positive attributes, the psychopath thus commences to deploy the weapon they have spent an entire lifetime perfecting: the chemical assault on the physiology of their potential targets—literally, to create a zombie version of what these people once were, and then make them dependent upon the chemistry of the psychopath.

Indeed, it is very typical of a psychopath to continually make remarks such as, 'you and I have such similar chemistry…' or 'we share the same energy…' from the very start when they are working a target. This is compounded by endless flattery gushingly bestowed. These targets are being love-bombed with strategic precision; matters not if this is in a romantic relationship or via a cult leader or a politician whose spin doctors have millions chanting a repetitive phrase over and over again—you are being turned into an addict. The substance you are being addicted to is part of the chemical warfare being waged upon you by the predator and it is only understandable that you would confuse it with genuine love and bonding.

What is really happening is a chemical disturbance created within the individual's physiology which has been maliciously and perfectly crafted by the psychopath. Targets are not even bonding with actual psychopaths, either—but with the feelings and sensations unleashed inside them by the skilful psychopath. What you became enchanted with was a bespoke persona the psychopath designed to manipulate you for their purposes. In reality, the target is as much in love and in the same way as a heroin junkie is in love with the needle.

It matters not how astute or streetwise and mature the target happens to be. Their level of education, intelligence and instinctual, intuitive boundaries will have been bypassed as they are caught in the psychopath's web of deceit and love-bombing and often with shocking rapidity. Before you realise it you can find yourself discussing wedding plans with this person whom you know as much about as your car mechanic or your hair stylist.

A chemical cocktail in the form of romantic dinners, weekend rendezvous, avalanches of love letters, cards, romantic gestures, promises, lavish gifts and intensive sex is administered during the early idealisation and targeting stage of a relationship with a psychopath. The targets are not lovesick fools who are smitten by opportunist playboys or vamps; they are prey to emotional and psychological terrorism.

Once out of these psychopathic relationships, targets suffer from the same levels of Post Traumatic Stress Disorder as a returned front-line combat veteran or prisoners of war. These after effects are very real, and until recent times, targets remained silent or, if they spoke, their pain was trivialised by society. This carefully camouflaged emotional and psychological terrorism is constantly taking place in communities all across this planet; profound pain caused by the four percent of the population that are psychopathic mutations upon the ninety-six percent of the overwhelmingly empathic population. One can only imagine how many suicides were a result of encounters with psychopaths. We are dealing with a very real stealth genocide implemented with murder-by-suicide—the everyday psychopath's main method of killing others. It is terrorism—the real kind.

One American female psychopath named Bobbi Ann Finley—dubbed the 'Military Mistress' after she married at least fourteen American soldiers after targeting, manipulating, conning and stealing up to $100,000 each from each of these men—was even referred to as a 'homegrown terrorist' in court by her former targets. Finley—who, just going by her demeanour and general body language, is the poster woman for the classic 'white trash' end of the female psychopathic spectrum—had nine children with as many men, before taking their money and leaving them in financial ruin and emotional despair.

In a jailhouse interview with ABC television programme *20/20*, Finley admitted that she may have destroyed lives, but she claimed she was also a victim who has had a hard upbringing. Throughout the interview she constantly smirks and her pupils rapidly dilate. You can also set your watch by how predictably a psychopath 'defends' their actions and never admits any culpability nor ever issues a sincere apology. She went on to state during the interview that she wasn't running a con. Anyone who has ever encountered a psychopath will hear such platitudes over and over again, at first to win your pity, and later to justify their actions after you are disposed of and they have moved on.

"I wanted protection, the protection that I should have had growing up. I married these guys I couldn't love. In many of the cases, you look and you started out and you get married and you're thinking, 'Oh, I'm going to live happily ever after,' and then you realise it was a mistake."

For almost two decades, Bobbi Ann Finley preyed like a feral animal on various military bases (these days psychopaths prefer Internet message boards, on-line social networking and dating sites) where she lied to servicemen, claiming to be a wealthy heiress, the daughter of a general or an injured veteran about to get a large pay-out. Her targets all expressed the same story upon initially encountering her: that she appeared to be charming, sexy, smart, funny, witty, and beautiful. In every case, right after the wedding things would quickly change; with money disappearing from their accounts, the honeymoon period was over as quickly as it had begun. After they were devalued and discarded, many of these men discovered that Finley had a history of fraud and bigamy, and had given birth to children and never told the fathers.

In most cases, these men were too embarrassed to tell anyone how easily they had been manipulated by this woman. It was usually the concerned relatives and friends who ran background checks on Finley and discovered who she really was—or wasn't. As is the case with many developing psychopathic relationships, a close friend or relative will be the one who first notices the red flags that are missed or ignored by the intoxicated target when the idealisation stage is in full swing.

As incredible as the Bobbi Ann Finley saga is, what is most telling in all this is how these men fell madly in love with a woman who was most certainly not traditionally beautiful in terms of what society would decree attractive in a modern Western female. All these men spoke of how 'beautiful' she was to them upon first meeting, and how quickly they fell in love with her. This serves to demonstrate—with the correct knowledge and sense of discipline to effectively mind control the target—how an adept and driven psychopath can distort the reality of the target to make them believe literally anything. Once you have been locked onto as a psychopath's target you cannot even trust your own eyes.

An old and dear male friend of mine who was in a long-term relationship with a female psychopath told me that during the height of the relationship with this woman, he literally believed at the time that she was the most beautiful woman who ever lived. Having known this woman myself I would have to say she was attractive and certainly sexually appealing in a 'slutty' manner of speaking. She eventually dumped my friend; over the course of a twelve-hour period she completely and unexpectedly 'fell in love' with a man she met at a nightclub. He showed me a photo he had taken of her when they were about two years into their relationship. In the photo she looked disturbingly ghoulish and almost like her face was hanging off her skull.

My friend had taken the photograph of her waiting for him through the window of a restaurant while she was not looking and had no idea why he'd done so. When he entered the restaurant and she caught sight of him, in the words of my friend, "She literally shape-shifted! Her entire face changed to become the woman I was madly in love with." This persona-switching aspect of the psychopath has been well documented by myself and others. It is one of the early red flags noticed by targets.

Sometimes this chemical alteration of the target's sense of emotional and psychological perception can also be quite literal—as in targets having been drugged with medications and other substances. It is not uncommon for female psychopaths to slip a date-rape cocktail of Viagra and Ecstasy into the drink of a man with whom she is socialising while he goes to the toilet.

This will make her seduction much easier as the male target will not only be more 'loving' and submissive to her suggestion due to the Ecstasy—with its induced euphoria, sense of intimacy and increased self-confidence—but also, with the Viagra he will maintain a sustained erection for the sexual encounter afterwards, no matter how much alcohol he has had to drink. The male target is then confusing an Ecstasy high and Viagra arousal with a meaningful emotional and physical attraction to the female psychopath. On the other hand, male psychopaths, particularly ones who are not very attractive to the individuals they are targeting, will administer date-rape drugs to female and other male homosexual targets.

## OXYTOCIN

Due to the nature of the male aspect of human sexual intercourse, the psychopathic phallus directly delivers his own organic drug: oxytocin. Known as the 'love drug', oxytocin (Greek ὠκυτοκίνη, ōkytokínē, 'quick labour') is a hormone found in all mammals which performs the function of a neuromodulator in the brain. In women, it is manufactured in large amounts during stimulation of the nipples, and in terms of the predatory male psychopath, manipulating female targets via orgasm, social recognition and bonding. More crucially for psychopathic mind-controlling purposes, oxytocin is also related to anxiety in women.

This is one of the reasons why male psychopaths keep their targets in a state of fear and insecurity—much like our psychopathic leaders in politics do to the entire society. It makes control and dependency on the psychopath easier to achieve and maintain. Newspapers are filled with scare stories about all the dangers possible and potential—real and imagined. This makes the readership more loyal, as they come to find a strange sort of comforting dependency upon the editorial pages. 'No news is good news' is a very powerful and deep statement when you begin to think about it in the context of how much of our behaviour is governed by chemical changes brought about by our emotional states.

These effects of oxytocin are mediated by protein-coupled receptors in the brain, evoking feelings of contentment, reduction in anxiety, and feelings of calmness and security around mates. This is what male psychopaths have skilfully developed to control their female targets since they first became sexually active in their early teens. It has now been determined that there is a powerful and profound correlation between oxytocin with human bonding.

All this leads to implementing inhibition within the brain partitions generally associated with psychological modification, fear, and anxiety—thus allowing female orgasm to occur more frequently and intensely. This is what has been done to the female target of the psychopath: she will constantly be indulged with flattery, love-bombing, paperback novel style romantic performances and high-intensity sex sessions. The female victim has then been successfully chemically altered by the psychopath, whereby she is now a highly-addicted junkie of the psychopath's brain chemistry-altering sleight-of-hand.

However, this is all a sham. There is no love. There is no romance. There are no 'soul mates' in this malignant coupling and pathological dependency.

### THE LOVING-REJECTION MIND CONTROL CYCLE

What happens next is the unleashing of the main purpose of the psychopath's 'soul mate' performance that was planned from the instant they took notice of the potential target—this being the loving-rejection-loving-rejection cycle. This is designed to create the perfect mind-control slave the psychopath wanted all along. The target will then be entering into what may well be the most significant, traumatic, and life-altering situation they will ever experience in their entire lives. A situation so personally convulsive that it will literally tear them to shreds psychologically and emotionally, right to the very depths of their soul. They will never be the same person again.

Due to the psychopath's obsession with ritual, such as using the same pet-names for targets from relationship to relationship, or putting obsessive symbolism on dates and times where they relive the rush of having pulled off one of their past 'wins', the psychopath is also a highly predictable predator. Since they are incapable of true creativity, they need ritual. They can only cunningly improvise based on tried and tested methods they have developed since childhood.

This is also why psychopaths tend to seek out government job-for-life employment or join Freemasonic organisations and other fraternities. They can even become Catholic priests. The magical rites of the mass are a very powerful ritual of mind-control which is subsequently destroying the convictions of the genuinely faithful within the Church of Rome. Naturally, the cultural aspect of the society and class system into which the psychopath is born will also supply them with a certain angle of attack they can play off and manipulate.

For instance, psychopaths within the Sicilian and Italian-American communities will aspire to join the Mafia and then wreak havoc upon their own kind (in reality, these 'goodfellas' are not even kin to other humans let alone anyone else of Italian extraction). Psychopaths become Mafiosi not only for the sense of power it provides, but for the ritualistic nature of the Mafia. People often forget that at its very core the Mafia is a Freemansonic-style organisation. La Cosa Nostra, with its culture of 'made men', 'burning of the saints' and with animal sacrifice and ritual murder proves most appealing to a psychopath, even more than any ancillary benefits derived from extortion and protection rackets.

This is also one of the reasons why psychopaths make up stories about being members of or connected to powerful/influential institutions and organisations; it feeds their sense of grandiosity and narcissism. Many of these psychopaths become politicians for this very reason alone. However, the key marker in all this is the predictable and ritualistic nature of the psychopath. Be it in a personal relationship, at the workplace, or running a country—they follow very specific predatory pathways.

This also gives rise to one of the Five Absolute Traits of every psychopath on the planet which I outlined in *Puzzling People*: Missing or Cryptic Past Histories. The reason for this is that people who are fully aware of a psychopath's past will easily be able to predict the psychopath's future; it is for this reason they strive to obfuscate, prevaricate and outright lie about their pasts. In the eyes of others the psychopath very often has missing years with little or no explanation for it, or perhaps an explanation for their past that comes off as contradictory. There is nothing inside the psychopath other than the usual pernicious, pathological ritualistic cycles repeated over and over again.

The psychopath always implements more or less the same modus operandi on targets, as they have to seek out a specific type of individual or organisation to target and manipulate over and over again. Prior to the current explosion of knowledge about psychopathology which is now sweeping across the globe, they enjoyed remarkable and essentially unrestricted success. Michael Woodworth, a psychologist specialising in psychopathy at the University of British Columbia, stated during a press conference in New York in October 2011 what interviewing psychopaths is like; "You can spend two or three hours and come out feeling like you have been hypnotized."

When the psychopath begins their chemical warfare upon a carefully selected target, they are placing a consciousness parasite inside that person's psyche. Once this parasite begins to feed upon the target's psychology, it can cause even the most sensible person to behave in ways they would never have believed possible.

*Katie's Story*

"I met this person who I have now come to realize is an emotionally manipulative psychopath when were both teenagers. We attended school together from the seventh grade all through high school, but were just classmates and never really close friends. I remembered him as being nice, shy and a little nerdy. Fast-forward twenty eight years and like many others these days we re-connected on Facebook.

For several months we were just casual friends and didn't interact any differently with each other than we did with casual Facebookers. Looking back though, and knowing what I know now, he was slowly getting to know me better and I didn't have my guard up, because it never occurred to me I needed to.

At some point I realized he was flirting with me and I have to admit, I enjoyed it. I was flattered by the attention. Anyway, one thing led to another and before you know it, the 'innocent' flirting escalated into major flirting. He started 'poking' me constantly. He sent me romantic 'Hearts,' 'Hugs' and eventually 'Kisses' every day with sweet personal messages of how gorgeous and sexy he thought I was. How much he liked my body and that he'd had a crush on me all through school. He was always complimenting me, making me feel special, and beautiful. He also started posting love songs on his Facebook page for me, which I thought was so romantic.

We started talking on the phone and during those initial conversations, I remember my face literally hurting from smiling so much. I felt like a teenager again with all the butterflies, hormones and feelings of infatuation that go along with that. It was intoxicating and we ended up having a long-distance, emotional and sexual cyber affair. I couldn't eat or sleep because of the constant adrenaline rush I felt from all of this and thinking about him all the time. Within six weeks of when the flirting really escalated, I found myself taking a trip to visit family and friends where he lives (where we're both from), and we met up and the affair became physical at that point.

Now, you would think that the reality of that first meeting would not live up to the fantasy that had been building for weeks between us. Isn't that what they always say? I even said it to him several times beforehand. Well, not only did the reality live up to the fantasy, it surpassed it! That's because I had been divulging all my secrets, everything about myself, and pouring my heart out to him over the previous weeks. *Talk to me,* he said. I had unwittingly given him the road map and key to my heart, mind, body and soul—and he studied me well. He was exactly the kind of man and lover I had always wanted and been looking for. I had never been with someone so romantic, tender and affectionate. The kind of stuff you only read about in fairytales.

That should have been a big red flag, but I was too busy being swept off my feet and ignored it. He made sure to point out that my life would be empty without him afterwards—that nobody would ever be able to give me what he did. And that's certainly the way it felt. I had never before experienced the kind of chemistry, intimacy and passion with anyone else like I had with him. He was the 'missing puzzle piece.' Yes, we even talked about that.

Having to return home and be apart from him was painful and I missed him constantly. We talked on the phone literally all day long on days I didn't have to work. He has the kind of job where he can talk on the phone at the same time, so we would go about our daily lives 'together' on the phone while we did other things. And all these phone conversations were on top of Facebook interaction, emails, and texting. On days I had to work, he would call every morning at the same time just to hear my voice and leave a sweet message. Even though I couldn't answer, I came to expect and love those daily calls. Just feeling my cell phone go off in my pocket made me smile, knowing it was him and that he was thinking of me. There was never a day we didn't talk on the phone and communicate in some other way as well.

Within a very short time, he told me he loved me. I wanted nothing more than to be with him and soon found myself taking another trip to see him. That weekend was the most romantic memory I have of our relationship. Everything was perfect. We spent four days and nights together and it was heartbreaking to leave. We didn't know how long we could continue, being long-distance like we were, and whether or not we would ever see each other again. After I returned home, we continued to get closer and he said he not only loved me, he was IN love with me. He led me to believe I was 'The One,' the 'Love of his Life.' We talked about having a future together. He said and did everything 'right' until I fell head-over-heels in love with him and started talking about moving there to be with him.

Then he started pulling away a little bit at a time, for no apparent reason. It started with little things, that separately would not have meant so much, but added up together, made me question his feelings for me. The Hearts, Hugs & Kisses that he had sent daily became fewer and farther between. Sometimes they were just texts, but gone were the terms of endearment. He also stopped interacting with me as much on Facebook. He went from commenting on my posts constantly and 'liking' just about everything, to rarely, and then never at all. Even my friends noticed and were wondering if we were still in a relationship.

At the same time he started interacting more and more with other women 'friends.' He stopped telling me he loved me when we hung up the phone. At first he would only say it in response to me saying it first, and eventually not even then. Emails that used to each be individually answered in complete paragraphs, became lumped together so that only a few would be acknowledged with brief, monosyllabic words and incomplete sentences. Texts I sent that were not responded to. Deleting comments I made on his FB page about his profile pictures, but leaving other women's comments up. When I questioned him on these various changes I noticed in him, he accused me of being too demanding. The next six months became a constant roller coaster of mind games, mixed messages, baffling hot and cold behavior, the silent treatment, gaslighting (as I now understand it), and lying.

His entire Facebook persona changed from what it had been when we first started interacting. He went from this sweet, church-going, family-guy going through a divorce from a terrible marriage, to a ladies' man leading the bachelor life. He would flirt with other women on Facebook, while practically ignoring me. He would go out to bars or parties on weekends and then post outrageous stories of escapades that supposedly took place involving women coming on to him. I say supposedly, because later on I learned how much he lied about everything.

Every time I reached my limit and tried to break things off, he would come chasing after me again with all the sweet words and sending me love songs to reel me back in. I don't know how many times this happened but it got to the point I was always waiting for the other shoe to drop. I started to dread weekends when he would basically 'put me on a shelf,' ignoring me and giving me the silent treatment. Wondering what he was doing and who he was with. Waiting for some dreaded post to show up on my Facebook wall.

In spite of all that, I kept trying to make the relationship work because I couldn't imagine my life without him at that point. On my third visit to see him, I planned a trip around his birthday in October, when he also had vacation time. I remember him not seeming all that excited by my arrival like he had been for the previous visits. A week before I was to leave, after I had already purchased airline tickets, he sent my best friend (also a mutual friend) a text saying he felt he should call things off and end it. She told him to man-up and let me know before I flew all the way out there to be blind-sided, if that's the way he felt.

A couple days went by and he didn't say anything, so as I was happily packing and preparing to leave, my friend ended up telling me herself and even forwarded me the text. I was stunned and completely heartbroken. I felt he basically sent her to do his dirty work and I told him so. When I spoke with him, he denied what he wrote and said we had misinterpreted what he meant and he was 'just venting.' I had the text in front of me and there was no way to misinterpret him saying it—it was just too much trouble for him to say it to my face.

So I flew out there anyway to see my friends, not knowing what was going to happen once I got there. We had continued communicating throughout the prior week, again with the hot and cold mixed messages from him. My first night in town, I was talking to him on the phone and asked if I was going to see him the next day. I told him I needed a definite time to plan my day or to forget it. When my friends saw the mind games he was playing, they told me to ignore him and quit talking to him. I left him a voicemail that said I was changing my ticket and returning early since he didn't want to see me. Well, true to form, when I did that, he couldn't track me down fast enough. Numerous phone calls, text messages, apologies, *I love you, please don't go,* etc.

This went on all week. Seeing him one day and having amazing sex, but wondering if it would be the last time. At one point he said, *What if we never talk again after you leave, are you going to be OK with that?* Of course I wasn't OK with that. On my second to last night there, he broke it off with me and said we would never talk again. He sat there emotionally detached and watched me sob hysterically, bawling my eyes out for I don't know how long.

Then the text messaging and phone calls started again. *I don't want this, I'm sorry... I'm already sad and missing talking to you on the phone every day. I want to have a future with you.. I love you...* I ignored several calls and texts before finally answering. It was my last day there and he wanted to take me to get something to eat. I told him, no, I already had plans with my friends. Later on that evening, as my friends and I are hanging out in the backyard, he shows up unannounced. He played broken-hearted. Gave me an 'I love you' little teddy bear and a card—giving me false hope, and reeled me back in again.

I returned home, things were fine for a few days, but then started going downhill again. It wasn't even a roller coaster anymore with highs and lows, but a continuous downward spiral over the next three weeks. I tried to break things off again and quit talking to him, but that only lasted a few days. Every day I didn't talk to him only got worse, not better. I still didn't have any idea of what I was really dealing with then. I was just very confused and trying to figure it all out. I was still clinging to the memory of the first six months and trying desperately to get back there.

I had to go back out there in December for a wedding. Somehow the relationship had 'improved' in between this time by returning to a roller coaster instead of a steady downward spiral. I know now that he was just stringing me along until he found my replacement. I not only went for the wedding, but stayed for the entire month and through the holidays to spend them with him. The first couple weeks of that trip were pretty good, except for his mind games and drama that had become a regular part of our dynamic. I had been making plans and trying to do everything I could to move out there to be with him earlier in the year, but then he started pulling away. He took me to a New Year's Eve party where I didn't know anyone, and basically ignored me the whole time. At that point, it was obvious I wasn't very happy.

Later he pointed this out to me, told me I was pessimis-
tic—before him I was very happy and positive. I used to be
a lot of fun and the life of the party, but he sucked the life
out of me. I broke it off with him AGAIN after he humiliated me at the New Year's Eve party, but on New Year's
Day and throughout that night, he continued calling me. At
some point though, as was typical, I found myself wanting
to believe he still cared about me. He was persistent and
managed to reel me back in for another round. The last
two days of my trip, things were good between us again.
That's always the way it was. A roller coaster of incredible
highs with unbelievable lows, but things ended on a good
note. And that's exactly what he wanted. He wanted things
to end on his terms, not mine. To leave me with a positive
memory, false hope, and wanting more. I was already planning my next visit, and he already knew it was the last time
he would ever see me.

Four weeks later, he dumped me 'overnight' when a
former girlfriend of over 25 years ago reappeared in his
life and they immediately picked up where they left off. He
let me know by posting it all over Facebook. Pictures of
the two of them kissing and holding each other at a party,
along with status updates that were heartbreaking to me.
He pretty much announced to all our mutual friends this
was his new girlfriend. It wasn't enough that he broke my
heart by dumping me the way he did, he had to crush me
in the process.

He had already de-friended me so I couldn't see what he
was posting. How my replacement was the life of the party
and how he slept with her that same night. On the anniversary of the exact same date that we had consummated our
relationship just one year before. He changed his profile
picture on Facebook to one of the two of them, along with
his relationship status within the following week. Telling
her how special and gorgeous she was, calling her all the
pet names he used to say to me. He started sending her
the same Hearts and posting the same love songs to her.
He even cleaned up his page to change his playboy, ladies'

man image, to that of a church-going, dedicated, one-woman man who had found 'The One.'

I realized in horror that ALL of it, EVERYTHING, the ENTIRE RELATIONSHIP from the very beginning had been ONE BIG LIE! NONE OF IT was real! Devastation doesn't even begin to describe it. I was annihilated. I have never been so hurt by anything or anyone in my entire life. For several days I couldn't eat or sleep and was literally sweating from every pore of my body. I couldn't wrap my head around the idea that someone could be so sadistic and intentionally play someone else like that.

Even though he had a new girlfriend, whom he was now displaying as the 'love of his life,' he kept calling and texting me for the next several weeks, even calling me 'sweetie'! When I didn't answer, he left voice mails saying he enjoyed talking to me and missed me, because I had been such an important part of his life for over a year. I would ignore him for a few days, but he would eventually wear me down, if only to fight with him some more. He knew exactly which buttons to push to make me respond. He only wanted to keep me around as a 'friend' to continue torturing me—to talk about the new woman and the previous woman.

On the very last day I spoke to him, he wanted to know when I was coming back for my next visit. I said I didn't know, that I wouldn't tell him anyway, and that I would never be able to see him again. He had the audacity to say, 'Oh, I'll know when you're here. You'll let me know.'

The final text I received from him told me to never contact him in any way, shape or form. No phone calls, texts, or emails. I sent one more text telling him I hadn't been out to visit since the last time I saw him, and only said that to see his reaction, which was interesting to say the least. I told him not to worry, it would be the last he would ever hear from me, because he was dead to me now.

He responded with, *How could you not know it was over? I was ready for a new chapter in my life.*

After I read *Puzzling People* I discovered that the 'new chapter in their life' is a classic line used by psychopaths to try and justify their treatment of others as they invent a new persona to work their new target. I had sensed he was looking for a replacement for a couple of months and was stringing me along.

I wrote him a letter about it back in November, but he of course denied that any of it was true. On the day before he officially announced my replacement, he told me he wasn't interested in anyone else and that he was going to that party alone. He completely set me up. It's been over eight months since he discarded and humiliated me so brutally and painfully. I have made significant progress, but I am still trying to heal and put the pieces of my life back together. I have suffered from major anxiety and depression, and find that I am now hyper-vigilant and startle very easily. I am not the same person I was before I met him—this experience has forever changed me.

I lost myself in that relationship and became someone I didn't even recognize at the end. A shell of my former self. I had never in my life allowed anyone to treat me so badly and then gone back for more. Some of the things I did were crazy! Things I would normally never do or think I was even capable of.

He was slowly making me insane. I had always been very strong-willed and never anybody's doormat. I'm not the type to settle for mere crumbs from someone. Where did my pride go? What happened to my backbone? The more I stood up for myself, the more he used it against me and punished me. Sometimes I wonder if I will ever fully recover.

It takes about two years to detox from the effects of having been infected by the psychopathic consciousness parasite and NO CONTACT EVER AGAIN (NCEA) is the key to this. Recovery does indeed happen, and you will regain your life and your health once more. Having knowledge of psychopaths and how they operate is a huge advantage towards speeding up recovery from the trauma. Most people who have had a psychopath pass through their lives and are unaware of what was done to them can sometimes spend decades attempting to understand just what happened.

Many even blame themselves for what took place in order to come to some kind of closure. Constantly trying to rationalise how such and such person could have been apparently so loving and supportive one minute and then instantly become heartless and cold the next by demonstrating a complete turnaround in their personality—suddenly unveiling an emotionally apathetic, smug, arrogant, indignant, manipulative, heartless stranger before them; an impostor of the comrade or soulmate you trusted with everything. They move on without a care in the world, dismissing you as though you never existed.

There is indeed something powerful, healing and restorative when the realisation that one was dealing with a psychopath all along finally hits home. This is when the noetic epiphany of some primal truth becomes apparent and one regains that native wisdom our modern culture and education systems have indoctrinated out of us.

As knowledge and awareness of the predatory nature and tactics of the socialised psychopath gain a foothold among the general population, this will help towards limiting and cutting off the hunting grounds. Even so, for recovering targets, it is a long, hard road to full recovery. Recovery not only happens in time, but it is very much a valuable life lesson when one looks back upon the experience.

Katie's testimony above demonstrates how in the early days psychopaths do everything to try and pretend they are just like their current target. In her case, the pathologically-driven sycophant frantically clicking Katie's Facebook 'Like' button, being the same demented parasitic parrot they all are during the idealising stage of their pathology. The psychopath always has the same tastes, values, viewpoints and interests as the target they are trying to bond with. They order the same food and drinks as you do when you both go out. They constantly quiz you about your sexual desires/fantasies so they can fulfil them. You get the 'soulmate' treatment to a T.

Often when the target has been instantly and brutally disposed of, the chemical crash they endure will cause them to act like junkies craving the drug the psychopath is now sadistically denying them. The target will often write a heartfelt letter—pleading with the psychopath to return to them. If the discarded former target is artistically minded, then a poem, song or painting will be created to try and express what the relationship means to them. All are a complete waste of time—they are gestures which only feed the transitional psychopath's rush of excitement as they relish these trophies of their 'win'. All the while you are composing that poem, they are busy establishing their relationship with the new target, and sucking in the energy from you, the devastated and discarded. one for sport and one for ego polishing.

Targets get the obsessive 'love' reaction from the psychopath only during the idealisation stage. It is during this phase when the psychopath is completely obsessed with every aspect of the target's life—if the target writes a cheque, the psychopath will announce, "Wow! Anyone ever tell you how beautiful your handwriting is? You are so good looking and special in every way and all you do! Everything about you is amazing!!!! I am just like you!!!!! I repeat and agree with everything you say—as I am your best friend!!!!! Just say and do something … ANYTHING … so I can agree with it … I will!"

Then, when the parasite finds a new host, this INSTANTLY changes to, "For Fuck's Sake—you need medication to deal with your abandonment issues…"

The effects of this appalling treatment drives decent people all over the world towards social isolation, suicide and temporary madness—to the point where some have tragically ended up jumping up and down while urinating on their beds in mental hospitals trying to convey to the doctors and nurses what was done to them. Others suffer on in confusion and emotional turmoil—enduring years of alcohol and/or anti-depressant abuse.

And all for no other reason than they thought they fell in love and were convinced they were loved in return only to end up feeling abandoned, discarded, discounted, violated, tortured and alone.

## WE'VE ALREADY BURIED AND MOURNED YOU

Targets are going through the same mourning and grieving process as though the psychopath had suddenly died. In a sense, they have. This is why people who have been abused and discarded by a psychopath and who later find out the psychopath has a terminal illness or has actually died show little if any emotion upon hearing the news.

Many will be satisfied that the psychopath has died, and some will be very happy to hear the psychopath is dead—especially if the psychopath had experienced a miserable, painful demise. Does this sound cold and vindictive? That is the point. The target's healing is the primary focus here and not the fate of the predator. The 'love' that one experiences with a psychopath is just a chemically-induced delusion—the hate that the recovering target feels afterward is the real emotion.

It is far more healthy to indulge in hatred of the psychopath than to reminisce about a relationship which was nothing more than a carefully crafted illusion implemented by the parasite and which could have easily destroyed you. Where was the psychopath's compassion, understanding and concern for you and your needs and emotional turmoil when they so casually changed persona out of the blue? Most likely, you were told to 'get over it, and move on', or heard the very commonly reported remark from the psychopath following the discard, 'Well, what do you want me to do about it?'

So when you hear of a former psychopathic abuser who is in the process of dying or has died, feel free to delight in the thought of dancing on their grave, or digging a hole in the ground all the way to Hell so you can hand-deliver them personally to Satan. These feelings are healthy and a sign of your emotional well-being and road to recovery. Other humans who have never gone through the horrors of psychopathic manipulation and mind games have no right to judge targets for indulging in this valuable healing experience. No matter how empathic the target is, you can't experience the death of someone twice and you can't pretend that you are not happy that the consciousness parasite is finally and completely out of your mind and out of your life.

Dracula won't be rising from the grave again. The psychopath already chose to 'die' once when they killed the persona that convinced you that you were loved by it. This is why, when a psychopath commits persona suicide, it is so deeply traumatic for the discarded target to stumble upon this individual alive and enjoying manipulating their current target. This is the origin of the vampire motif—Nosferatu—the 'undead', constantly rising from the grave over and over again to suck the life-blood out of spellbound victims.

This is also one of the reasons why psychopaths are essentially on a life-long downward spiral to social isolation. The previous targets and sometimes even the entire social circle of the target have no use for a self-made corpse; hence, why psychopaths are often amazed when people like Katie do not even want to be friends with them afterwards. Being reptilian in both nature and brain chemistry, the psychopath lives in the predatory moment—without any due consideration to the old skins they previously shed so casually, along with any resulting negative social and economic consequences which result. Unless they are from wealthy families, psychopaths generally die alone and even if they do have family around their death beds, most will be glad to be rid of them.

We must not only identify these predators correctly, but we must banish this psychopathic consciousness parasite from society—one psychopath at a time. NO CONTACT EVER AGAIN kills all known psychopaths dead. A world without clueless enablers waiting to be targeted is a world without psychopaths. They are so demented that they simply view love as a peculiar construct, a method—or more succinctly, the means to control others.

On no other level does the psychopath comprehend the notion of love other than as something other people want for reasons which are completely mysterious to the psychopath. However, the psychopath is not only aware of what they are doing to others, they take great pleasure in destroying decent and loving people in order to rob their target's energy while feeding the psychopath's ego.

Bizarrely, when the psychopath swears that they cannot live without you, they are being somewhat genuine in terms of their needs and desires of the moment. You are the 'soulmate' for now. Psychopaths do not value your personality or your humanity and the only thing they find special or unique about you is the specifics of the payoff to be gained by manipulating you. You may be entertainment or a place to stay or their beneficiary when you leave all your worldly goods to them in your will; these are all extras to their ultimate thrill: picking the lock on your insecurities in order to exploit them.

The target will 'do for now'. But that is not what the target will be told by the psychopath; instead it's quite the opposite. The psychopath makes sure to mention things such as 'growing old together' and so on and the promise of eternal devotion will be offered up very early in the relationship. However, it is just for now. In the same way a child wants the latest toy and then loses interest once the batteries are used up, then starts looking for their next favourite new toy, a psychopath sees no difference between a human life and a material object. The target is treated like a disposable lighter, and is valued as such.

## BAD KARMA CHAMELEON

Psychopaths will go to almost comical and absurd lengths to prove they are 'just like you.' They will suddenly take up smoking, vegetarianism, become pretend homosexuals, have instant religious conversions to your faith or branch of radical atheism, instantly change political views and so on. Exactly what you have told them you want is exactly what you will get. Because the psychopath has nothing real about them to offer other than their underlying predatory nature, that is the only thing about them that is or was ever sincere. Everything else on top of their true nature is just window dressing in order to find enablers.

The early encounter with the psychopath is always about them mirroring the target as part of a hybrid idealisation/camouflage strategy, and the target believes they have encountered a kindred spirit.

Very common with a psychopath—before they move in to live with a target—they will come out and ask the target, 'is there anything about my life which annoys you? Just let me know and I will change it.' Other successful behaviour modification which resulted from previous relationships will have been already implemented for the next target. The psychopath literally does not know how to be a human being—their entire lifelong existence is to disguise this inner predatory emptiness with an outer skin of a plausible facsimile of a wonderful and amazing person. Ultimately, they are ham actors in a string of off-Broadway flops.

"After a lifetime of people-watching, I can smell vulnerability like a bloodhound. The people I ingratiate myself with are the type who are happy to just have someone to talk to."

*- Dispatches from Psychopaths*

## CHAPTER THREE

# NATURAL DISORDER

Although the psychopath gets a 'rush' from manipulating and fooling people, this is borne from the fact that inside the psychopath there is nothing 'in there' but an internal emptiness which cannot be filled. This is also expressed sexually as the psychopath translates this emptiness into a hunger to have every orifice filled. This is why the psychopathic male is fascinated with getting women to wear straps-ons, or to have a threesome with another male involved.

The female psychopath is obsessed with the male penis for the same reason. The pathological asexuality of the psychopath is another manifestation of this copycat nature. They need to know how to please men and women sexually as they will need to become 'gay' and 'straight' on demand. They develop the skills necessary to adapt to any prey and the desires of that prey even to the point of becoming a form of biological sex toy. The well-noted obsession with pornography observed in many psychopaths is driven more by their desire to learn how to manipulate people sexually rather than for arousal or titillation.

A friend of mine who was in a relationship with a female psychopath told me how she once admitted to him that when she was in her teens she would go to pornographic movies with her then boyfriend in the same way a normal couple of that age might go to see a romance movie in a conventional cinema. Afterwards, she would 'practice' what she had seen in the pornographic film. Male psychopaths will likewise do the same. People who have been with these men will often remark that sexual encounters were more like something learned from a porn movie; mechanical, scripted, and that there was no natural ease or spontaneity or inspiration in making love. Everything seemed rehearsed. Everything was a race for the finish line. There was no apparent enjoyment in the moment. Ever.

## DEVALUE AND DISCARD

As the relationship deteriorates, the same psychopath who purposely mirrored and celebrated every aspect of the target's own lifestyle will become the most ruthless critic of their entire existence. These psychopathic, parasitic, imbecilic, fraudulent half-wits will then assume a pedestal of ethical and intellectual superiority and begin talking down to the target. One minute you are a genius—the next, a simpleton. Planning to have a baby with you on a Friday—calling you ugly and disgusting on a Monday. Then it's time for the psychopath to 'move on' as the relationship 'just didn't work out.'

## THE SMOKESCREEN OF PROJECTION

Since my last book on psychopaths, I have researched and given much consideration to the psychopathic technique known as projection. There is something profoundly insightful in how they use this constantly and at the drop of a hat—without any consideration or consequence. It is truly mystifying that these individuals can be claiming that what they are doing to you, you are doing to them!

It makes no sense, and perhaps this is the purpose. A form of morality thought-salad, whereby the psychopath plants this seed into the target's mind with the intended purpose that when the truth comes out, the target will be so bewildered and mesmerised by their own confusion in the face of something that is on another level beyond hypocrisy. That is because the internal psychology of the psychopath is so twisted that in their own minds they are infallible. Because the psychopath you are talking to was not the same one who played with your mind, projection affords the psychopath the ultimate 'get out of reality' card.

I have come to the conclusion that when the psychopath is projecting, they do so via a transitional version of themselves which jumps out of the bespoke persona currently being used to manipulate a target, does the projection, and then jumps back in again. Later on in the psychopath's own mind, it was not them who damaged you, but rather the temporary version of themselves who did it. When back in the bespoke persona being used to work you in the present the psychopath feels unaccountable for their actions and then goes on to project their actions onto their accuser. Hence, no reason to say 'sorry' or feel any kind of guilt. Another version of themselves caused the offence, while you get the blame.

I can recall one psychopath telling me, "I am not doing this out of guilt", after it had approached me again soon after the projection which took place on the eve of the discard. For decades, I had wondered precisely what the psychopath meant by this and I now realise that what it was telling me was the other version of themselves was responsible for the manipulation, mind games and emotional damage, and that this new persona they were now using was not at fault for anything that had gone before; therefore, no reason for them to feel guilty. This goes a long way to explaining how psychopaths are capable of passing lie detector tests; *someone else did it.*

This multiple personality aspect of the psychopath to 'pick and mix' different versions of themselves (including transitional versions) to utilise as needed is the reason why they have no concept of guilt. Quite literally, someone else was responsible, and therefore they can project the blame upon and onto others with a straight face. When a psychopath is telling you that they did not lie when they made you all the promises they did and then broke them, they are, believe it or not, in a perverse way, being honest with you.

What is actually happening is that the psychopath is creating a completely new version of themselves and is not moving to any new stage in their lives—in just the same way a reptile sheds its skin for a new one. However, this is taking place on a psychological level. They are wiping their hard drive of the old operating software and files, and this includes you (but not completely, as we shall see).

The previous version which they self-annihilated with their persona switching is the one who made the promises, took the wedding vows, undertook a 'gentleman's agreement', and so on. You are talking to 'Mr. or Ms. In-Between' now. That is to say, the crossover, transitional entity metamorphosing from the psychopath persona used to work you, on to the new version of themselves, and in the mind of the psychopath this new version is no longer responsible for the previous actions and commitments they made. So what's your problem?

## NOT HUMAN. NOT EVEN CLOSE.

This is the moment. This is the point at which the target comes to realise that this is not a normal one-to-one human interaction between two people. This is something very different altogether indeed. One is inclined to think they are dealing with a liar, or perhaps someone who has suffered brain injury and somehow lost their memory, but still the puzzling pieces just won't fit together to complete that picture. The lie is so staggeringly surreal that you think they are trying to make you believe you imagined it. Even with you presenting them with complex audio, video and email print-outs, text messages of things and events which involved the psychopath, they will still insist these events never happened. Or worse still, you are misinterpreting them and twisting the psychopath's words.

The non-disordered person can literally lose their minds trying to deal with a psychopath. The psychopath looks like the person they knew and can even act like them for a momentary spasm, yet even though they physically seem the same—except for perhaps the automatic feral smirk, dead eyes and unconvincing remorse—'Mr. or Ms. In-Between' psychopath is standing in front of you, denying everything they said up until the moment they moved into the transitional psychopathic state between what was and what's to come. Experiencing the psychological trauma of the new persona before you can be a recipe for a nervous breakdown and/or Post Traumatic Stress Disorder.

If there is one moment of illumination when the psychopath

demonstrates their unbridled pathology, it is in the pathological pregnant pause between the personality that worked you and the not-quite-fully-evolved bespoke persona designed to work the next target. It is almost impossible to describe the psychological and emotional confusion it creates—to wreck your head, play with your mind, distort your perceptions, and place you in a state where you might just grant the psychopath anything they need to make them return to the persona they used on you.

This is when psychologically damaged and discarded targets look back upon as the moment they realised they were not dealing with a normal human being and that something very different was 'in there'. This stranger could be the person you were married to, your own child or parent or your former best friend—when you look at them now they are unrecognisable.

What is taking place during the transitional stage: the psychopath is like a ball of modelling clay which is currently being reshaped into the bespoke persona needed to work their next target. This process is by no means a smooth transition for the psychopath; they are continually assessing if the new target really is an improvement on the previous one, as well as possibly keeping a weather eye on the advantages of a third or fourth target. The psychopath is driven by their own needs and requirements and are constantly hedging their bets, working the best angle, looking for the best odds to deliver what they require.

At a certain point they can actually be a hybrid of the persona they used to work you while still rapidly cultivating a persona to manipulate the next target. At the same time the psychopath is telling the new target they are in love with them (whilst protesting they 'are not sure it is a good idea for us to do this') and telling their new target's children and pets whom they only just met that 'they love them' and 'they are the most beautiful in the world' (in order to cultivate the concept that the psychopath will complete his or her family) the psychopath will be still playing with the previous target by suddenly telling them they miss them, or 'you are the one

I really love' or trying to imply in some way that all is not lost completely in the relationship.

Although on the surface this may seem like a form of doubt or procrastination on the behalf of the psychopath, it is nothing of the sort. The psychopath knows exactly what it is doing: harvesting energy and attention from both targets at the midpoint of transition from one persona to the next. Both the former target and the new target will be subject to the hot-and-cold treatment.

The former target is being tortured with the hope that the relationship is not doomed after all, while the new target is becoming increasingly infatuated due to a manipulation of their brain chemistry with lovebombing and flattery. The psychopath then withdraws attention in order to train the new target by means of a psycho-sexual Pavlovian reward system, coaching the new target to become completely dependent upon the psychopath.

While the previous target is being manipulated with a 'Will they/won't they come back to me?' mind-control game, the new target will be subjected to a 'have I or have I not won their love … ?' mind-control game of their own to get them to work harder for their reward. Little do these unfortunate individuals realise that they are essentially constructing the weapon that will eventually be used to destroy them.

All the while, the psychopath is having non-stop rushes of energy charging and invigorating them. They are literally jumping around in a fit of giddiness and tap dancing to a song in their hearts as they are 'winning' on several levels. Two dummies are feeding the parasite—one is near suicidal with grief while the other is already out looking for an engagement ring or wedding dress. The psychopath has successfully managed to completely dupe two individuals simultaneously and this situation, this alignment of bodies to produce a total emotional eclipse, is the biggest high of the psychopath's existence.

Imagine a tapeworm which has the ability of bilocation inside two separate humans and feeding off both at the same time. This is what the transitional psychopath feels like. This is why they cannot maintain a monogamous relationship of any kind, nor can the psychopath remain loyal to any individual, family, organisation or group. This consciousness parasite is eternally insatiable in attempting to fill the empty void within them. Knowing about this eternal hunger is good news; it is one of the primary traits to detect what you were dealing with all along and can also help you spot a psychopath from a great distance, buying you plenty of time to establish the psychological and emotional firewall you need.

### PSYCHOPATHS AND SEASONAL EFFECTS

I have received many emails from people who have given me the history of their targeting and discarding by psychopaths in romantic, familial, personal and professional relationships and along with describing the usual traits all psychopaths share, useful anecdotal evidence seems to be emerging: interesting seasonal and even possibly moon phase-related material which should be worthy of further study.

One of the more intriguing similarities in the stories include the discovery by targets of what they were dealing with during springtime in the northern hemisphere. Time after time, a majority of psychopaths jumped ship during this period and embarked upon their next psychopathic feeding frenzy.

A male psychopath will finally pounce on the female target he has been grooming all winter on the Internet. A female psychopath will move into a target's house as soon as she can rent a delivery truck and promise to 'put Viagra in your Alzheimer's medication when we are in the retirement home together.' This to plant the notion that she is in this for the long haul in the subconscious mind of the target. As soon as the buds of spring appear, the psychopath responds to the change in the weather in much the same way a bacterium or virus requires warm temperatures to activate and destroy the host from within.

Things to watch out for with psychopaths during springtime:
- An increase in the sob stories
- Mentioning of new friends out of the blue

- Subtle passive-aggressive attacks on current hosts and targets
- Clandestine business meetings and trips to see sick relatives
- Money issues which suddenly arise
- Suddenly taking a very enthusiastic interest in subjects they never bothered with before or even ridiculed previously
- Condescension, ridicule and a general downgrading of previous partners and organisations.

Then, some time between late April and late June, our hero or heroine jumps like a tape worm in a piece of undercooked pork into the intestinal tract of their new 'beloved', 'soul mate', 'special one' or 'belief system,' and the parasitic cycle begins all over again.

It is hard to say for certain if this psychopathic springtime can be scientifically validated, but one thing that has been conclusively shown is that psychopaths are more feral and animalistic, thereby having a very real connection to natural cycles markedly different to that of non-disordered people. While a normal person might make contingency preparations in terms of fuel and food to deal with the cold winter months, the psychopathic consciousness parasite will generally use the long winter nights to source and groom the next target who will then feed, clothe and house them the following winter.

This seasonal aspect of psychopathology also appears to be more prevalent with ones lower on the socio-economic ladder, as well as psychopaths with minimal education and IQ. It's also very common within the social-climbing 'white trash' end of the psychopathic spectrum.

## PSYCHOPATHS AND PROTO-PSYCHOPATHS

Proto-psychopaths emulate the pathology of the psychopath not because they are driven to do it out of excitement or a need to control others but as an externalisation of the environment in which they feel trapped. Proto-psychopathic children emulate the pathology, ultimately becoming deeply dysfunctional, anti-social human beings who originally only desired to please a psychopathic parent.

Proto-psychopaths cannot and never will be genuine psychopaths, as the chemical and electrical make-up of their brains is the same as any other empathic person. Group therapy and cognitive behavioural therapy appear to offer the best results in delivering the proto-psychopath into a healthy state of cohesion with the social and morally acceptable culture around them. Often, simply removing them from their abusive situation and exposing them to a better quality of life yields miraculous results. Think of the anti-social street kids who are introduced to new cultures and lifestyles and how this has been enough to de-program them away from their pathology imprinting.

On the other hand, the natural psychopath cannot be reformed. They are essentially a sub-species which can no more learn to become empathic than a Mac software program can function on a Windows operating system. The challenge remains in accurately assessing the difference between a psychopath and proto-psychopath, particularly if the proto-psychopath has been made deeply disordered by sexual and psychological abuse, war, or having been a victim of excessive racism/sectarianism.

However, the underlying drive behind the proto-psychopath and the genuine article can be best explained by considering impulse versus planning. Psychopaths are target-driven and any impulsiveness is skilfully contained within their meticulously crafted predatory agenda. They know precisely what they are doing and why, even when they appear to have a 'daredevil' aspect to their performance.

More often than not, proto-psychopaths are almost exclusively driven by impulse, poor social and sexual boundaries and lack of control. Even their most horrific acts are generally a result of 'lashing out' in the guise of revenge, sexual and romantic frustration, or due to simply not knowing how to deal with complex emotional and ethical situations.

With a psychopath, there is always an element of ritual, practice, planning and eventual implementation of a tactical plan of action towards the carefully selected target or specific goal.

## COMPARATIVE TRAITS AND BEHAVIOURS

*A natural-born psychopath will go to incredible lengths to avoid culpability,* and if forced to make an apology it will be only as a tactic to extricate themselves from a sticky situation or to manipulate a target more effectively.

When the full impact of the damage they have done to others hits home within their psyche, *proto-psychopath will admit their guilt and be capable of genuine remorse for their actions.*

Even if they achieve a good level of proficiency or artistic ability, *a psychopath will never be capable of producing anything original* or unique from their own imagination—they are always copycats.

*A proto-psychopath will show evidence of genuine talent* in coming up with original concepts and creative expressions.

*A genuine psychopath will have the most bizarre music collections.* Everything from Doris Day to death metal, there will be no consistency based on actual emotion regarding a particular sound or style. To the psychopath, it music merely serves as potential props to manipulate others; bespoke tastes for their bespoke personas. The chameleon tastes of the psychopath are usually noticed by others as fickle, or that the psychopath is easily swayed in their tastes, interests and hobbies but make no mistake—psychopaths are simply inventing a highly-customised persona which they will deploy in order to hit the target they are aiming at.

On the other hand, *a proto-psychopath will have meaningful tastes in music* and other forms of popular culture for which they will feel and express a real affinity, enthusiasm and inspiration.

*A psychopath will laugh on cue when others laugh,* cry when they think others expect them to cry but can't properly grasp the notions of metaphor, allegory or any form of contextual underlying meme or subtext to anything. It just is what it is; almost akin to a malignant form of autism.

*A proto-psychopath will understand and fully appreciate complex and satirical humour and jokes,* or subtle resonance within a movie or book plot line or dialogue. They can be capable of grasping deeper insights. Often this approach is a useful method to condition them out of their disorder and reform them.

Genuine psychopaths never dream. When they say they do, it is a lie based on a recollection of having listened to others talking about their dreams. Real psychopaths most certainly never have nightmares while a proto-psychopath will dream and often have nightmares.

## STEALING YOUR LIFE AWAY

A friend of mine within the Irish arts scene built up a highly successful gallery business following the ending of her marriage. Eventually, she was swept off her feet by a psychopath who sauntered into the gallery one day and who seemed to have a very good understanding of art and the art business. They started dating. She was lonely and looking for someone to share her life and success with, and so—in no time—he professed his 'soulmate' ambitions towards her and as is tragically the case, she found herself married to him very quickly. This was basically a classic 'rebound' relationship situation after her divorce, not long before the psychopath entered her life. This is a very common target type for a predatory psychopath to seek out.

The story of how she eventually came to see he was a psychopath is a classic example of how they prey upon a specific target to meet their requirements; in this case, a vulnerable but highly successful and empathic businesswoman. She relayed to me that while looking through a desk drawer he had left open in his haste she was horrified to discover that her signature was written out dozens of times on blank pieces of paper using his pen. She knew well that he always used a blue pen (ritual) and consistently refused to use any other colour.

Right in front of her was proof he was developing the skill to forge her signature. After further investigation she discovered he had already begun writing cheques made out to himself for cash and that he had been doing this for some time, to the tune of several tens of thousands of euro, placing her previously booming business in danger.

He was also selling paintings behind her back which he had taken from the gallery under the guise that he was returning them to the artists who painted them. When confronted, he denied it completely and claimed that she was doing this herself, and that she was also going senile (gaslighting). Then he exploded into a rage, claiming that the art gallery and all the paintings in there belonged to him now and that she was psychologically unfit to run the business any longer.

A psychopath is incapable of admitting any wrongdoing. When all the evidence is stacked against them, they still try to gaslight and project their way out of the situation. This is due to the fact that the psychopath can disconnect instantaneously and with alacrity from the persona who told the lies, stole the money, played the target. As we have seen with the transitional psychopath, there is an element of 'this version of me is not responsible for what previous versions of me have said and done…'

## PSYCHOPATHIC SPYING AND PRIVACY

Psychopaths are natural spies—this is why they are sought out and highly valued by espionage agencies the world over as they are able to operate free from underlying ethics and any sense of genuine morals. A real life James Bond is much more likely to be some socially inept psychopath using his government job as a means to legally download child pornography rather than indulging in a jet-set life of beautiful women and fast cars. I suspect one of the reasons that this glamorous image of spies being womanising mavericks who can kill without consequence is put out there in order to attract psychopaths into the secret services.

The author of the James Bond series of books, Ian Fleming, was a very highly connected member of the elite. Fleming was employed to essentially future-build society through popular fiction (propaganda). In much the same way, H.G. Wells was assigned by the political and social think-tank—The Fabian Society—to do the same with his novels *Things to Come* and *The Time Machine*. The first mention in popular culture of drinking Coca Cola and eating a Big Mac was Fleming's 007 character in the book version of *Dr. No.*

Modern popular culture is in many ways a scientifically-designed system used to gaslight the masses with crass entertainment and mould them into commercially viable roles and stereotypes. We are encouraged not to protect our privacy. Some movie theatres in the USA now openly boast about being 'cellphone and video-conferencing friendly'—while the movie is showing. We are socially conditioned to disregard our own emotional, personal and especially our sexual boundaries.

'Bond Girls' are essentially 007's own private harem—disposable enablers for a psychopath with a flash car and an unknown past. He places these women in constant danger and sees no worth in their humanity except for what he can get from them in the moment. Quite often they die (most often as a result of him barging into their life) and then 007 casually moves on to the next woman just as though the female corpse laying at his feet never existed. Sound familiar? The rationale for all this is that James Bond is a spy—*On Her Majesty's Secret Service*—and this somehow makes psychopathic behaviour both necessary and justifiable. The writings of Ian Fleming are a tour-de-force of psychopathic rationale and pathological justification.

Psychopaths also relate to the male characters in movies about hitmen and gangsters. Women out of relationships with psychopaths have often related stories of how describing themselves as 'a maverick' would be the main way their ex-husband rationalised his own pathology, and why he proudly displayed a framed poster from the movie *Scarface* in their living room.

## THE SPY WHO NEVER LOVED ME

Psychopaths stalk their present target all over the Internet to see who the target is talking to, what hobby and interest groups the target is posting to and reading, all in order to acquire in-depth knowledge of what the target requires on an emotional level. A target in the research stage has no privacy when a psychopath is on the prowl. This sniffing out can also extend to family members and friends of the target.

In the attempt to compile a complex dossier on their life, targets will have their names obsessively typed into search engines by the psychopath. As they project their own pathological drive for control and information, the psychopath trusts no one—not even your own word regarding what you like or don't like. Psychopaths prefer instead to rely upon what they can learn from online sources. There is no concept of trust in a relationship with a psychopath and only a limited amount of information about the psychopath's past, present and future will be forthcoming. There is also very little point in safe-guarding your own privacy; by the time you are in an actual relationship with a psychopath they will have already thoroughly trawled through your personal history without you ever discovering it.

At the same time as the psychopath is obsessively following every movement you make in order to find out if you are betraying them, another version of the same psychopath will be fishing online for their new enabler. The psychopath will be gathering data and grooming their next target so when the main approach takes place the new target thinks they have encountered a soul mate—just like you did.

In this Internet age, the gaslighting and manipulation very often begins before the target is even aware of the psychopath's existence. It is indeed a very disturbing thought that somewhere in cyberspace a psychopath is busy putting your name into a search engine in order to excavate your life history and everything that makes you the person you are so that they can at some point in the future arrive unexpectedly as your dream come true. This is what is happening to millions of people all over the world, every single day of the week.

None of this could happen without the human decency and sense of respectfulness the target applies to others. Psychopaths depend on their target's respecting the psychopath's personal boundaries—while it constantly monitors the target and everything the target does online and elsewhere. One male psychopath I have known for most of my adult life literally knows the detailed business of everyone within his social circle, neighbourhood and at work to a level that is actually uncanny. For example, he is aware if one of his relatives was in a certain nightclub on a certain day of the week and talking to a particular person. This psychopath has a network of information-enablers and from these people he can garnish staggering levels of personal information into the lives and business of others around him.

Yet his own life is a closed book. There is no sense of hypocrisy or indulging in double standards—that is for other people to worry about, not the psychopath. Psychopaths can function as two (or more) different personas at the same time and one persona is never responsible for the behaviour of the other.

## THE ART OF NO CONTACT EVER AGAIN

As I have been stressing for a few years now, there is only one rule in dealing with a psychopath, and that rule is: NO CONTACT EVER AGAIN.

It is empowering to the former target on so many levels once NCEA is established and once the deluded sense of missing the psychopath has passed something truly remarkable occurs. The target turns the tables and the 'hunted thus becomes the hunter'. The beauty of NCEA is that targets can undertake this fantastic tool of emotional liberation with no overt action towards the psychopath. Therein lies the simple, but extremely effective beauty of the NO CONTACT EVER AGAIN rule. Do nothing, achieve everything.

I continue to receive emails and messages from countless numbers of people who have escaped from the overwhelming sense of emotional and psychological torture the psychopath had inflicted upon them by simply having nothing to do with them ever again, making sure the psychopath was aware of this without ever informing the psychopath. They tell me of the delicious sensation of deep satisfaction they feel at the moment when the psychopath sent them a friends request on Facebook and the target just clicked 'ignore' and 'block this person' and the feeling of personal empower-

ment when they casually hung up the phone when the psychopath
called them out of the blue.

That is the moment you go from being at the mercy of the predator to imposing your absolute and total domination upon the psychopath by depriving them of the only deadly weapon most of
them ever have: the ability to become the parasite in your head.
NO CONTACT EVER AGAIN puts the parasite in permanent quar-
antine, where it is helpless and driven to extreme frustration after
cutting off its energy supply for good.

The fact that you have done this with as little fuss as possible is
a double blow for the starving vampire. It wants you, at the very
least, to scream something along the lines of, 'FUCK YOU, AND
GET OUT OF MY LIFE!' at the top of your voice as you slam down
the phone. This would still be providing them the energy they
crave. They expect you to write them long, tormented, angry letters telling them what you think of them so they can keep it as a
memento of when they sucked the life out of you, but by implementing NCEA you are imposing upon them the one thing they
fear and loathe the most: nothing. Nothing at all. Then you casually walk away as if they never existed. You can still write that letter
telling them how you feel, and not post it. Better still, put it in an
envelope, place a stamp on it and post it back to yourself.

The purpose of NO CONTACT EVER AGAIN is not to hurt the
psychopath—get that idea out of the way right now. How can
you hurt something which does not have valid human emotions
to begin with? Nor is the purpose of NCEA to make the psychopath come to terms with what they did to you—they have no conscience, guilty or otherwise. You mean nothing to them other than
free energy when they need it.

The primary purpose of NCEA is two-fold: first, to protect yourself from any further manipulation or mind games that the returning psychopath may be planning to use on you, and secondly, to
take charge of the situation. Get the power play out of the hands
of the psychopath and back into yours. This changes everything.
You are back with a vengeance. Wanting the psychopath to return

to your life is like wanting cancer twice and ensuring you remain in lifelong remission is the objective. Nothing accomplishes this as effectively as NCEA.

NCEA is so emotionally and psychologically empowering that it is difficult to describe in terms of just writing about it, but it is. It is simply the most beautiful moment one could imagine when you apply the rule. It is delicious and empowering knowing that you had the most profound and important 'final word' in the end. The word was unspoken, yet stated something more than all the books in all the libraries in the world combined could ever relate. The silent final word becomes the unwritten manifesto of your escape from slavery and the shocked and bewildered psychopath knows it. The one thing no psychopath is ever prepared for happens to them—they become a non-entity to the target.

As you casually ignore them in the street when they greet you and you continue on your way, or casually put down the phone, or nonchalantly close the door in their face or block them on your social networking site, what you don't experience is the reaction of the psychopath on the other end; they collapse internally. They are so completely frustrated at not being able to get anything more from you that it undermines everything—from their sense of narcissistic perfection to their cocky sense of arrogance.

The smug grin is wiped right off their faces as they know they have been usurped and there is NOTHING they can do about it. At this point, the psychopath ceases being the consciousness parasite in your head and you become the mind parasite within their own cesspool of resentment, unfulfilled fantasy, failures and frustrations. They will be unable to grasp how casually you have dismissed them. It will torment them for years and, in many cases, for the rest of their lives. They will never get over what you did to them. Talk about ironic punishment.

Your implementation of NO CONTACT EVER AGAIN becomes something of an irritating obsession to the psychopath. Especially if you carry on with your life as if they never existed and particularly if you become happy and successful without them. How can they ever justify walking away from a winner? How can they claim the former target is a loser? They can't. Your success and your lack of interest in them completely undermines their smear campaigns.

The satisfaction they enjoyed by sucking the energy out of you during your demolishment in the downgrading and abandonment phase of your relationship will always be with you to some extent. You will still feel angry at the humiliation. You are human. However, this will be nothing compared to the effect it will have on the psychopath when you become a contented success, fully confident that you can never be hurt again.

It will drive them mad knowing that they jumped ship too soon and made a huge mistake polluting your consciousness. NCEA means they have not a hope in hell of weaselling their way back into your life. All non-elite psychopaths are on a long, slow downhill slide into ruin. As they continue to fall apart they will be sickened and revolted by any successes in your life, knowing there is no invisible umbilical cord to pull you back into their toxic and devious agenda. You won.

## NO EYE CONTACT EVER AGAIN

In the case of individuals who have to maintain contact with a psychopath, either through the workplace, living in a small town alongside them, co-parenting children, or having to deal with them as family members, the strategy then is to avoid making eye contact with them (NECEA). The psychopath's predatory stare can be extremely unsettling to people who have to deal with them and do not want to be reminded of what the entity behind their eyes did to them.

If you are confronting the psychopath in court, look away from them at all times. They will smirk and make faces at you as you are giving your statements in order to rattle you—don't be tempted to look. If you are sharing child custody and dropping kids off to them or collecting them, keep your eyes on the kids at all times. If the psychopath says something to you and you are obliged to respond or acknowledge it, casually look away or past them when addressing them verbally.

This will infuriate the psychopath, even if they do not visibly demonstrate it. The eyes of a psychopath are like the needle of a syringe full of heroin to a recovered addict. They will use eye contact to burrow into your soul and tear your emotions and psychology asunder if you let them. They will attempt to confuse and disorientate you; if allowed, you will lose your concentration and make mistakes. The psychopath always wants you to recall the pain, heartbreak and suffering they caused you. They want to suck every last drop of energy out of you if they can.

If they have limited time to deal with you in a particular situation, this consciousness parasite will try everything to get into you. The eyes are indeed the windows of the soul. A psychopath may not have a soul as such, but they certainly know Route One to get into yours. It is always with the eyes first, then verbally.

Former targets constantly make reference to how the psychopath's stare mesmerized them in the early days of the relationship and haunted them afterwards. The psychopath was energy-harvesting the targets in both cases. They will take your energy any way they can get it and eye contact is generally the first and last method of attack for the psychopath. Take a note from Ulysses, the legendary Greek king of Ithaca and hero of Homer's epic poem *The Odyssey* when he escaped from the captivity of the Cyclops by blinding the monster. Cut off the energy supply with no eye contact ever again.

## THE BALLET OF ABSURD IRONY

Following successful implementation of NO CONTACT EVER AGAIN or NO EYE CONTACT EVER AGAIN, the psychopath will—with their legendary capacity for hypocrisy and absurdity—try to imply that the former target is the one using emotional manipulation on the psychopath. Incredible as this sounds, this is precisely what they will do. They will tell others how you are ignoring them or pointing out their pathology as proof that you are emotionally blackmailing the psychopath. I have personally heard this from several targets who have experienced this. The same psychopath who used gaslighting, projection, Stockholm Syndrome, the silent treatment and emotional blackmail on the target will then begin to portray themselves as the 'real victim'.

This absurdity will be apparent to all. For starters, how can the former target be using emotional blackmail on the psychopath when they want nothing from the psychopath except for them to stay out of their life for all eternity? This reaction is indicative of how effective NCEA and NECEA being used on them. They simply cannot handle it. More worrying for the psychopath is that they will be very well aware that your shunning of them in an emotionless manner will be setting off red flags in the eyes of other people who know both of you.

The psychopath will be the one acting outraged, even hysterical and paranoid, and searching for anyone to listen to their side of the story. All this will achieve—and this is very important—if the target does not react to the psychopath's smear campaign in the same hysterical way—is that the psychopath will be the object of suspicion and ridicule. No smoke without fire. Then, when they realise your emotions and psychology are no longer available to the psychopath for plundering, they literally have to die. Not in a biological sense (although the sudden loss of energy often has profound health implications for mind parasites in general). The psychopath's feeding ground for energy, pity and attention has dried up and they will leave, and most likely will never be heard from ever again.

Always, the psychopath will be agitated, frustrated and angry at you for turning the tables on them and getting your dignity, self-respect, sense of self and, most important of all, your life energy back from it. Then you can go on to achieve the potential you are capable of in your own life—while the psychopath occasionally types your name into Google during moments of desperation or when another target has gone NCEA on them. It's a beautiful thing, really.

NCEA also includes:

*No typing the psychopath's name into Google or looking them up on social networking sites.* They will always portray themselves as having an amazing life with a wonderful relationship even when they are sleeping in a homeless shelter and hanging around the bus station performing fellatio on strangers for spare change.

*Looking up their new target's photo or details.* You will only end up comparing yourself to them, or doing something stupid like trying to warn them; you will only be supplying the psychopath with energy since they will take it to mean you still care about them. It is not your business to interfere in the life of this other new target, unless you think (which is highly unlikely) that their life may be in imminent danger. If this is the case, do not contact the new target; contact the police. You must move on with your life. Something to also think about is that perhaps the new target may need to go through the same experience with a psychopath in their own life in the same way that you have had to in order for them to learn the things you know now.

Discarded targets will constantly ask themselves who exactly was the real person they were involved with… the persona at the start who seemed so kind and loving, or the heartless, cold-blooded, manipulative sadist at the end? The answer to this is self-evident: the pathological actor who said goodbye. That was the real person.

## THE NO CONTACT EVER AGAIN SOCIETY

With the growing awareness of how these Intra-Species Predators operate and how relating to them as other than human is rapidly becoming common knowledge, it serves as a perfect set up to introduce the true post-psychopathic society. A psychopath cannot hide their true nature any longer nor are they able to prey with their accustomed clandestine opportunism. Many are being driven to the margins of a society where they once worked center stage among the oblivious. The eventual fate of the psychopath is extinction as the targets are developing the survival skills needed to detect and avoid them.

The collective consciousness of the human race is now coming to terms with this enormous danger. We have the means and the knowledge to move on from the Psychopathic Control Grid at both the macro and micro level, but we are not there yet; we must remain vigilant and informed to bring this transition to its eventual fulfilment.

My ultimate message is that people who have been targeted by a psychopath need to stop hating and blaming the psychopaths and instead, at some point, go to work on themselves. With psychopaths, what they do and how they function is 'just business'. With my own work, it is the same approach. I am not out to oppress psychopaths any more than I am out to oppress sharks, bacteria, rats, wood lice or Wall Street bankers. I fully acknowledge and accept their place in society for better or for worse. I am just helping people to cope with psychopaths and then move on with their lives.

Psychopaths only see their reality in terms of a power struggle: their needs against the entire world. They view everything outside of what they identify as 'themselves' as either the means to achieve, or the obstacle that blocks, their desires. Psychopaths place zero importance on developing and maintaining any relationships which are not based on a power play. They do not even really care about the pleasure of sex—it has more to do with the power they gain from using sex to manipulate others. When they return offering sex, you are being used for something you have that they want, and it could be as simple as playing with your mind in order to kill their boredom.

All I do is coach the other team. For me, it is 'just business', too. My business is that I am playing my very small part in protecting and uplifting the human consciousness in which dealing with the psychopathic issue has become one facet of this project which also includes my other writings, art, music and public speaking. A world without psychopaths is a win-win situation for everyone, including, as we shall see, the implementation of far-reaching social, political, economic, evolutionary, spiritual changes in human consciousness that benefits the human race as a whole. Yes, that's right—I said spiritual.

"What people think of me matters a great deal. It's the people themselves who don't matter."

- *Dispatches from Psychopaths*

## Chapter Four
# Hell's Belles

*"After a five year relationship, where I was devoted and faithful, gave her my love, supported her career and education ambitions, showed her compassion and caring while she was sick, depressed or grieving, she sends me an email out of the blue one day telling me that she and I were finished.*

*It came as a monumentally painful shock to me. I had no idea our relationship was even in trouble. She did not approach me in person or even call me. She sent me a half-assed, barely worded 'Dear John' type email with no explanation as to why. I was heartbroken, angry and above all completely bewildered as to the sudden change in our relationship.*

*Then, within five minutes of ending a relationship with a man she claimed to have loved right up until she dumped me, there she was on Twitter laughing and joking about Paris Hilton's dress sense. That wasn't how a normal person behaves while claiming to be 'too hurt to speak to me'—yet she wasn't too hurt to continue on with every other aspect of her life as if nothing had happened."*

Within ancient Greek mythology, there is a tale of the Libyan queen who became a child-eating daemon by the name of Lamia. The name Lamia is derived from the Greek word for gullet (*laimos*) and refers to her insatiable appetite for innocent human flesh. The term 'lamia' later metamorphosed into a north African and middle-eastern archetype representing a predatory female entity. Along with cannibalism, the lamia are notorious for their uncleanliness, their gluttony, and their stupidity and are often associated with caves and damp places. They are also depicted as having a serpent's tail and being sexually feral. Later, the motif of the lamia became the folklore of the vampire and succubi—seducing men and then feeding on their blood. Very often, she is portrayed as being hermaphroditic in nature.

There is something not fully 'woman' about the female psycho-path. No matter how hard she works at promoting the 'girlie girl' image or her coquettish personas, she is always either lacking in or overcompensating for something essentially feminine. Her com-passion is fake. Her relationship towards children (if she has any) is a big show for the gullible. She brings up strange events—which may or may not be true—as cover stories for a life of non-stop pro-miscuity. These include pity-harvesting sagas involving being raped by a neighbour, or some other hair-raising event such as a paedo-philic assault which she relates in an almost homespun manner.

The psychopath female loves *The Vagina Monologues*, as for her, what is between her legs and what it can do for her is ALL that makes her a woman. A female psychopath is just not cut out for certain professions such as nursing because ultimately, she is incapable of nurturing others. She projects her barely-female state upon other women. She becomes a fashion editor for a newspaper, or writes ar-ticles for parenting magazines where she speaks out against breast feeding, as she does not want saggy boobs, and how she finds Bill and Hillary Clinton's relationship inspiring and 'kinda sweet'.

The Psychopathic Control Grid celebrates and promotes the fe-male psychopath archetype not only because she is more likely to shop than place her priorities on concern for others but because her high testosterone levels mirror their own asexuality agenda. The absolute total and complete destruction of the feminine is a core goal of the psychopathic elite, particularly for the ones in me-dia and fashion. They have been gaslighting women for decades now, the agenda being to make women hate their own feminin-ity. From the flat-chested Flappers of the 1920's to boyish Twiggy in the 1960's—they have tried at every opportunity to asexualise women.

The Psychopathic Control Grid goes on to gaslight women fur-ther by encouraging them to also be 'try-sexuals', who will hand themselves over to any man who wants them. In the middle of all this are perfectly normal, well-adjusted women under colossal pressure from mainly male psychopaths who gaslight and confuse them constantly in order to keep them spending money and not have children. In order words, to make them proto-psychopaths in Prada.

Now, the psychopaths in the fashion industry are taking it to the next level. They are using men to model for women's clothes. Just in time for Christmas, 2011, the Dutch department store Hema used a male model, Andrej Pejic, to model their Mega Push-Up Bra for a poster campaign. The images, featuring Pejic wearing the bra under two dresses and a sweater, became a trending topic on Twitter in a matter of hours.

Most likely, the people working for or employed by Hema were frantically posting on social networking sites about how 'amazing' and 'ground breaking' using a man to model for a bra was. One even Tweeted: "Andrej Pejic is the prettiest man woman known to man." Andrej Pejic had previously modelled for fashion designer Jean Paul Gaultier's womenswear haute couture show in Paris wearing a bridal gown—he also ranked number 98 in FHM magazine's '100 Sexiest Women in the World 2011' feature. Did I mention that he is a man?

Hilary Alexander, Fashion Director at *The Telegraph*, made a very telling statement to the BBC—which really says you all you need to know where this is heading in the context of the Psychopathic Control Grid. "Andrej is obviously beautiful and he has the most amazing figure. When you consider that a lot of designers are designing for this impossible ideal for someone who is 5ft 11in, no hips and no chest." Either these people are completely insane, and/or misogynistic beyond comprehension, or they are working towards a common psychopathic gaslighting agenda of distorting women's minds to the point where they consider men to be more feminine than women. First, we are presented with starved-looking fourteen-year-old girls as supermodels—now we have men modelling bras. They might as well just start murdering baby girls at birth. The BBC took it one step further in 2011 when they announced that a panda in a Scottish zoo was the 'Female Face of the Year'.

Women are now taking second place to animals within the mass media.

We need to wake up and get wise to this social re-engineering. It is only a matter of time before some middle-aged 'brave' Hollywood star shows up at a movie premiere with his eight-year-old 'girlfriend' (or boyfriend) and the Common Purpose-trained repeaters in journalism will no doubt compare him to Ghandi.

## MORE THAN A WOMAN

Steven first heard the term 'cunt' when he was eight years old. Like most normal children of his age back then, he had no idea what the term meant, except in the context of his mother screaming it at the top of her voice—"Ya fucking yella cunt!"—as she was smashing his face repeatedly against the door of a wardrobe until the bridge of Steven's nose burst open and blood spewed from it, leaving a scar to this day. The child's alleged crime was that he did not win the fight that took place in front of the drab Dublin block of 1960's flats where the family lived.

Steven's mother casually observed the fight from the balcony of the flat where the profoundly dysfunctional family resided. That was, until the thug who had been bullying Steven at school finished punching and kicking him, and Steven started to sob. At the time, Steven had no idea why his mother—who was considered the other half of the local 'headcase family' in their building, was doing this to him. It took Steven many years later to discover and understand why his own mother—as disturbed as she was—essentially took part in a group assault of her own eldest son.

The truth was that Steven's mother was infected by a consciousness parasite that had entered her mind and which was, at the time, hollowing out her sense of self in order to fulfil its own long-term strategy. Being subconsciously aware that she had no other way of winning the fight against the consciousness parasite in her own psyche, and no other outlet for her incredible internal turmoil, she verbally and then physically attacked her eight-year-old son for his 'failure' to win a fight against a neighbourhood street thug, as her own form of a psychological safety valve.

## FIRST, WE GET THE WOMEN...

This consciousness parasite was Steven's father. A belligerent and narcissistic low-level psychopath who had infected an uneducated and ignorant woman and slowly, over time, removed her personality and replaced it with a facsimile of his own distorted, absurd agenda in order to make her the perfect enabler that he required.

In nature, there is a biological parasite called the lancet fluke, which waits on slime-covered cow dung for an ant to come along and consume the dung so it can take control of the ant's nervous system. It does this in order to guide the ant towards a patch of grass which will be eaten by a cow—so the lancet fluke can continue on its life cycle. In the human context, the consciousness parasite does much the same to the psyche of an individual, family, workplace, community and entire nation. In the case of Steven's mother, it went much deeper than just her young child being an outlet for her unresolved rage towards her own personal consciousness parasite—or "King Ted", as he liked to be called.

The Psychopathic Control Grid of Irish society at that time was itself infected by the political and social consciousness parasite of the Vatican-controlled government and social order. Women did not have a chance in such a society unless they became baby machines for the Pope. In the same way, women today in modern Western society are forced to struggle to survive unless they become credit card courtesans for the psychopathic consciousness parasite that is the mass media.

Steven once recalled his father saying, "I am a great husband—I let your mother have friends and work at a part-time job." Steven recalled his mother with a black eye (from 'walking into a door', of course...) announcing that her husband was indeed a great man. As the smashed optic nerves around her suborbital bone twitched in a spasm of agreement.

The term 'cunt' has been in common usage to describe the female genitalia since about the twelfth century on. Of Anglo-Saxon origin, the term was not considered obscene during this period. London even had a street named 'Gropecunte Lane.' During the Middle Ages, streets were often named after the various trades, goods and services available on them and so Gropecunt Lane was a red light district. At the time of Geoffrey Chaucer (c. 1390) the words 'quaint' and 'cunt' were interchangeable terms and were probably pronounced the same way, too.

Following the Classical era, a woman's vagina was generally looked upon as appealing and delightful, then something interesting happened: the English language was re-engineered into a form of primitive Neuro-Linguistic Programming (NLP) towards a more pernicious method of social control. The likes of John Dee and, to an extent, William Shakespeare (whomever this individual actually was) began to groom the consciousness of the masses towards the increasingly imperialist agenda of the English ruling classes. Babylon was on the move again.

The development of the British Empire from Elizabethan times onward can be viewed just as much in the context of the triumph of language and word-play as it can be considered a seafaring and military conquest. Ironically, it was during the reign of Queen Elizabeth (the 'Virgin Queen')—a woman who brilliantly created a new persona of herself as the Protestant Virgin Mary in post-Catholic England—that the term 'cunt' lost its charm. Elizabeth oversaw the transition of the term 'cunt' going from a harmless name for a part of a woman's sexual anatomy into an obscene, profane term. Women were being altered and this is on-going to this day.

In the late eighteenth century, the term 'cunt' was mentioned in *A Classical Dictionary of The Vulgar Tongue* as 'a nasty name for a nasty thing'. This is an interesting comment considering that the female genitalia—despite being the gateway of physical existence— then became a 'nasty thing' according to the Georgian intelligentsia parading around in judges' wigs, and of the society they defended which forced their women of the time to wear powdered lead make up and be imprisoned inside bizarre dresses featuring a complex cage structure to keep their 'nasty things' away from the mincing male dandies who made up the social elite of the period.

Why did the Psychopathic Control Grid take control of language in this way? Why were women especially targeted to a far greater degree than men for control? How did a woman's menstrual cycle become 'the curse'? For me, the answer is obvious. The ruling elites knew that men ultimately want sex with women. If the consciousness parasite could enter into the female mind and control them, then this could be harnessed to control all society.

Men could be made to spend more money, fight wars, climb the social ladder and obediently serve the system so they COULD GET LAID. Women, therefore, ceased being the mothers, daughters and creators of life as the outward manifestation of their femininity, and instead became the tools of manipulation for all society. Women became slaves and to this day they are still slaves. By extension (pardon the expression) this also made the man a slave to his own penis.

Women are more in bondage to the Psychopathic Control Grid these days than they have been at any other time in the past, as it is now their consciousness which has been enslaved following the women's suffrage/ liberation movements. Did anyone actually believe for a moment that the elites were going to allow women to just become free? As with all psychopaths, there had to be a trade-off and this would be that their consciousness would be taken from them as they became 'liberated'. Off with the chastity belt and on with the SlutWalk. Look at how feminism put women in helicopter gunships so they could be as murderous as men. What role has feminism played in manifesting psychopathic females making 'thumbs up' gestures over the corpses of prisoners they most probably murdered? The iconic image of Private Lynndie England smirking and pointing at naked Iraqis being tortured was one of the fully formed fruits of the tree planted by the Psychopath Control Grid centuries ago. According to journalist Lima Nabil, "In Abu Ghraib," she says, "women were tortured by the Americans much more than the men. One woman said she witnessed five girls being raped. Most of the women in the prison were raped—some of them left prison pregnant. Families killed some of these women— because of the shame."

Where is the western feminist movement in all of this? Where is the outrage and shame? The slightest bit of self-evaluation will show that the feminist movement has indeed succeeded in allowing women the same pathological opportunities in life as men.

The modern liberated woman doubles the taxation intake for the governments who freed her—thanks to her career-focused 'empowerment'. She is then also expected to be a perfect mother, daughter, wife and whore in order to prove herself as a 'modern woman'. Prove herself to whom? The answer to this is that women have to prove themselves constantly to the consciousness parasite placed in their minds by centuries of psychological and emotional conditioning. This same consciousness parasite within these women's psyches is also their own sexuality which is used as a control mechanism in the minds of men. The situation has been created whereby women have to market their sexuality to men who are then conditioned to commence lobbying for it. All for the sake of keeping the Psychopathic Control Grid in business. In the twenty-first century, we are now all beggars and whores on Gropecunte Lane.

## THE BASIC HUMAN RIGHT TO BE A SLUT. JUST LIKE ON MTV.

Anyone who is aware of my work knows that I consider the number of female psychopaths in Western society to be on par with male psychopaths. One of the reasons why the stats are so skewed is that most female psychopaths are diagnosed with the bogus Borderline Personality Disorder (BPD) and hence, why there is a common misconception that male psychopaths greatly outnumber the female variety.

In this book, I would like to concentrate more on the cultivation of female proto-psychopathology by mass media, the entertainment industry and the fashion industry. Otherwise intelligent, empathic, sensitive and dignified women are being re-engineered into 'bitches' and 'hos' to the point where many of the young women today are quantifying their own feminine nature on little more than a comparative study of the other women around them based on a 'bitch-to-ho' ratio. The purpose of this self-evaluation is to deduce whether the men in their social circle 'wish your girlfriend was hot like me ...'

I was recently told of an eighty-year-old woman who still thinks she is 'hot' and claims that 'sexy young guys' in their twenties are checking her out at the supermarket 'check-out' line. Apparently, this woman states this in all seriousness and honestly believes that these young men are trying to get her into bed. What on earth has brought a woman—who at the age of eighty should be considering herself a wise leader and maven of the community—to become so deluded that she can only see her own worth as being a sex object for young men thirty years after her last menstrual cycle? The tragic reality is that many women believe they have no other choice—as the mass media has created a situation where they demand that women view themselves as obsolete beyond their ability to be a sex object. The psychopathic males in charge of all this, with their young trophy wives stroking their husbands' liver spots, have projected their own pathology on to all women. The message is clear: 'either you're sexy or you're not worth keeping alive'.

Things have become so completely absurd that now being a slut has become a symbol of being a liberated woman. The surprisingly well-orchestrated SlutWalk Movement began in Toronto, Canada in April 2011 when Constable Michael Sanguinetti suggested that to remain safe, 'women should avoid dressing like sluts.' His off-the-cuff remarks created a global movement—literally overnight—of women walking the streets of Western cities dressed like sluts, marching in angry protest.

Let's allow this to sink in for a second, shall we? An obscure Canadian police officer makes a throwaway comment making a statement that was hardly that offensive. He did not say 'women deserve to be raped for dressing like sluts'. Rather, he pointed out the dangers of drunks assaulting scantily-clad young women in downtown areas on weekends, and then he later apologised for the remark. Perhaps his comments could have been phrased better, or demonstrated a little more erudite sensibility and sensitivity. Lo and behold, within no time, his pointless remarks manifested into a global cause for affluent, mainly white women in the West, known as the SlutWalk Movement.

You couldn't make this up. It is so obvious that some serious strings are pulling this movement along just going by how quickly and well-organised it all became in no time. Considering the past history of such similar 'grassroots' movements, it is safe to bet these strings lead to the top of the pyramid.

In Iran and Saudi Arabia, women are being beheaded for falling in love with the wrong man. In India, women have to live with issues such as female feticide, infanticide, dowry murders and honour killings. In Africa, there is female genital mutilation. Yet some women in the West are whipped up into a frenzy of mass global protest as THEY DEGRADE THEIR OWN FEMININITY in order to make a point about being allowed to be sluts if they choose to be so, by marching in public and deliberately dressing provocatively—like 'sluts.' The consciousness parasite of MTV has trained these 'liberated women' so well, don't you think?

Putting my tin foil hat on, I am inclined to think that this is all very well-orchestrated and planned behind the scenes by men who are no doubt pissing themselves laughing over having altered the notion of womanhood to the point that many of the women attending SlutWalk events dress their own prepubescent daughters as 'sluts' as well. These 'Lil Sluts' will no doubt be standing in supermarket checkouts at age eighty winking at startled young guys in their twenties. Once again, they have fallen for the bait and have been trained to be reactionary and impulsive (much like natural female psychopaths tend to be) and run right into the arms of their own psychological annihilation.

I came across an image of one overweight SlutWalk protestor holding up a sign saying "My Daughter Has the Right to Be A Slut if She Wants"—charming. I also came across the following ironic comment about the SlutWalk events on a message board: "Sounds like a great idea whatever guy came up with them parades."

The fact that the so-called feminist movement are championing the likes of SlutWalk tells you all you need to know about who is setting the agenda here. One of the champions of the modern women's movement, Gloria Steinem, spied on Marxist students for the CIA, compiling dossiers on them, and helping to provoke riots. In 1958, Steinem was recruited by the CIA's Cord Meyers to direct an 'informal group of activists' entitled the Independent Research Service. One of Steinem's CIA colleagues was Clay Felker, an editor at *Esquire* magazine, who published articles by Steinem, building up her cult status as a feminist leader.

When Clay later became publisher of *The New Yorker*, he hired her as a contributing editor, and in 1971 made her editor of *Ms. Magazine*. Considering its anti-establishment identity, *Ms. Magazine* became a darling of corporate America, filling Steinem's pages with their advertisements while the magazine's editorial pages ignored the plight of women political prisoners in Chile who were being tortured and murdered by General Pinochet's brutal junta … ah, Pinochet, another CIA employee.

Feminism never had anything to do with empowering women. It had everything to do with changing their personas to acquiesce cohesively into the agenda of the Psychopathic Control Grid.

The female proto-psychopath who hates men is good for business. In most developed nations she pays hefty income tax rates. She likes shopping and getting into debt with 'retail therapy' and she will pay to put the softest part of her body on a mammography machine and allow herself to be blasted with massive doses of radiation in order to avoid getting cancer.

Psychopaths—both male and female—have a strange obsession with cancer, and this has been projected onto the rest of us. It is practically their religion in some ways. They love 'talking cancer' and indulging in something called 'cancer awareness'—boasting about family members who have died of cancer. Also interesting is how psychopaths demonstrate visceral hatred and ridicule towards anyone who questions the motives of the modern cancer industry and expresses an interest in alternative cures and prevention.

Many psychopaths fake cancer to raise funds and garnish the pity and attention which they crave like a drug. Martha Nicholas, a 42-year-old mother of two, said she was diagnosed with Stage 4 ovarian cancer. She told a group of supporters in July 2011 that "each night, I wonder if it will be the last"—while holding back her tears. She was arrested shortly after for fraud. There were no hospital or other records of her ever having had cancer. Several fundraisers were held to supposedly help Nicholas pay for her treatment. At one event, she raised over $10,000 selling orange 'Cancer Sucks' t-shirts. Even her two children, aged 10 and 13, thought their mother had cancer. In a TV interview, an associate of Martha Nicholas stated she had Borderline Personality Disorder and was not responsible for her actions.

Nicholas is not the only fake cancer 'hero'—in 2010, Ashley Kirilow, a Canadian woman, pleaded guilty to one count of fraud after she lied about having cancer to raise money. Male psychopaths also fake cancer. However, illnesses such as breast and ovarian cancer are so central to the public perception of cancer as being more 'emotional' when connected to women. Couple this with cancer being considered an almost ancillary aspect of the feminist movement—female psychopaths faking cancer receive donations more readily.

As with the SlutWalk Movement, there is an emotionally reactive element in any discussion having to do with the plight of women with cancer, and this inspires female psychopaths to find all manner of ways to jump on the bandwagon, while women who have been genuinely impacted upon by cancer are often overlooked. Another reason for the reactionary self-destruction of the proto-psychopathic modern female psyche (and most certainly the rates of cancer) is diet. All these low-fat diets and low-fat products have resulted in a lack of saturated fats in the diet of Western women today (as well as in men and children). The human brain needs fats and proteins to constantly maintain and regenerate its form and structure, and to optimise bio-electrical and bio-chemical processes. A low-fat diet devoid of saturated fats not only leads to obesity, but reactive and hostile emotional irrationality, as well.

Hence, why the most partisan of the SlutWalk protestors encountered at these events tend to be overweight and incapable of any kind of intellectual debate on the matter, but instead become angry and defensive, just like a real female psychopath would be. Can you see where this is taking us? They want all women behaving like female psychopaths. Women are being attacked first in order to manipulate, confuse and frustrate the men so we all become dependent on the Psychopathic Control Grid. Just business.

## THE PRINCESS PROGRAM

Another aspect of this attack on women by the consciousness parasite of mass media is arguably the products of the Walt Disney organisation and similar entities which bombard the psychology of young girls with the 'Princess' archetype form of mind control. While young boys are being groomed by computer games towards eventually being killed or disabled in future oil wars for the Psychopathic Control Grid, young girls are being given unrealistic notions of expecting to be 'treated as a princess' when they become adults.

Child psychologist Jennifer L. Hardstein authored a fascinating book entitled *Princess Recovery: A How-To Guide to Raising Strong, Empowered Girls Who Can Create Their Own Happily Ever Afters*—in which she lays out an excellent case demonstrating that the minds of young girls today are being distorted by the modern fairytale fantasies churned out by the likes of Disney. Hardstein points out that children as young as two are being bombarded with unrealistic ideals from Disney cartoons promoting the idea that if a girl is pretty enough and has fancy clothes and shoes, she will then find love and popularity—a form of mind control which has a profound impact on a young girl's failing to understand as they grow up that intelligence, generosity and passion are more important values to cultivate.

One can easily see the underlying psychopathic resonance in all this. Young girls are getting this message everywhere: that their entire worth is based solely on how they look and the material possessions they manage to attain. Dr. Hardstein warns of the influence of toys such as scantily-clad Barbie dolls and teenage celebrities in heavy make-up—resulting in a situation in which a children's store, Kids'N'Teens in the Greeley Mall in Colorado, was forced to pull its range of crotchless underwear for children that were for sale next to the princess dresses.

The crotchless panties, sized to fit a seven-year-old, caused outrage when some parents complained about them. The store defended their selling junior pink and leopard-print thong panties with no crotches by explaining that around 25 percent of its range is targeted at teens (as if crotchless underwear for teens is perfectly acceptable). Add to this a story out of the north of England about a pole-dancing school for pre-teenaged girls. Jess Leanne Norris, who teaches the youngsters, insisted that "nothing rude is going on". Norris also claimed that photos on the Web of little girls—some as young as eight—pole dancing, were, 'not inappropriate'.

The psychopaths who are running the show know precisely what they are doing. One woman wrote to me about her psychopathic ex-husband who bought her a tiny lingerie outfit into which she had no chance of ever fitting into. When he suddenly walked out on her and his daughter months later, his rationale was that she would not wear lingerie for him. Upon hearing this, she embarked on a diet involving bulimic episodes in the tragic hope of winning him back. Ironically, he actually left her for a much larger woman than she was at the time. Her psychopath ex just wanted to enjoy his power and control by being entertained by her suffering and degradation. This story alone provides an advertisement for the importance of NCEA if ever there was one.

Psychopaths manufacture chaos/absurdity and then capitalise on this to get what they want. They are the supreme merchants of nonsense. However, it is nonsense with a desired end result: a controlled demolition of the target's psyche. Among all this personal misery, disruption and breakdown—along with destroying social and economic stability—the psychopaths flourish, unbridled and free. They can thrive amidst the noise and the distortion, preying more effectively when camouflaged by social chaos when there is less chance of anyone noticing and a greater chance of manipulating people who are already stressed and unstable.

Nazi-occupied Paris was a prime example of a place and time which became a psychopathic free-for-all during the waning days of World War II—with Jews and other terrified and vulnerable citizens all hoping to survive the turmoil. Disappearances became so common they often were not investigated by the authorities. One psychopath took full advantage of this chaos in order to unleash the full potential of his pathological need for power and control over others.

Dr. Marcel Petiot, a respected physician who turned into an opportunistic mass murderer by night, preying largely on Jews who were desperate to leave Paris by luring them with promises of escape. Petiot killed perhaps as many as one hundred and fifty people—until police found body parts scattered around his elegant townhouse. He had plotted out very detailed plans on how he was going to take advantage of the terror all around him. Petiot was described as very intelligent and charismatic, and before the war enjoyed a respected social position and an enviable collection of art and antiques.

Most male psychopaths portray themselves as heroic figures. Likewise, Petiot claimed to be a member of the Resistance, promising the people he approached safe passage to South America in return for payment. The victims were told to write letters to their relatives, telling them that they were safe and would return once the Nazi occupation ended. Then they were killed by lethal gas, and dismembered or burned. Petiot was eventually captured and executed by guillotine after his trial in 1946.

Petiot was a microcosm of the Psychopathic Control Grid— social upheaval is never seen as disruptive for business—quite the contrary: it allowed the psychopathic mind to run free and take complete advantage of others. Laws and moral codes are just barriers standing in the way of the psychopath attaining everything they covet. Take these morality safety valves away and you get everything from mass-murdering medical professionals to crotchless panties for eight year olds.

## GIRL POWER, OR SOMETHING

The psychopaths who place these consciousness parasites into the collective mind of women in order to destroy their self-esteem have been doing this since the time of The Whore of Babylon, the earliest record of women portrayed as being a problematic gender. As Babylonian civilisation metamorphosed in Classical and Imperial times, it carried the consciousness parasite along with it. Women since then have been considered the source of various human strife, anguish and temptation to do evil. At the same time, they were being gaslighted with ideals of purity and motherhood to make them as dependent upon their manufactured low self-esteem as possible.

In all popular culture since Babylon, women are constantly shown of as vengeful, manipulative and disruptive. The underlying drive of this manufactured fear and resentment of women is to manipulate them. Constantly gaslight them with conflicting messages of what they should or should not be. Then, when they attained these standards which culture demands of them, completely move the goalposts.

## THE 'LADIES' OF SEX AND THE CITY

Our society is the most manipulated and controlled in history because of the programming and conditioning we're all exposed to by virtue of mass media. We're living in a virtual reality, a totally controlled environment created by and benefiting only the controllers. Via non-stop indoctrination, television nourishes an obsession with collecting meaningless trinkets, fashions and possessions, and shapes how the viewer sees themselves as part of humanity. Most of all, it has robbed people of their ability to think critically and objectively.

Mind-control is not a recent phenomenon—it's ancient. What's different about the times we live in is the technology that allows for simultaneous hypnotic programming and mind-control on a global scale, shaping the thinking and behaviour of large numbers of people.

There's a reason why television networks, the music industry and various other media companies have 'programming' departments. The programming with which we are constantly assaulted throughout our lives conditions us. It programs us to a particular world view: a corporate world view.

If I could cite one programme which serves as a full-on projection of the psychopathic mind of the creators, writers and producers, I need look no further than the *Sex and the City* movies and television series. Psychopathic traits ran through every aspect of this production like a cancerous vein through otherwise healthy tissue. This show had it all: projection, gaslighting, the covetous psychopathic mindset, psychopath asexuality, promiscuity, the confusing of sexual organs with love, addictions, word-salad and above all else, a not-so-subtle transsexual-paedophile mind control program, designed to turn young girls and women into materialistic male drag queen archetypes who based their entire sense of self-worth on how many men they have had sex with and how many material possessions they could acquire.

The female cast of *Sex and the City* were women playing the part of homosexual drag queens, with a sprinkling of the sexually active pre-teen theme thrown in. I have nothing against either gay men or drag queens, but I can spot a Psychopathic Control Grid crazy-making mind control tactic in order to psychologically re-engineer women in order to sell more products. This was the ultimate agenda of *Sex and the City*—to get women to twist their notions of what being a woman is in order to purchase as much bling as possible.

Maybe, if they were promiscuous enough to also become infected with HIV/cervical cancer from having as many sexual partners as possible and if they could afford the chemotherapy after all the retail therapy they could then instil these new values of 'female empowerment' into their daughters.

One of the more farcical aspects of this agenda was the marketing of cupcakes during some episodes. It came across almost like an in-house joke by the producers just to see just how stupid the fans of this show actually were. The Magnolia Bakery, a real place located in the heart of the affluent and gay West Village neighbour-hood of Manhattan (the writer of the show is a gay millionaire), was featured in some key scenes throughout the series. The cup-cakes themselves became a metaphor for semen ejaculating from a male phallus—being devoured by the female cast who groaned in orgasmic delight. Within days, Internet baking blogs—often writ-ten by women who proclaimed themselves as 'Christian moms' in their profiles—featured the *Sex and the City* 'Cumcakes' craze.

The psychopathic social engineering around *Sex in the City* reached its most absurd heights when it was indirectly decreed—via the usual half-witted radio talk show hosts, journalists and mag-azine editors—that this was a show which men and women could sit down together in front of the TV and enjoy as a couple. News-flash: any woman reading this who was a fan of that show, if your husband was genuinely excited about the latest herpes-swapping escapades of these women—you are married to a gay man. Either that, or he was a psychopath who could relate to the endless themes of asexuality and promiscuity viewers were indoctrinated with.

Paedophilia was also central to the subtext of *Sex and the City*, as the hyper-sexualisation of children was a core motif in the opening credits of the show. The lead drag queen archetype of the show, is seen walking the streets of Manhattan in a pink tulle tutu, more similar to the kind that toddlers wear than to any ballet gear. Carrie is a sex columnist for a newspaper. A bus displaying a large adver-tisement of her in a tiny dress passes by—a clear portrayal by the advertisement photo as a drag queen/transsexual infant. In other words, the perfect sex partner for any psychopathic male. The slo-gan on the bus reads, 'Carrie Bradshaw knows good sex', and in-stantly the viewer is presented with unbounded asexuality of the psychopathic mind before a single line of dialogue is delivered.

If that wasn't enough, when this monstrosity finally ran its ob-noxious course, the producers and distributors invented one more final fiasco in the form of worldwide *Sex and the City* farewell parties, whereby cinemas all over the world were to be filled with Kleenex-dispensing 'empowered' women saying goodbye to their best friends. Such media circuses are so insane that it is hard to comprehend how people actually fall for this, but they did—in their millions. Tragically, this is what a large demographic of the Western female population has been reduced to by the Psychopathic Control Grid.

Then there is classic gaslighting—*Sex and the City* fans are then told to feel fortunate by comparing themselves to women in the Islamic world, who are told where to go, how to think and what to wear by men. The message of *Sex and the City*—and nearly every product promoted via the medium of this show—is concepted, designed and marketed by men... Ironic, don't you think? But that is the entire point—they do not want you to think. They want you to shop till you drop and then expose yourself to every disease known to man with as many sexual partners as you can possibly locate.

Just when it seemed as if the *Sex and the City* scourge had finally ended, like all psychopaths they just don't go away easily. They always return to mess with your head for old time's sake. The *Sex and the City* producers came up with yet another marketing angle in order to hype the premiere of the second movie in the series. *Sex and the City II* was launched with another round of carefully-orchestrated 'fan club' mass hysteria events, but this time the producers of the show indulged in a bit of crazy-making and pity-playing with the cast of the show finally 'growing up' and entering a more mature world of semi-respectable forms of materialism, fashionable lesbianism and black diamond engagement rings—which is interesting since the previous plan for the premiere was to be a series of bling cocktail parties for 'cancer awareness'.

Cancer? Never heard of it—good thing the producers raised 'awareness' about it, otherwise we would have been taken completely by surprise. In reality, the psychopaths and proto-psychopaths behind the likes of *Sex and the City* had planned to retain the services of real-life victims of cancer as part of an emotive PR campaign to attract cinema goers. All I can think of is they finally succumbed to an attack of good taste and decided otherwise.

## IN THE COMPANY OF SHE-WOLVES

Apart from personal relationships, be they romantic or familial, the most common scenario which leads a person into direct personal contact with the psychopath is often in the workplace. As psychopaths constantly generate new versions of themselves with résumé featuring faked credentials, moving from job to job is very easy for them compared to a human. While the rest of us are driven by economic necessity and pressures brought about by paying bills and providing for our families, a psychopath views the workplace in the same way a hyena or other predator will see a herd of wildebeest. They will seek to find the prey least likely to notice them, and then attack. The reason for doing so is to move up the corporate ladder by emotionally and psychologically destroying potential rivals.

In the case of a mainly female-dominated workplace, a female psychopath entering into the situation will go about their parasitic and manipulative games in a very different manner than a male feral psychopath would. Even if they are driven by a desire to move up the ladder, female psychopaths tend to not work alone. If the female psychopath is attractive, she will have sex with the senior managers. Mainly the married ones—as a form of eventual blackmail. In the case of an unattractive or uneducated female psychopath, she will develop a network of proto-psychopathic hyenas around her in order to assist them in the attack.

Often, this pack of easily-manipulated women will be encouraged to target and attempt to destroy another female in the department for no other reason than the target may be more attractive, in a happy relationship or just simply because she is a good worker—all at the behest of the dominant female psychopath within the social dynamic. As is the case with the male psychopath, the female psychopath always sees other humans as either potential enablers or obstacles to be removed. Fully aware of the many insecurities ravaging the psyches of women today, the female psychopath capi-

talises upon these to develop her posse of proto-psychopathic females ready to do her bidding. In time, the women who assist these
predators in bullying another female will be used, discarded and
often destroyed by the same female psychopath, once they have
served their function.

### Diana's Story

I took a factory job with a local high-tech assembly company a convenient distance from where I lived. Although it
was unskilled labour, the pay was surprisingly good for the
effort involved. The work was straightforward assembly of
small computer parts and in many ways it was the perfect
job for me at that time.

My previous job had been as an assistant art director in
an advertising agency, and there I enjoyed a well-paid and
interesting lifestyle in a world of glamour and big salaries.
But having moved to a much smaller town, I was content
to set my sights lower in order to make an easy paycheque
with a no-brainer assembly job. I also realised that since
my husband and I weren't locals who'd lived here all our
lives, I was somewhat of an outsider. There was a part of
me that both expected and accepted that for a little while I
was going to be treated differently in this small town environment. I also sensed from the other workers I'd already
met on the first day working there that as soon as I'd been
at the job for a while and they got to know me and I got to
know them, I'd fit right in and be just 'one of the girls'.

I have to say that apart from the culture shock of having to clock-in and deal with the 'factory mentality', I was
perfectly content there. The other women I worked with
were pleasant, easy-going, helpful, friendly and overall,
very nice to me as well as to one another. Everyone got on
pretty well and we often had a lot of fun. The supervisors,
who were generally male, were nice guys, too.

There was a little bit of pressure now and again when
there was a deadline to fill a specific order, but overall, it
was not a stressful place to work. As I was on a weight-loss
programme with one of the other women in my department
named Eileen, we would spend our one-hour lunch break

going for walks in a nearby park if the weather was nice. Although Eileen was divorced, she was living with a man who worked nearby and who was much older than she was. Eileen had left her previous husband—she told me he was an alcoholic and she suspected him of being somewhat of a womaniser, though she couldn't prove it. She asked me about my own husband and how our marriage lasted so long.

She also asked why I moved from the big city to a small town, how many children did we have, and so on. The questions seemed harmless enough, and besides that, I enjoyed having what I felt was the start of a new friendship. In fact, looking back on that time, I really do not think there was anything suspicious in Eileen asking about my home life and my husband. Just normal girl talk. We got along quite well, I felt, and it made going to work all the more pleasant.

After about six months of my arrival, the company had an upsurge in business and with this came a need for more staff for all departments and positions. One day, a new woman came to work in our department named Agnes. As this was a small town and most of the women of our age group had grown up together, Agnes coming into our department was like kids returning to school at the end of the summer holiday. She knew everybody in the department personally. So her first day was more like a reunion than starting out at a new place of work for her. Almost immediately, I could see she was interested in me. She kept staring at me from across the department with her beady eyes. I could see her in the corner of my eye watching me and then muttering to the other women in the department. There were also three German girls working with us, but she had no interest in them—only in me.

The few times I spoke to Agnes personally, she asked me all sorts of questions about my home life. While similar to Eileen's curiosity as far as the questions themselves went, her interest felt more invasive than simple pleasant chit-chat or wanting to get to know me better in a friendly way. All she ever seemed to want to do was boast about her sex life and always wanted to know about mine. She told the most perverted and absurd stories about her teenage daughter finding her and her partner having sex in the living room and would burst out in the most obnoxious laugh.

None of her stories sounded plausible. They sounded like something she'd either seen on TV or read in some trashy chick-lit novel. She was also starting to get on my nerves with her cackling laugh and piercing voice, and she never seemed to shut up. How she got any work done, or reached her daily or weekly quotas in the department was beyond me, and something I could never figure out. What with all that constant talking—not just to me, but to whoever was there or walked by our area—she never appeared to do anything work-related—except, of course, when the supervisors came by, which was when she appeared as the perfect, serious, dedicated worker. More importantly, she realised the effect she was having on me.

Then for no reason that I could make any sense of, Eileen stopped wanting to go on our lunch break walks together. Instead, she started taking them with Agnes. She did not seem to understand why I was hurt by this, but I just put it down to parochial bonding or something like that. Agnes was in her mid fifties but dressed like a teenager from the 1970's. Sleeveless tops in winter, and the cold never affected her, which always amazed me. Even in the depths of the winter months, and in the mornings when the factory was warming up in the first hour or so after opening, she would be wearing, at best, a lightweight sweater over her sleeveless top.

She laughed and made odd faces at me if I complained that I was freezing. She strutted around the factory as though every man on earth was not only eyeing her but wanted her sexually, too. Yet she looked almost like a gorilla, with her muscular upper body and overall physical strength and ability to lift heavy boxes, and she never seemed to stop moving. I have never seen any human being constantly in a state of movement! If there was a pause in her work, she would move boxes around the department from one side of

the facility to the other, and then later in the day move them
back again for no apparent reason.

It was agitating and obnoxious to be around her. Her re-
lentless loud-mouthed boasting about her sexual escapades
was enjoyed by the other women who laughed right along
with her and continued non-stop all day until we clocked
out. It was draining the living life energy out of me. It
wasn't a hard job or a physically demanding job, but at
the end of each day, after listening to that motormouth for
eight hours I was exhausted. But not as drained as when I
would look up and see her whispering to the other women
in the department and noticing some of them looking at
me. Things then began to change for the worse.

One morning, Eileen, who normally came to work in
sneakers, track suits and comfortable casual wear, arrived
in practically identical fashion to what Agnes normally
wore. Super tight jeans, the same type of shoes, the same
sleeveless tank tops, large tacky earrings and even her hair
was the same style as Agnes'! They had now become a
team. The old Eileen had been somehow merged into looking and acting like Agnes. All day long, Agnes kept telling
Eileen—who I already knew had deep self-esteem issues
due to problems with her former husband—how sexy and
amazing Eileen looked and how all the men would be lining up to fuck her now.

I have never witnessed such overblown, full-on, clearly
fake flattery in my life! Agnes would spend all day long
telling Eileen how hot and sexy she was. This carry-on
spread like an infection. Soon, the other women in the department joined in. It was like a virus. They all chimed in
together with Agnes, telling Eileen how great she looked,
how hot she was, how all the men in the factory wanted
her—even though all the men in the factory were ignoring
the pair of them. Then the bullying started.

Women in close working environments tend to menstru-
ate all at the same time after a while. What people never
talk about is how, when an evil influence enters a group
of women—in this case an evil employee—the rest of the
women become like a pack of wolves hunting. This is what

happened to me. They all began to act and treat me the same way Agnes had. First, whispering between themselves and quickly looking at me, then muttering and whispering once more, as well as making snide and catty remarks about my marriage. I never spoke about my sex life, yet they were all aware I was in a happy relationship with a man who loved me and had been with me for many years.

The bullying went on for weeks and weeks. I used to go into the ladies' room and cry constantly. I couldn't understand why it was happening, and wondered as I cried if it was me who had done or said something wrong—although I knew I hadn't. I even went over to Eileen in a private moment, away from Agnes, which was hardly ever because she was like Eileen's shadow, and asked her, almost pleaded with her, if she would please tell me if I'd done anything to upset her or any of the other women.

Eileen grimaced, almost physically contorted her face and disgustedly replied, "What? What's your problem? You're so fucking sensitive. Nothing's wrong. No one's upset. It's your imagination. Go take a pill or something and stop annoying me."

I was speechless. As she turned to walk away from me, she almost ran straight to Agnes to talk to her. The two of them then began snickering again. This went on pretty much every day—their ignoring me, only speaking to me if I asked a question or needed something that was work-related, and only in one or two-word answers, at best.

An overall dismissive attitude towards me in general. I felt like a pariah, a leper. No one in my department, with the exception of the three very quiet and shy German girls who spoke very little English anyway, even bothered saying good morning to me when we first clocked in or good night at the end of each working day. I felt isolated, alienated, extremely distressed and exhausted mentally and emotionally. It got to the point where on a Sunday night, I'd ask my husband if we could please just go to the local pub for a glass of wine in the evening so I could relax enough to sleep, then get up, go back to work and face the misery once more.

One day, another woman from another department found me in the ladies' toilet and for the first time in months was the first woman in the factory who showed any form of humanity or decency. When I told her everything that was happening in my department, she smiled, put her hand on my shoulder, gave me a tissue, then laughed and said, "Sweetheart, do not be bothering yourself with 'Insane Agnes'! She is considered the biggest lowlife in this town. I'd say pretty much everyone knows her and hates her. She has messed up so many lives and made so many enemies. You've no idea because you're not from here originally. We all know her from school and into our twenties and thirties. All you have to understand is she hates you for being beautiful and classy. There's your crime right there. She can't be you, she can't be like you, and she hates you for that."

At the time, it shocked me to hear all this. I had become so conditioned to thinking that the small pathological circle in my department was my entire world. It even encroached on my home life and affected my marriage—which was just what Agnes was trying to achieve. She wanted me dead—I could feel it. If she could have murdered me and gotten away with it, she would have. More importantly, I began to discover that Agnes had a lifelong history in the town of doing this to other women. I was just the latest target in a long line of her twisted and evil mind-games.

I realised there really was no hope of this nightmare ending so decided to quit the job. Besides, Agnes was looking to be promoted to department head, thanks to her amazing ability to turn on the charm coupled with putting on the hard-working woman mask when she needed it. I quickly found another job working as a copywriter with a small publishing company in another town not too far away.

When I handed in my notice at the factory and underwent my Human Resources exit interview, I spilled the beans completely. Even though Agnes had projected this image as the department's top worker, the management were well aware of my professionalism and said they were sorry to see me go, as well as a bit perplexed, as they had understood that I liked working there. Then, the head of the company came down and asked me about what was going on with Agnes and Eileen in our department. I told them everything. How Agnes claimed the managers were all paedophiles and 'queers', how she gaslighted me into not going to Human Resources to complain about the bullying as she constantly made statements such as, "When you become a rat in a small town it is a reputation that stays with you forever and only weak, pathetic people go crying to Human Resources".

I left the building and had all the senior managers shake my hand and wish me well. Later that night, some people arranged a farewell party for me at a local pub. Dozens showed up and I got the same stories about 'insane Agnes'... I had lived in terror of this pathetic psychopath and her enablers while I worked there. I felt like I had been trapped into a false version of the world by this creature.

Soon after, Agnes was fired from the factory. Then she took over the ownership of a store in town and the business instantly collapsed. Nobody in town wanted to buy anything off her—even though the business was thriving before she bought it with her enabler boyfriend's money. The last time I saw Eileen was in a local supermarket— dressed in a track suit and sneakers again. She looks as if she had aged forty years. I did not speak to her, nor did I want to. My life has moved on.

I recently heard that Agnes is suffering from breast cancer and I was surprised when I heard from a former coworker that even Eileen doesn't go over to her house to see her. It is sad when that happens to anyone of course, but at the same time, I think I could've gotten cancer from all the emotional stress and misery she enjoyed putting me though if I had stayed at the factory much longer.

I can now clearly see all her games and manipulation and using of people. For all her narcissistic boasting about being 'so well loved' in the town, and her endless tales of her amazing life and of course her 'incredible sex life' at the top of her obnoxious shrill voice all day long—for all that, Agnes is dying—all alone except for her daughters who come around now and again out of obligation. All her other enablers have moved on.

Looking back, I see that it was an experience I needed to go though. I was too trusting and too open about myself, assuming that others all had the same innocent mentality as me. I now keep my mouth shut and choose my friends very carefully. Now I am the only woman working in a room full of men—I feel safer and more respected. Maybe one of them could turn out to be a psychopath in time just like Agnes was, but at least I know I will only have to deal with one man and not a pack of wolves coming at me under the leadership of a single female psychopath.

"Society was my greatest teacher. I spent my life observing who it shuns and embraces. I moulded my life on the latter."

*- Dispatches from Psychopaths*

CHAPTER FIVE
# TWILIGHT

As knowledge becomes more universal regarding what psychopaths are and how they function within society, it becomes increasingly difficult for this particular consciousness parasite to prey upon gullible victims as easily as they once did. It now seems that hardly a week goes by without a major media outlet running a story on socialised psychopaths of one kind or another. The days of this term being applied exclusively to serial killers and axe murderers appears to be waning. The collective consciousness is presently reclaiming the term to identify the original nature of the condition, while softer terms which had co-opted the impact of the word psychopath—such as narcissist, sociopath and the absurd anti-social personality—are losing their popularity. Being a free-range psychopath just isn't as easy and productive as it once was and they have to work a lot harder for their prey these days. Considering that no psychopath will ever reform or change their ways once they get a taste for the lifestyle, we most certainly cannot expect them to enter into respectable society with good intentions. Once a psychopath, always a psychopath.

So now the predator must look towards more complex and devious methods of avoiding detection, while at the same time trying to source a supply of targets and enablers. Over the last few years during my research—not only into psychopaths, but also into my other fields of interest, such as the occult and esoteric history—I would occasionally come across various historic personalities whose life stories screamed *Psychopath!* straight off the page.

Some of these case studies are significant in that not only do they provide us with proof that the consciousness parasite has been a prevailing aspect of social traditions going right back to Babylon, but in terms of how psychopaths target and manipulate others we can determine that they haven't progressed at all over the centuries. It has very much been a case of 'business as usual' for thousands of years.

The psychopath is always at the centre of paradoxes, be this via chemically-induced love and hate, or between intuitive critics and infatuated enablers. The psychopath is the pivot in the middle of the see-saw, manipulating both conditions up or down accordingly, lifting the enablers and dropping the discarded, yet always striving to hold the overall balance of power by playing off one side against the other.

Any historic figure who cultivates a network of devoted enablers to protect them from the consequences of their actions always sets off my historical red flags. This is particularly strong for me when reading how the psychopath is made to pay the ultimate penalty for their lifestyle, and how some enablers refuse to believe anything is wrong with these individuals no matter how much evidence is presented. Even worse is when high-profile psychopathic public figures later become a kind of revisionist enabler—excusing the pathology of the individual in question and putting the blame on the victims (implying 'envy', 'ignorance' or 'hysteria'), rather than on the psychopath.

## THE PSYCHOPATH PRIEST
## & THE ETERNALLY SPELLBOUND ENABLERS

When I first stumbled upon this remarkable piece of socio-religious history I dismissed it as another example of religious intolerance and superstitious hysteria in sixteenth century France, but the deeper I dug into the life story of Urbain Grandier, I realised I had stumbled upon a historic example of a classic remorseless psychopath believing he could take on anyone and win, no matter how powerful and influential. The failure of the authorities to take action against his machinations led to a degradation of all.

What follows is the story of an influential psychopath running amok with power, arrogance and sexual escapades wrapped up in an air of supreme hubris and cloaked by the auspices of the Catholic Church, but what makes this extra special is other psychopaths were revealing their true colours at the time. Add to this the general levels of paranoia, self-preservation and hysteria which humans are prone to during intense social and political pressure, and you have a situation where everyone becomes a kind of proto-psychopath and enabler. This is the reason why I am against witch-hunts during episodes of emotional critical mass as it's often difficult to tell the enablers from the proto-psychopaths from the psychopaths themselves while it's unfolding. This is one reason why psychopaths try to kick off episodes of unrest—terrorist attacks, assassinations and wars all serve as excellent camouflage/distraction for secondary agendas.

Ultimately, this is a tale of humble folk triumphing over evil and a profound lesson for us all regarding psychopaths as it resonates with the present era and the war against the consciousness parasites. Another interesting side note to this story is that some of the most ardent defenders of Urbain Grandier are also some of the most influential defenders of the Psychopath Control Grid, such as Aldous Huxley.

Born in Bouère, Mayenne, Urbain Grandier was a French Catholic priest who was burned at the stake after being convicted of witchcraft, following the events of the so-called 'Loudun Possessions'. Regardless what his defenders claim as the reasons why Grandier was brought up on charges of witchcraft, one thing is certain: his main downfall was his own limitless hubris, womanising and arrogance.

The son of a lawyer, Grandier was the nephew of the powerful Canon Grandier of Saintes. Raised in a world of power and privilege, he was sent to the Jesuit College in Bordeaux to complete his education. After a decade, he was ordained a Jesuit novice in 1615. At this point, Grandier should have embarked on a promising and comfortable life. Instead, he used his background and status to further his own pathology. By the time he reached his late twenties,

Grandier had accumulated many influential benefactors who wrote of his 'charm' and 'flattery'. Appointed as a priest in the church of Sainte Croix in Loudun in the Diocese of Poitiers, Grandier found himself on the front line of the Reformation. Loudun was a town torn apart by sectarian conflict between Catholics and the powerful Protestant sect, the Huguenots. Even so, Grandier found himself in the highest social circles within the community, where his flattery and charm of the good and great of Loudun continued unabated.

As with all psychopaths entering a particular social circle, there was a sharp division of opinion about his arrival. The women of Loudun were enchanted by his silver tongue and air of self-confidence, and found in him a distinct improvement over his elderly predecessor. Disregarding his vow of celibacy, Grandier was known to have had sexual relationships with a number of women, both single and married, as well as helping himself to the nuns at the local convent.

In more relaxed times, Grandier would have been able to get away with his womanising. However, within the social and political tension of the Reformation, the Protestants were looking for any opportunity to point out the hypocrisy of the Church of Rome and Fr. Urbain Grandier was a dangerous liability. Not surprisingly, in 1632 a group of nuns from the local Ursuline convent accused him of having bewitched them, specifically sending the demon Asmodai, among others, to commit evil and impudent acts with them.

Asmodai (Hebrew: Ashmedai) is the demon of lust and was therefore the fall guy responsible for twisting people's sexual desires. In a pre-scientific age, demonic and other supernatural and folk archetypes were used to symbolise various human pathologies, in this case a demon which represents one of the aspects of what later became known as psychopathology. It is very easy for us to look back with twenty-first century eyes and deride these people for claiming demonic possession, though we should bear in mind that it was a pre-psychology world and they were accessing the only explanatory option available to them at the time.

Aldous Huxley—that proponent and defender of chemical

slavery of the lower classes—has made the argument that the accusations of demonic possession began after Grandier refused to
become the spiritual director of the convent. According to Huxley, the Mother Superior, Sister Jeanne of the Angels, had become
sexually obsessed with Grandier.

Enraged by his rejection, Sister Jeanne then accused Grandier
of using black magic to seduce her. The other nuns gradually began to make similar accusations (which Huxley dismissed as peer
pressure). Grandier was then arrested, interrogated and tried by
an ecclesiastical tribunal, which acquitted him. This was due to his
charm under testimony as well as support from influential family
and political connections. Huxley's defence of Grandier—accusing the Mother Superior of being a sixteenth-century version of a
bunny boiler—should set off all the alarm bells that this is a case
of one famous historical psychopath defending the actions of another.

I believe that Sister Jeanne had no other option than to bring
these witchcraft charges against Grandier in order to protect the
younger nuns in her convent from his insatiable sexual appetite.
Huxley's agenda, on the other hand, is clearly to protect the psychopath Grandier by means of an attack on his victims.

The extent of Grandier's womanising was boundless and undertaken without consequence. This included targeting Philippe Trincant, the daughter of Louis Trincant, who was the public prosecu-
tor of Loudun and one of Grandier's staunchest allies. This affair
added to Grandier's god-like arrogance and sense of invincibility.
Being a typical psychopath, Grandier, who could have had (and
often did) sex with any woman he desired, self-sabotaged his relationship with Louis Trincant, revealing his incredible arrogance.
When Philippe became pregnant by Grandier, who subsequently
devalued and discarded her, Trincant led an informal but growing
group of citizens who understandably were driven to bring Grandier down for one reason or another.

Charged by his growing sense of power and invincibility, Grandier then set his sights on Madeleine de Brou, the daughter of a

wealthy nobleman who enjoyed a high-standing in the community by living a pious life. Within a matter of weeks, Grandier had
persuaded her to marry him. Grandier's enemies then complained
to the bishop, Henry-Louis Chastelguier de la Rochepozay, that
Grandier was out of control. Grandier was arrested on charges of
seducing married women and young girls, amongst other crimes,
and imprisoned. For murky reasons, the case was then adjourned
and he was given time to clear himself with his superiors. At this
point, any normal person would have been thankful for avoiding
the charges and sought to mend their ways.

Instead, following his release, there were even more incredible
accounts of his continuing predatory nature. He was accused of
having sex with women on the floor of his own church. He inde-
cently fondled women when talking to them in public. Following a
plea bargain with the bishop, Grandier was arrested once more and
taken to jail. Grandier petitioned the bishop for his release, claiming that he had repented. The bishop's response was to increase his
punishment, and Grandier was forced to fast on bread and water
every Friday for three months and was stripped of his vocation—
more or less putting an end to his once promising career in the
Catholic Church hierarchy.

Grandier then had the audacity to announce his intention to
appeal the case. His growing list of enemies appealed to the government in Paris, claiming he should be tried by the non-secular
court—as it would deny him the protection afforded by his many
defenders in the Catholic Church. During the trial, accusations
from the townspeople were dismissed while Louis Trincant decided to protect his daughter's reputation by keeping silent about her
illegitimate child fathered by Grandier. The archbishop remained
supportive of Grandier. A classic example of a devious psychopath
knowing what he had to do to get his way, Grandier was reinstated
as priest, (of course) once again considered himself to be invulner-
able. He was advised by many to behave himself and leave Loudun.
Grandier refused and went back to his serial womanising—mainly
with married women.

This is when he encountered his nemesis, Sister Jeanne des Anges, the Mother Superior of the Ursuline convent at Loudun, when she invited him to take the vacant post of Canon. Historians use this as proof that the Mother Superior was a sexually frustrated and neurotic woman who took out her frustrations on Grandier. Personally, I find this reasoning to be unfair and sexist. She eventually appointed Canon Mignon to fill the vacant post, a conservative priest who deeply disliked Grandier.

Becoming aware of the sexual secrets of the nuns and their idiosyncracies, mainly as a result of their institutionalised lifestyle, Mignon conspired with Grandier's enemies to let it be known that Grandier's influence was responsible for the nuns' strange antics within the convent after dark. Grandier laughingly shrugged off these accusations, confident that no one would believe them, but it didn't really matter; Grandier had collected so many enemies at this point that they were going to use whatever option within their means to bring this psychopath down. Another factor at work here was that Grandier was becoming a liability and needed to be made an example of in order to off-set the growing political danger posed by the Huguenots who were taking the Grandier story and running with it as it provided the perfect anti-Catholic propaganda to promote the Protestant Church as the less corrupt alternative.

In anticipation of a guilty verdict and execution, thirty thousand people had flocked to Loudon to witness the spectacle. Before sentence was passed, Grandier made a speech proclaiming his innocence to the stone-faced judges. So moved were the spectators that many burst into tears, forcing the judges to clear the room. The prosecutors, pushing Grandier's alleged guilt to the maximum, insisted that when he said the word God, he really meant Satan. Grandier was convicted and sentenced to be tortured and burned alive at the stake, and his ashes scattered to the winds. The sentence also stated that he would be forced to kneel at St. Peter's Church and the Ursuline convent and ask forgiveness.

After hours of brutal torture, during which Grandier refused to atone for his actions, he was dressed in a shirt soaked in sulphur and a rope was tied around his neck. He was then seated in a donkey cart and hauled through the streets. At the door of St. Peter's Church, he was lifted down and urged to beg pardon for his crimes. Due to the brutal torture he was subjected to earlier, Grandier could not kneel because of his crushed legs and fell on his face. He was lifted up and held by one of his supporters, Father Grillau, who prayed for him.

Approaching the Ursuline convent, Grandier was ordered to ask for forgiveness from Sister Jeanne and all the nuns. He replied that he had never done them any harm and could only pray that God would forgive them for what they had done (gaslighting to the end). At no point during any of his arrests, imprisonment, trials and torture did Grandier issue an apology for the people he used, manipulated and discarded. This later made him something of a folk hero to the 'Free Love' generation of the 1960's as Grandier was eventually immortalised as some kind of Reformation-era Jim Morrison by the British movie director Ken Russell in the movie *The Devils*.

Father René Bernier, who had testified against Grandier, came forward to ask for Grandier's forgiveness and offered to say a mass for him. Grandier was tied to a small iron seat fasted to the stake. He had been promised strangulation by the noose around his neck prior to the start of the fire—this was then denied. His death was to be as excruciating as possible. Grandier screamed as his body was consumed in flames. A flock of pigeons appeared, wheeling around the fire. Grandier's enemies took this as a sign of demons, while his supporters took it as a sign of the Holy Ghost.

Back at the convent, Sister Jeanne and the other nuns were remorseful about Grandier and worried that they had sinned. Soon, however, the priest was forgotten until later on in history, where he was elevated to the level of almost a rock star of the sixteenth century. Certainly, his execution was horrific and sadistic, but while modern historians make reference to this as somehow a sign of his repentance, they use his death as a smokescreen to hide the very real psychopath which Grandier most certainly was.

Even in death, and also afterwards, a form of retroactive pity play has been utilised by his revisionist enablers to portray him as a man ahead of his time with a harmless taste for the ladies, while ignoring the many women he targeted, used and abused while he was a wealthy and well-connected Catholic priest supposedly subject to an oath of celibacy. More than anything else, the horrific death of Grandier brought about by a maelstrom of revenge teaches us that a psychopath will never reform and will continue to push his machinations further and further, as long as he can get away with it. When the psychopath's arrogance collides with the built-up resentment of the ones who have been damaged, it can make protopsychopaths of us all. A more sensible and pragmatic approach is to become aware of how psychopaths function—so we can get away from them in the early days, rather than be pushed to extremes of sadistic vengeance, which degrade us all—later on.

The lesson to be learned is this: recognising psychopathic traits as early as possible, paying attention to the red flags when they first appear and taking action to establish NCEA from the start can save us from becoming inhuman ourselves out of the desire for revenge.

## THE DISABLED OR 'FAKING IT' PSYCHOPATH

When I first brought up the topic of the disabled psychopath, I was met with shock and amazement. The very idea of whether or not a disabled or handicapped person has a real or overblown disability is an uncomfortable concept for most people. But we have all met them, and some have had their lives destroyed by taking care of them. Think of the Andy and Lou characters from the TV series *Little Britain.*

A psychopath is more likely to drink alcohol and drive, take daredevil risks, get beaten up in a fight, have severe migraines, suffer from AIDS and become addicted to drugs to a far greater degree than a normal person. Their pathology will not end once in the wheelchair or treatment clinic—on the contrary—it will provide them with an extra guilt leverage to manipulate enablers. This is also why psychopaths fake cancer and will overplay real or imagined diseases, disorders and disabilities they may or may not have.

Ironically, their true disorder—being a psychopath—remains even more deeply masked under their 'handicap'.

Imagine you want a free ride—to 'be taken care' of so you would never have to work, avoiding all the responsibilities of the modern world in terms of feeding, clothing and housing yourself. Now consider if you were a psychopath and were either genuinely disabled to some degree, or worse, faking a disability. Imagine how much power this would give you over others, both personally and in a social context, not to mention abusing government disability payments and services. Finding round-the-clock enablers would be extremely easy; your local social services/charity organisations may even provide you with a professional carer. All you have to do is nothing, except use guilt, sympathy and play on people's good nature to exploit them to your own ends.

*Gordon's Story*

"I first met Alan in person at a music festival in 1994. We were both in relationships with other people at the time; I was gay and he was still living a straight life. We even worked in the same large hospital in New Mexico, but were unaware of each other's existence. I have to admit that at first I found him physically unattractive and even ugly. But he was funny and so much more outgoing than my more scholarly partner at the time. I had entered into a long-term relationship when I was younger and our time together had been financially and emotionally difficult, including two failed businesses. It was a case of two nice people who should have remained friends and should have never have become a couple.

Looking back now, I can see that Alan had picked up on this. Within no time, we were going to lunch constantly and I found his company a wonderful respite from my job as an accountant. I used to love meeting him in town for a coffee or sandwich. Made going to work fun for a change. I was also loving his attention and his ability to listen to me talk about my own life. Boy, did he listen! He would stare into my eyes as I spoke about the disappointments in my own life and especially my relationship. Yet he was still straight and—as superficial as this may sound—I enjoyed having a straight friend. Many of the other male nurses at the hospital were gay and he presented himself with a more interesting and fuller life.

Alan's wife at the time was—according to him—a cold, emotionless, hard and jealous woman. He fed me constant stories of how she changed as soon as they were married, and how she was always criticizing him, calling him fat, a dummy, worthless and stupid. One weekend, the hospital softball team was playing in Las Vegas and we both went there independently and alone. We were staying in a really nice hotel and Alan and I went for a walk on the Strip to check out the casinos and drunken tourists after dinner one evening. He was so nice and considerate. Listened to all my stories of my own unsatisfying relationships, as he always did. How alone I felt that weekend as my partner was not interested in coming to Las Vegas with me. At this point, I still just considered him a good friend—nothing more.

Then, as we were walking up the steps from the hotel's underground parking lot, completely out of the blue, Alan pushed me up against the concrete wall and kissed me with incredible passion! No man had ever kissed me like that before. I should have been shocked, but I was instantly head-over-heels in love with him and could hardly believe it. How a single kiss from another man I did not even consider being gay or very attractive could change my whole life in an instant. To this day, I can hardly accept that this had happened, but it did. I fell in love because of a single kiss and that kiss changed my life completely.

After a passionate affair which lasted a month, Alan told me he was leaving his wife and asked me if I would end my own unhappy relationship and become his partner. I am ashamed to admit that even then, in the gestation of that moment, I knew this was a mistake. I was also feeling guilty about becoming a 'home wrecker,' but he continued to plead with me about there being only one chance of true love in this life and how he could not stomach the idea of me in the same bed with another man. Everything was unfolding so fast, so passionately and I had no time to think.

I was completely caught up in the intense romantic energy of the experience.

I told him that I needed time to think about all this. Even though I knew I loved Alan at this point, it was a major decision. Being an accountant, I was aware of the legal and financial consequences for both of us, not to mention the change in lifestyle which comes with such a decision. I went home that night and thought about it for a week, while Alan was away visiting his mother in Tempe. Eventually, I decided I was going to leave my partner and be with Alan.

When he returned from visiting his mother, I called him back on his cell phone, and to my amazement, he was having second thoughts! This was after non-stop weeks of begging me to live with him and 'complete our great love story together'. Sending me constant texts from Tempe with 'ALAN AND GORDON FOREVER' and other similar sentiments. I was being brainwashed and I wanted to believe I was being wooed by my prince charming, but now I was now getting procrastination and sudden reluctance off him.

Like a fool, I drove over to the town where he lived and arranged to meet him in my car. It was completely crazy, looking back on it now. I was suddenly the one begging him to make a commitment to me and he was now the one having second thoughts! He said he needed more time and we then had sex in his car. Then I went home, literally shaking, and as I drove the car into the driveway, I received a text message. It was from Alan and it simply stated. 'SPEND YOUR LIFE WITH ME OR I WILL DIE WITHOUT YOU'.

Within eight months, we were both living together in a rented apartment, with Alan divorced and now openly living as a gay man. He relished coming out of the closet. He became 'super gay' and behaved like a new person. He seemed so alive, so youthful and even beautiful to me now! It all happened so quickly. Neither of us were in a good financial position following his divorce (which I paid for), and then a 'honeymoon' in the Bahamas which Alan insisted on, but I was happy and Alan seemed happy too.

Then things changed when we began to look for a home

to move into. I wanted somewhere near the hospital. Alan, however, wanted to live in this beautiful restored Spanish-style adobe church which was about 80 miles from our work. With Alan on shift work at the hospital, we would need two cars for commuting. I think I would have enjoyed commuting that distance if we both did it together. But that was not possible. When I expressed concerns about the mortgage repayments on the converted church and the distance from work, he became like a child—went into 'a mood' and sat in front of the TV watching stupid wrestling constantly and saying nothing. It was almost like he was sending me the message that he was going straight again...

Like a fool, I sat down and even though it was going to be a struggle I reluctantly agreed that yes, perhaps we could just about afford it. No sooner had we taken out the loan from the bank and signed the papers did Alan then proceed to get himself a brand new, fully-loaded Porsche. I was shocked. We could not afford it. But he then continued to explain how his wife denied him any material happiness and how he 'needed to spoil himself'. Then, a few days later and out of the blue, Alan quit his job as a nurse. He simply walked off the job one day, leaving his supervisor to come to my office and asked what happened. I was shocked, embarrassed and outraged. I went home and could not find Alan. He was missing. I was terrified something had happened... and it had. He had driven to Tempe to see his mother without telling me.

When he came back, he gave me the violin and tears story about how nursing was killing him, watching people die—especially children. Then he told me he was becoming a target of homophobia. Other members of the hospital staff who were making lewd comments about his new lifestyle and about me was 'torture' for him. I asked him to submit a formal complaint of homophobia and bullying to the hospital administrators, but he refused. As we worked at a Jewish hospital with a strong equal opportunity policy, his complaints would have been taken very seriously. Alan still refused, claiming he did not want to 'bring me into it', which was ridiculous. What could I do? Force him by hand

and drag him back to work? Alan then promised me he
would get another job in no time.

He then spent the next month sitting at home all day on
the computer talking about wrestling and playing online
games until I came back home from work and cooked our
dinner. I put up with it—but I wasn't happy. I can see now
how I was being primed for what was to come next. One
night, after coming home from work late, I found the back
door left opened and my three house cats had wandered
off. I exploded in anger and fear. After thankfully locating
the cats safely and bringing them home from a neighbor's
yard, I demanded to know why he had not looked for a job
and his overall lack of responsibility. Then he came out
with the 'truth' about his 'disability'.

For the next hour, Alan told me a story of having been
raped by a priest when he was an altar boy. How the psychological trauma of the event caused him to develop a
weakness in his legs that made walking difficult. It had
gone away when he met me as he had become 'reborn'
but now the weakness was coming back. I suggested we
visit a doctor or specialist the next day. I was informed he
had 'seen them all and none of them were able to help'. I
then suggested some psychological therapy to deal with the
trauma and perhaps this would help. He refused, saying the
pain was 'in his soul but living in his legs'. It is very difficult for me to type this now—I feel like the biggest fool in
the world. Without any kind of medical or other legal proof,
Alan had convinced me he was disabled and he could no
longer work and so I was now the sole breadwinner for
the pair of us. I cringe looking back on it now—holding
him with tears in my eyes, telling him that we would get
through it and then finding out it was all a lie! I was the
one feeling guilty and heartless. I was being made slowly
insane by him.

In the next few months, I managed to get an evening
teaching job to supplement my position at the hospital. The
money was good, but between the two jobs and volunteer-
ing for a local animal shelter, I was exhausted. Alan did
nothing around the house. Not a single thing, not even a

simple gesture to try and make things easier for me. He either spent all day on the computer, or sat in front of the TV. All the while he pretended he could not move his legs and many a night I carried him to the bed. Our sex life was practically nonexistent and I became his full-time provider and home nurse.

Then something incredible happened. Alan made a temporary recovery. His mental and emotional state improved dramatically for no apparent reason and he was walking around again. I have to admit, he did seem more positive and he even managed to start to do things like taking out the trash, changing and cleaning the cat litter boxes and washing the dishes. Small things like this meant so much to me at the time. He was able to walk around the house without having to stop for a rest every few steps. I was delighted.

Alan then produced this website which told stories of people who recovered from disabilities by going to places such as Lourdes, Disneyland and so on, and how some scientists explained that this can heal psychosomatic trauma. Then Alan suggested we go for a vacation in Hawaii and how I needed it as much as he did. I was desperate to get him back to what he was before we moved to the old church. I used to sit alone by myself in the living room looking up to the roof and wonder if God was punishing me for being gay or breaking up someone's marriage. I was also drinking a lot more than I normally did. I was at my lowest and I needed 'something' too. So when Alan suggested a vacation in Hawaii I happily agreed.

As soon as the plane touched down in Honolulu, he was back to his old self! Instant miraculous recovery! He ran around the airport terminal getting our bags with a spring in his step. Staying in Waikiki, we drove and hiked all over the island and danced in clubs until the early hours. We even started having passionate sex again, which I had missed so much. It was a miracle! My old Alan was back. But then something happened on the night before our return home. He changed into a different person while in a club and he let me see a different side of him. He started a fight with a waitress over a mix-up in the order, being very degrading and rotten to her. He called her 'stupid whore'—and threw the tip at her. It was like a mask or something had come off him. He was so dark and so intense.

We left the club and he told me it was because of the 'medication' he was on, mixed with booze… an over-the-counter muscle relaxant he used for the pains in his legs. Still I fell for his tales of woe and forgave him again. The next morning upon waking he announces, right after telling me how much he loved me, that his legs were feeling strange again. No sooner had the plane landed at Albuquerque than Alan was 'unwell' again. He shuffled around the building with a sad-sack look on his face. With me pushing the luggage cart and with him in tow behind me—stopping every few steps to deal with the pain and weakness. I still believed his condition was real!

For the next six months, life went on the same way. I worked constantly while he continued watching TV and playing online games. One night, coming home from work, I noticed a large dent in the fender of Alan's Porsche. He claimed he could not drive it anymore—so it sat in front of the house until he was 'well again.'

This time I went to the neighbors next door and asked if they had seen anything happen to the car before I went to talk to Alan about it. It looked as if the car had been hit while it was in this location. To my amazement, my neighbor tells me that Alan hit another car in town after he drove through a STOP sign intersection that afternoon as she had seen the police taking his details. She then told me that Alan constantly drives back and forth into town while I am at work. She also then went on to say that she had no idea he was unwell as she saw him running back and forth to the car all the time. I did not go into the house. I sat in my car and sobbed for over an hour. Half hoping Alan would come out to see if I was okay. He never did. I went back inside and there he was at the computer. Never asked why I was late. Then he came out with, 'Hey, you'll never believe what happened in the driveway today… some clown reversing a delivery truck…'

I went into our room and packed my bags. I put the cats in the car and never said a word to him. I returned to my parents' house. As he was in the back room on the computer the whole time I guess he just assumed I was doing my usual chores around the house. In a way, I was, but this time I was cleaning up the mess my life had become since I encountered this most devious and manipulative man.

It has been almost a year since I left the old church with the cats. Alan today lives with his sister in Atlanta where he is a Salsa dancing instructor. Now I spend most of my days wondering why an educated and strong person like me was so blinded and so easily manipulated for so long. I have come to doubt my own abilities as a person in so many ways. Now I am the one who feels disabled."

## CHARITABLE PSYCHOPATHS

In the run-up to Christmas, our landscape is filled with large billboards put up by various charities looking for our donations. Most of these will be designed to tug at your heartstrings with photos of actors (often from minority groups) with a forlorn look of hopelessness on their faces, complete with tag lines about how they once used to build homes but now they are homeless. Actresses and models are shown with mascara-ed tears running down their cheeks and a painted-on black eye to indicate domestic abuse. In most cases with these large charities, you are being gaslighted into giving your money to a greedy corporation or religious institution playing on your human decency in order to take your money. Most of these charities are slick operations, with CEOs and other directors on huge salaries, working out of plush high-rent office buildings, and enjoying lavish benefits and travel expenses including first class flights and accommodations for themselves (and often their partners and families) to attend conferences all over the world within easy reach of a top class golf course and five-star restaurants where they rub shoulders with other high-flying altruistic parasites.

The environmental and climate-based charities appear to be the ones who are the most fond of burning fossil fuels to fly to exotic locations while demanding the rest of us take our vacations at home. One recent case here in Ireland involved the head of an environmental action organisation who had their wedding party use public transport to get to the church on time, with bride and groom in their nuptial best to serve as an example to others to save the environment. Reading further down the story, the happy couple met in Thailand during an eco-holiday and the bride's family flew all the way from Australia to Ireland for the wedding. Then, in order to get some opportunistic self-publicity for their cause, they travelled the last few miles on a suburban train.

It is impossible to comprehend such staggering levels of self-righteous hypocrisy, but we have to bear in mind that consciousness parasites are bombarding our psyche with dissonant information to the point that our critical thinking collapses under the load. The guilt that is activated by playing on social responsibility is very often the crowbar they use to break down the door to your humanity. This will then provide a direct route to your pocket. After their 'operational costs' are paid for what is left goes to the needy. In the case of donations for cancer and other medical research, the money sent in by well-intentioned folk will be funnelled into pharmaceutical corporations and universities for drug research and animal cruelty—so another new miracle treatment can be announced by the media and which never manifests beyond the newspaper headline. The people who are dying of these illnesses will not see a penny of it—even though they are the ones who need it the most.

I have gone into detail in my previous book about how psychopathic manipulators will give money to charity in a very public manner in order to win trust with potential targets during the ice breaking stage. It is a form of material flattery. Psychopaths can at times seem incredibly charitable and will lavish large amounts of money and gifts upon others. But we have to keep in mind that a psychopath sees this 'altruism' purely as a strategic investment in public virtue and nothing else. When a psychopath states they are trying to level their karma, they mean it literally. They are not on any kind of path of spiritual enlightenment. It is just business—charity to them is not a selfless act of kindness.

A psychopath will weigh up the options and then make a large donation to charity, or give a house away to a homeless family and do it in a very public manner so that when others are finally wising up to what this predator is really all about, someone will remark, 'How could he be a psychopath? He gave $10,000 to AIDS research!' or 'How could she be a psychopath when she gave her house to a homeless immigrant family!' This is the only reason the psychopath ever indulges in this generosity: it is virtue insurance for the future which looks great in court and also discredits any gossip right at the point people begin to realise there just may be a parasite in their midst.

During the idealisation and targeting stage, relationship psychopaths will also spare no expense in wooing a potential target (and sometimes their children or close family) with lavish gifts and even large amounts of cash. But this is exclusively viewed as an investment towards the overall agenda of altering the target's consciousness in order to make them easier to manipulate. At the end of the day, when all is said and done and every possible option has been exhausted, this 'charity' and 'generosity' is just a ruse to con others.

This could be anything from a psychopathic, suddenly 'gay' husband coming out of the closet and leaving his devastated wife to pick up the financial mess while he plays the gay rights hero, to an elderly psychopath who needs a place to live and reminds you about the time they did 'this and that for others'. They will cough, suddenly feel faint, twitch or shiver on queue, or bring up their heart condition or cancer just to add more emotional punch to their devious agenda. Just business.

A psychopath is a cunning and ruthless financial speculator and like every other aspect of the psychopath's existence, this ability is misdirected towards manipulating others with an eye to the short term gain rather than becoming a legitimate successful business person for the long run. This is also why psychopaths are drawn to professions such as veterinary health, nursing, elderly or special needs carers, overseas aid workers, missionaries, religious orders and so on; these professions promote a persona of a selfless, compassionate 'carer', when the reality is a shifty grifter on the prowl looking for easy targets under a cloak of superficial piety. With a psychopath, there is no such thing as genuine giving and caring—it is always taking and using.

## A GOOD DAY TO DIE

In 1979, John Mills played the role of the well-known British sci-fi character Professor Quatermass in the TV movie *Quatermass IV*. The story revolved around a breakdown in British society with anarchy and gang violence becoming the new social order. In amongst this chaos, a group of hippie-type individuals begins walking in large groups across the countryside towards various megalithic sites. As the modern world sinks further into misery and violence, 'The Planet People' start to gather in large numbers all over the world, prepared to meet their expected transport to a better life on another planet.

As the story develops, it becomes apparent that a pathological alien force is harvesting the energy of the Planet People when they arrive at these sites on specific dates ready to be 'transported'. Amongst the cult is an individual who proclaims himself to be the leader of the group. Capitalising on his apparent invulnerability to the hypnosis under which the rest of the cult operates, he eventually manages to coerce the Planet People into murdering local farmers and rural inhabitants for their belongings, along with anyone who refuses to follow his leadership.

What makes this story so interesting is that although the psychopath leads people to their destruction, he himself is never actually harvested by the aliens.

The New Age movement, with its denial of reality and lifelong celebration of infantilism, represents a lucrative target for any psychopath who wishes to present themselves as a 'lightworker'.

Some of the most appallingly resentful and toxic individuals I have encountered in my own life have referred to themselves as 'healers' and 'empaths', when in terms of their actual behaviour towards others they were driven by nothing other than taking advantage of other people in need of hope and offering bogus cures for cancer. This is not to say that the New Age movement is exclusively filled with nothing but charlatans—there are good and bad in all groups. Sadly, though, the childlike trust and suicidal notions that 'all is love' which run through the New Age movement make it a perfect hunting ground for psychopaths who learn all the correct clichés and superficial gestures of 'oneness'.

One of Oprah Winfrey's New Age gurus, James Arthur Ray, received a two-year sentence in 2011 for reckless endangerment while hosting a sweat lodge vision quest in 2009. This millionaire charlatan's irresponsible behaviour caused the deaths of three people and serious injury to dozens more at his 'Sun Warrior Retreat' in Sedona, Arizona. He charged disciples an estimated $10,000 each to spend thirty-six hours in the Arizona desert without food or water in order to connect them with their higher selves. During this tragic farce, James Arthur Ray crammed fifty of his followers into a small lodge for a two-hour ceremony. Using manipulative speeches as the heat became more unbearable, he talked his followers out of leaving and then demanded more steaming rocks be brought in as participants reported pain and began vomiting.

The wife of one of Ray's assistants, an organiser of the ceremony, removed one of the dying from the intense heat of the lodge. Upon returning to save more 'warriors', James Arthur Ray told her it would be 'sacrilegious' to save the rest. He was then heard announcing, "it's a good day to die" as one of the participants, experiencing a heart attack, began shouting, "I don't want to die, I don't want to die."

Prior to this event, James Arthur Ray was something of a superstar within the New Age movement. His psychopathic smirk and unsettling eyes managed to fool an army of followers into joining his cult and making him rich and famous. He was the author of the book *Harmonic Wealth*, which became a bestseller and he was frequently featured on US mainstream media. James Arthur Ray also starred in the absurd New Age movie *The Secret*, which presented the science of quantum physics in a distorted manner, presumably designed to reap the greatest material benefit from the gullible. He also taught at Stephen Covey Motivational seminars while claiming he was still an employee of AT&T, although the company could find no record of him as an employee or contractor.

## SECOND LIFE PSYCHOPATHS

The fantasy on-line role playing game Second Life® is a 3D virtual reality world where the participants, called Residents, can explore this virtual world called The Grid, meet and interact with other Residents, socialise, have virtual sex and participate in activities, along with taking part in commercial pursuits from property to services trading. As Second Life commercial and social functions can also cross over from the virtual world to the real world, it provides a lucrative hunting ground for psychopaths garnishing real life enablers and money from this virtual world.

Users create their own avatar and make it look how they wish, so anyone can be beautiful and/or interesting. In many ways, Second Life provides the ultimate latter-day, metaphorical expression of the psychopath and the evolution of the consciousness parasite. Along with social networking and other message boards, I am being contacted by more and more people who have been targeted on Second Life. Even though Second Life can seem absurd and pathetically escapist to many people, it also provides an escape for lonely, housebound and depressed folk.

From the feedback I have received from people who were targeted on Second Life—just as in real life—the psychopaths function using more or less the same modus operandi with each target they begin to work. They meet and 'friend' the avatar, and this is followed with being love-bombed and flattered. They first obtain your trust by telling you how honest they are and how important honesty and integrity is to them. Then the psychopath begins to gaslight the target, moving from their artificial, self-contained avatar life and into the target's real life.

Just as in real life, psychopaths differ in how they proceed to use jealousy, lying about everything and attempting to isolate users from other Second Lifers. As an example, psychopaths in Second Life refer to conversations that never took place and remind the target of something they claim the target said, but didn't, as well as citing adventures which they supposedly shared on the Grid but which never actually took place. Even so, targets can be bowled over by the intensity of it all and fall in love with the psychopath's avatar. It has been known for a while that it is not uncommon for people to fall in love online with a complete stranger. Once the psychopaths have determined that the target has become infatuated with them, they begin to take it from Second Life and into the real world. This will be in the form of moving the relationship to Skype or some other instant messaging service. This then leads towards the psychopath wanting to meet the target in the real world.

*Clara's Story*

"I agreed to meet him away from Second Life eventually, but he pressured me to meet him sooner than I would have liked. This is a common experience—they want to meet you quickly before you find out what they're really doing. You see, most of them have other avatars (called alts) in Second Life, and they've got other girlfriends who they're telling the same things to ('I love you', 'I've waited all my life for you') and in some cases lining up to meet outside in the real world.

This was the case with my little charmer and I'm glad to say that when I found out what he was doing I told the whole harem and he was dumped in one go. Sadly, one of the women has gone back to him—but we all understand why. We all feel like we're recovering from having been on some bad addictive drugs. Of course the inevitable happens if you kick up a fuss. He begins to slander you. This would seem to be a universal experience in Second Life when the victim tries to fight back.

He would repeat the same pattern over and over again in Second Life—leaving a trail of broken hearts down the years. It's a dangerous and wicked game they play. Some of the victims have chronic illnesses and they succumb to the stress and relapse into worse health. Some inevitably become depressed or the depression they were seeking to escape in Second Life gets worse.

Some of the women have told me that in post-relationships they have had repetitive thoughts and nightmares about their Second Life psychopath—just as one has in real life. They feel like he got inside their brains. They report that it feels different from the end of a normal love affair. Mine used mind control techniques on me because certain 'trigger' words will start off repetitive thoughts.

Some people have been dismissive with me about the problem of psychopaths in Second Life. They say 'you knew it was a game' and things like that. Well, yes I did know it was a game and so did the others. But the psychopath on Second Life says things to take it outside of the game such as 'I know this is a game but my feelings for you are real'. The one who targeted me played the following game, typical of what goes on:

1. It's a game.
2. I'll convince her that we've gone beyond the game and it's now real.
3. I'll continue to 'play' her as a game but she won't know.
4. She's found out! I'll tell her it's just a game.

I've talked to a lot of women in Second Life over the past few months. I believe that there are a disproportionate number of psychopaths online and that Second Life in particular is teeming. Ageing psychopaths in particular love it in Second Life because they can be young and beautiful again and attract women. As they age, they can't do this as easily in real life. There are also lots of potential victims in there because many people go in because they've got health or other problems and they want to escape from real life. So you've got a high number of ill, disabled and depressed people—easy prey.

When avatars have sex (and they do) the man can secretly impregnate the woman with a pregnancy programme. If she tries to have sex with another man he will get a message saying that she is pregnant and I think it will say who the 'father' is. If she wants to get rid of the programme that is inside her avatar she has to have a virtual abortion at a Second Life abortion clinic. If she decides to have the baby she can go through a 'birth' or just buy a baby and the programme is removed. All this costs money of course. I feel ill just thinking about it."

## CHILD PSYCHOPATHS

Perhaps the most traumatic event a parent can encounter is coming to the realisation that one of their children may be a psychopath. It poses many difficulties, from loving the unlovable to finding a way to resolve the dilemma for the safety and security of the family as a whole, particularly the other children. There are also legal obligations which parents are obliged to and should fulfil. I won't make any bones about it; if you have a psychopathic child you are stuck with them until they reach legal age. After that, the primary thrust of your role as a parent and as a family is to keep this monster away from you.

The first possible sign that a child may indeed be psychopathic is that it will demonstrate a lack of emotional and interactive bonding with his/her mother, similar to children who are considered to be autistic. In and of itself, this is not a potential red flag, but it must be taken seriously in any case. Parents may notice certain anti-social manifestations within the child between the ages of five and ten, including an inability to share common experiences with other children; a self-centred mindset when playing with other children; doing whatever it takes to win and being incapable of recognising that cheating is unfair and wrong. An example of this would be where two children are racing one another and the psychopathic child pulls the other one's hair, trips them or pushes them into an object along the way and then throws their hands up in the air announcing 'I win'! When playing games like Monopoly, the child steals money from the bank, or when playing with toy soldiers the child would capture prisoners and mutilate them.

Other anti-social manifestations include not sharing their candy and sweets with other children; showing little or no concern for other children who fall or are injured; making fun of other children's clothes, socio-economic status, or a disability they may have; hoarding their toys and not allowing other children to play with them or stealing the toys of other children; not demonstrating sorrow when a pet dies. Also, they will almost never, if at all, talk about dreaming or dreams they've had.

On the eve of puberty, more signs will begin to manifest. Animal cruelty may be carried out to an almost industrial level of sadism. Most young boys (probably as a result of a 'hunter' evolutionary drive) do torture and kill animals, although it rarely moves beyond insects and small rodents. Psychopathic children, if they do show an interest in animal cruelty, will kill thousands of animals and will not refrain from targeting all and every species available to them. If they demonstrate an ability to formulate and execute complex methods of torture and murdering of animals, then parents should be very concerned.

When puberty arrives, their sexuality will manifest long before the children around them become sexually active. They will at this stage immediately understand that there is a sense of power and control over others using sex. A young teenaged female psychopath will have lost her virginity before age fourteen, and by the time she is in her mid-teens could be living with an older boy who may live alone in a house, or with an elderly relative. The early teen psychopath has an instinctual prostitute mentality—not driven out of economic necessity, but from fully intuiting how much control it gives her over others.

She will completely ignore the wishes and demands of her parents—often travelling long distances to have sex with older boyfriends in the military and in college, all before she reaches her late teens. She will express a desire for breast implants or other cosmetic surgery at the earliest possible stage and find someone to pay for this.

Generally doing poorly to average in school, the teen psychopath will often befriend a mishmash of seemingly incompatible peers, or have much older friends than their own age group, whom they smoke cigarettes and drink alcohol with.

As with all prospective homemade diagnoses of any psychopath, I am outlining a progression/cluster of pathological behaviours from early childhood to teens. I am not suggesting using individual elements of negative behaviour as an absolute indicator of a psychopathic child. Ultimately, any diagnosis should be (but sadly rarely) determined by a mental health professional.

In most cases involving parents dealing with a particularly feral male child psychopath, they will have to deal with their entire family structure being torn apart. Dealing with the psychopathic child takes up so much of their time, effort and money, that the other children are unfortunately not given the attention they deserve. The psychopathic child is fully aware of this and enjoys being the centre of attention. Constantly running away from home even before they reach their teens is commonly reported. Making up false allegations about having been molested by the parents or other adults in order to destroy the family from within is also commonly reported.

Some of these psychopathic children will even boast that this is their intention—to torment the parents and land their siblings in foster care. Often, they will play one parent off against the other. When caught and exposed as liars, thieves and manipulators, psychopathic children show neither remorse or understanding of the damage they have done to others. Nothing is his or her fault. Someone else is always to blame. Little Psychopath Johnny or Mary has absolutely no conscience and no remorse—a pathological trait they will carry with them for the rest of their existence.

When the distraught and energy-drained parents bring a psychopathic child to a psychiatric clinic or mental health practitioner, they are generally given a diagnosis of Conduct Disorder (CD) and/or Oppositional Defiant Disorder (ODD) culled from the pages of the *Diagnostic Statistical Manual of Mental Disorders* (DSM). It is next to impossible to get help when dealing with a juvenile psychopath. The police, hospitals and court systems are either unresponsive or ill-prepared to help. Mental health professionals refrain from any diagnosis of childhood psychopathy.

Until the psychopathic child reaches legal age of adulthood, parents and the rest of the family are doomed to suffer through this nightmare. This would be bad enough, but the psychopath almost certainly will be a burden upon the rest of the family for its natural life. These prodigal sons or daughters will always return with sob stories and other tales of having been redeemed by religion, or arriving unexpectedly with their children which they produced along the way. As the parents age, and there may be an inheritance or possible free house waiting for the psychopath to take advantage of later. The parents of psychopathic children have to deal with all the long-term impacts this savage spawn will have upon them and their other children.

One reader contacted me with a plan he and his wife came up with to deal with the long-term effects of having a psychopathic son. Along with the decision to cut him out of their will, he and his wife saved up a large amount of cash. When their son was of recruitment age, they told him they would give it to him in cash—on the proviso that he agreed to sign up for the Royal Navy.

Their son agreed, and enlisted. True to form, he went AWOL in Singapore on a tour of duty after he was caught stealing supplies from the ship and trying to sell them on the black market. He never came home again. The parents have since moved house to another country and started over. The last they heard, their son was working in a nightclub in Spain.

I have included this story to illustrate how similar methods of 'bribery' would probably be the best method to keep a psychopathic offspring away from the family once they reach legal age.

## THE PRO-PSYCHOPATH LOBBY

In December 2011, Peter Jonason, of New Mexico University—without presenting a shred of hard evidence—told *New Scientist* magazine that he believes psychopaths may have an innate, genetic component that explains why some people (especially men) seem unable to stop their impulsive, thrill-seeking and callous, Machiavellian behaviour. He then went on to announce that psychopaths, along with their deceitful and exploitative nature, "...may represent a successful evolutionary strategy," As usual, newspaper journalists presented Jonason's wild speculations as absolute scientific fact in newspapers the world over.

And so it begins...

The psychopath is no longer able to hide in the shadows, and so is currently being re-branded by corporate and governmental science as being a positive evolutionary force. This agenda, in tandem with other memes designed to cultivate and promote the myth that psychopaths are unwell people who are not responsible for their actions, is how the psychopaths in charge of our world will now proceed to deal with the avalanche of information about psychopaths which is now exploding into the mainstream. The consciousness parasites at the top are sending out their propagandists to obscure psychopathy with a smokescreen of pseudo-scientific babble and classic projection in order to convince the general population that these are the people to emulate.

Much of the correspondence I receive revolves around my description of what I termed the Psychopathic Control Grid, and how we should all be defending our consciousness from exploitation from the psychopathic elements within modern society.

One does not have to look very hard to see that many public figures—both contemporary and historical—display a plethora of uniquely psychopathic behavioural traits and these will be instantly recognisable to anyone who has experienced their own relationship with a psychopath. It does not matter if the psychopath was male or female, nor what social class they came from—there is always a common modus operandi which all psychopaths share.

I purposely played down this aspect of psychopathology in *Puzzling People.* I knew the book would be read mainly by people recovering from psychopathic abuse in a one-on-one sense and their primary need for knowledge, reassurance and recovery. I strongly believe that real healing for those coming out of psychopathic relationships is to build a firewall around their consciousness, in order to prevent further damage from all consciousness parasites (not just psychopaths) along with deflecting socially-invasive psychological and intellectual exploitation from major media.

The reason for this is simple: if we are aware of the nature of the all-invasive attempts at mind control by the Psychopathic Control Grid, then we can cultivate an equally powerful sense of psychological immunity resulting in a better quality of life and a greater sense of independence. We can enjoy a quality of personal security and contentment which no prescription-scribbling psychiatrist can prescribe.

Adepts of this knowledge can concentrate on the things in life which bring joy and fulfilment rather than on the things we are told we lack by advertising and mass media. This is the real reason psychopaths can permeate our lives so easily and proceed to destroy us from within: if you watch television, go to the cinema or rent movies, read fashion magazines, play video games or listen to commercial radio, you have been softened-up in advance to think that you may be missing the one essential thing that only another person or corporation can supply.

Don't fall for it anymore. If you're afraid, you're being played.

## AND THE PSYCHOPATHS MOVE IN

Having this knowledge allows us more time to concentrate our energies on following our true purpose in life (our dharma) while sharing it with the ones who deserve it the most. We need to start taking control of our own neural plasticity and begin rebuilding the brain and mind we need to serve us personally—and not have TV, magazines, newspapers, movies, MTV, vampire-porn dramas, *Family Guy*, *South Park* and video games doing it for us. If we reclaim our minds from these consciousness parasites, we can avoid sitting on the shrink's couch, or waiting for the latest psychotropic medications to smother the damage which the Psychopathic Control Grid has inflicted upon us.

## YOU HAVE TO HANDLE THE TRUTH

It is very difficult for the average person who reads newspapers and gets their world view from TV news to accept that they are far more mind-controlled than they realise. Even more difficult for them to accept is that the more formal education they have been subjected to, the more they find themselves trapped within a locked paradigm. Some of the most wise and knowledgeable people I have ever encountered were toothless sheep farmers on the sides of mountains, while some of the most ignorant clutch their PhD as if it was a non-transferable ticket to higher states of the human experience.

The only thing these highly-educated folks have proven is that they are very good at repeating what they were told to repeat. I am certainly not implying that people with PhDs are not brilliant, creative and vitally important to the advancement of the human experience on this planet. Many are—but many, many others are programmed vanguards of a psychopathic corporate system and in possession of a piece of paper declaring little more than what an obedient servant they have been. It matters not if the academic has a PhD in biology and knows nothing about politics; their opinion on the political system is portrayed more times than not by major media as that of an 'expert' by virtue of them having attained a PhD—any PhD.

I was one of the founding members of a political lobby group here in Ireland which tried to get the national rail system improved. We were the first public transport user group in Irish parliamentary history to formally address a government committee. It was very exciting at the time. I used my graphic design skills to create a slide presentation on why commuters' needs were not being addressed. I delivered a speech which was broadcast on national TV. The politicians praised us for our presentation. Then, nothing happened.

The reason for this was two-fold: the politicians overseeing public transport development in Ireland most likely never took a bus or train in their lives, preferring instead to travel by private government limos and first class air travel. Secondly, the un-elected, faceless senior civil servants behind the scenes—the ones who really control democracy—generally never use public transport either and also enjoy government cars and other perks. Not one of the ministers in charge of public transport, nor the senior civil servants at the Department of Transport used public transport, and they hadn't a clue about what the life of a bus or train commuter was really about. Yet, they were all experts in the field of public transport because they held PhDs and Master's Degrees in everything from Theology to Accounting.

And herein lies the problem: education today is geared far too much towards specialisation in one particular field. There is nothing 'universal' about a contemporary university education. I believe all these fields of academic, scientific and technical research are purposely kept compartmentalised so that they do not inter-communicate. This specialisation affords a greater level of control in order to safeguard the real drive of modern education, churning out servants to big business and governmental agendas, creating nuts and bolts and cogs for The Machine.

When big business controls education and learning, we are no longer advancing as a culture and a species. We are being conditioned to remain within selected paradigms and compartments which determine our economic potential and debt slavery. The Psychopathic Control Grid has a vested interest in keeping the talented individuals and innovators down.

Just look at our elites today. From George W. Bush to Tony Blair to Prince Charles—centuries of inbreeding among these Darwinian-obsessed 'favoured races' has created a gene pool at the top of the pyramid which is a long way off from their ancestors Alexander the Great, Charlemagne, Julius Caesar and the pharaohs of Egypt. These people have a vested interest in keeping the rest of us dumbed down, using everything from autism-inducing infant vaccines to media and celebrity obsessions, to educational systems which indoctrinate rather than nourish the full potential of the human mind, all to accomplish and maintain our slavery. Just like the psychopath you were in a relationship with had you thinking you were a dummy, a moron and a liability, the Psychopathic Control Grid eternally concentrating on their own needs and ignoring yours.

## PSYCHIATRY AND THE DARK ARTS

One of the most effective methods to spot a psychopath on an Internet message board or forum is when they are involved in a debate with an articulate, well-read individual and the psychopath begins to lose ground in the debate—the psychopath never yields ground. The psychopath never pauses to take stock of the flow or drift of the discussion, and will tell the other party, 'interesting, I will think this over and get back to you.'

The psychopath is never wrong—it has invested too much in the belief package its persona is currently aligned with to start wondering if it needs to develop a new one in order to portray himself or herself as wise and progressive in the eyes of others. This instinctual attack by the psychopath occurs when the other person is bringing up fringe or non-mainstream viewpoints or—heaven forbid -expressing an original idea or concept outside the psychopath's scope of reference.

As the psychopath starts to realise that it is running out of links to corporate and government propaganda websites to defend their side of the debate, the tone changes; a sense of holier-than-thou arrogance emerges alongside sarcasm and ridicule of the opposition. When the psychopath is no longer able to dazzle and impress with yet another link to a website, watch carefully, for this is when its true colours begin to emerge: word salad, scrambling to denigrate others' opinions, gaslighting, prevarication and often sudden disappearances.

This is no different than when a psychopath terminates your relationship out of the blue. Prior to abandonment, you will have become very familiar with the sudden condescension and arrogance of the psychopath as well as their tendency to avoid having to give you a straight answer to a simple question. Psychopaths don't debate—they twist, distort, patronise, condescend, accuse and word-salad you into a position where you begin to think you really are all the horrible and degrading things they are saying—that is, if you are lucky enough to actually see them face-to-face; chances are you'll be dealing with this in an email or text message.

The psychopath will go to extreme lengths not to deal with you on the phone and certainly not in person if they can help it. This makes them the perfect 'keyboard warriors'. Some even make YouTube videos when it is time to devalue and discard their devoted enabler. You are sent on your way with as little fuss as possible, as they need time to get back to working their next scam or target. You will simply be 'shooed away' like an insect of no consequence. This progression of pathology of devaluing, ridiculing and eventual disposal of the other party is common to all psychopaths, and stands out a mile on Internet message boards when you become aware of certain individuals on Internet groups who do this over and over again.

When the oh-so-clever Internet psychopath has worked their way through their fall-back options of *LOL! FFS! Troll! Shill!* or their favourite final card played in order to not lose face, *'HAHA You Tinfoil Hatter!'* They will accuse the other party of embarking on a 'hysterical diatribe' or a 'hate-filled rant' to deflect attention from the fact that the psychopath—who always considers itself to be the most intelligent and noble entity on earth—is out of its depth and losing ground. Even when the other party is expressing their viewpoint in a calm and collective manner with good references sources, they are dismissed as not having 'proper academic credentials'. This is because a psychopath cannot comprehend the idea of someone embarking on a knowledge path of their own for the sake of enjoying a personal learning and creative development experience.

A female psychopath I was once in a relationship with became very annoyed when she found me reading a book on Egyptian hieroglyphs. She smugly remarked, "Why are you wasting your time reading about that stuff?" Her phobia of my interest in Egyptian hieroglyphs was driven by two things: firstly, she could not grasp why I should attain complex new knowledge into a given subject if there was no perceivable financial or social benefit to doing so and, secondly, she had spent considerable amounts of time and effort 'working me' up to that point by pretending she was equally as passionate about the same subjects, interests and hobbies that I was. This, in her mind, would have represented one more thing she had to learn in order to keep 'working' me. To a psychopath, the acquisition of knowledge is only ever about manipulating others, ego-polishing and business.

A psychopath only enters the higher education system to make money and/or target an economically affluent enabler while feeding their need to be respected as the amazing individual they perceive themselves to be. Psychopaths are extremely wary of people who have studied independently and have subsequently published on their topic without having attained a degree. The psychopathic mind is terrified of non-mainstream views, novel approaches and new thinking to the point that it is fully supportive of mainstream education (indoctrination) as well as government and media's lock-down ability to keep most of society as potentially ignorant as the psychopath is. The irony is that the same psychopath accusing the other party of not being an accredited expert most likely never graduated college themselves.

## PATHOCRACY, THE PHALLUS OF OPPRESSION

In Andrzej M. Lobaczewski's remarkable book, *Political Ponerology: A Science on the Nature of Evil Adjusted for Political Purposes*, the author scientifically makes the case that totalitarian government is controlled and organised by psychopaths, and requiring low-level psychopaths to keep pathocracy running. Without the heads of the various government departments being psychopaths, or at least emulating the orders of the psychopaths above without question, the psychopaths at the top of the pyramid cannot maintain overall control of the citizens.

The kind of psychopath who would work toward achieving the status of moderator on an Internet message board could be best compared to the character of O'Brien in George Orwell's novel, *1984*. In a pre-Internet age, many of these types would be drawn towards employment in civil service/government positions (as many still are), where they do not care about the underlying ethos and morality of the system which they serve. Because, to put it succinctly, it is what they do. The Psychopathic Control Grid cannot function, control and push forward their agenda without these mediocre psychopaths 'just following orders'.

At the time of writing this book, both Ireland and Greece are being subjected to brutal economic austerity measures with large scale cutbacks in government services and funding. Many private sector workers are either facing unemployment or emigration. Along with this, both the Irish and the Greek public sector and especially the parliamentary employees are receiving pay increases and non-performance linked bonuses, while the rest of the people in these societies are struggling to make ends meet. On the surface, such actions by the Irish and Greek governments may seem insane, but they serve a very real political objective with the mediocre psychopathic public sector employees and managers being an integral part of all this. Now, before the reader assumes I am attacking government and public workers here, let me clarify that I am not. I am talking about a political system which—like the corporate sector— seeks to reward the O'Briens of the bureaucracy, as it does with the sharks on Wall Street. Often, the hard-working and devoted public servant is the first victim of the bureaucratic psychopaths.

Currently, the civil servants in both Greece and Ireland are being groomed to become the bulldogs of the establishment, with the aim of finding the psychopathic O'Briens who will serve the agenda of the State without question, and will revel in the status it provides. They will gladly oppress and torment the non-government employed/unemployed citizens whom they have come to see as animals. These 'Little Hitler' psychopathic types will see themselves as a superior proto-elite class, obsessively defending the authority figures and structure above them.

These civil servants desire to maintain this sense of status and immunity from normal economic fluctuations, and this will involve demonstrating their loyalty to the elites in government by pushing their agenda for them. Mindless policy-enforcing bureaucratic bots will maintain order over an increasing totalitarian society—which both Ireland and Greece are currently being re-engineered into becoming by the IMF and EU. Franz Kafka's novel, *The Trial*, illustrates a disturbing but no less realistic insight into the petty snobbery and mediocrity of equilibrium within the psychology of the psychopathic government employee that oppressive governments find so useful. A historical example of the mediocre psychopath with little or no real prospects in the private sector reaching a level of dangerous power would be Reinhard Heydrich—the Nazi 'God of Death'.

Heydrich, as the chief of the Reich Main Security Office (RSHA)—an official body charged with fighting all 'enemies of the Reich' within and outside German borders—was also one of the initial architects of the Holocaust when he had chaired the Wannsee Conference in Berlin. Heydrich's official role was that of deputy protector of Bohemia and Moravia, two regions in today's Czech Republic. In the weeks after he arrived in his new office, Heydrich ordered more than four hundred people who were living nearby to be killed, because he needed his 'quiet space'.

A classic psychopath, Heydrich showed little or no interest in the objective of the Third Reich until noticing the movement's spectacular success in gaining power and popularity which resulted in him joining the SS. This set Reinhard Heydrich apart from most of the faithful followers of Hitler whose views were shaped by Germany's humiliation at the Versailles Treaty and the resulting chaos of the Weimar Republic. Heydrich saw the Nazi movement as a good opportunity for social climbing—and if this involved mass murder, well… it was just business. His psychopathic credentials come even more into focus as he expressed his enthusiasm for the policies of National Socialism in order to impress his fiancée.

Now please pay careful attention to the rest of the Reinhard Heydrich story, as it illustrates a classic example of my 'as above, so below' approach to the subject of psychopathology. You will also realise that the psychopath you were in a relationship with will bear an uncanny resemblance to the pathological behaviour and life-trajectory of Reinhard Heydrich.

Heydrich had become engaged to nineteen-year-old Lina von Osten. He informed another girlfriend that he was breaking things off with her by sending her a copy of his engagement announcement to Lina von Osten. The discarded girlfriend's father was so outraged by this classic psychopathic devalue and discard tactic treatment of his daughter, that he officially went to the head of the Navy, who at the time was Heydrich's employer, and ruled that Heydrich's conduct had been unbecoming an officer. Subsequently, Heydrich was stripped of his rank. The soon-to-be Nazi 'God of Death', consumed with self-pity, locked himself in his room and cried for days.

As Heydrich couldn't come to terms with the loss of his social status as an officer, he then turned to his fiancée Lina von Osten as his new social enabler. Von Osten was publicly vocal about, and highly sympathetic to, the Nazi Party and its political and military objectives. In a 1970 radio interview, she spoke of how Reinhard Heydrich threw himself into Hitler's *Mein Kampf* in order to impress her and her family. The German historian Robert Gerwarth, Professor of History at University College Dublin, concludes that Heydrich's devotion to National Socialism was motivated by his desire to find a way back to a position of power. Through a combination of flattery and sycophantic devotion to the Nazi high command, Heydrich became a rising star within National Socialism. A typical psychopath who spent his life 'refusing to do the dirty work' (his own words), he rose to be head of the Reich Main Security Office until he was assassinated while sitting in the back seat of a convertible Mercedes in Prague's Libe by Czech resistance gunmen.

Tragically, it didn't end there. Hitler was so incensed following the loss of one of his more devoted and sycophantic bureaucrats, that following Heydrich's assassination, the Nazis wiped two towns off the face of the earth—Lidice and Ležáky. Thousands of innocent civilians, including children, were either killed or dragged off to labour camps in which nearly all died. Heydrich represented the classic government bureaucratic psychopath—carrying out his orders without giving consideration to any moral or ethical consequences. This is why totalitarian and democratic governments alike value such psychopaths so highly: They get the job done.

From strike busting to genocide, from enforcing draconian carbon and other unfair taxes to putting Sodium Fluoride in the drinking water, a government cannot function without this specific form of mediocre monster. What begins with cutting off a single-mother's allowance ends in labour camps. The psychopaths in governments have to always be watched, and not just the elected politicians. We enjoy the right to vote and what public services/ entitlements we still have access to because previous generations of citizens fought, went on strike and even took up arms against the previous manifestations of the Psychopathic Control Grid.

Just because they are no longer putting us in labour camps and working us to death in the mines starting at age eleven does not mean for a moment that the same elites would not do this to us again if we took our eye off the ball. In a 1962 speech at UC Berkeley, Aldous Huxley—another inbred aristocratic spawn from one of Darwin's 'favoured races' and the author of the novel (many would say blueprint) *Brave New World*—stated that, "If you are going to control any population for any length of time, you must bring in an element of getting people to consent to what is happening to them. We are in the process of developing a whole series of techniques, which will enable the controlling oligarchy—who have always existed and will presumably always exist—to get people to love their servitude... I think there are going to be scientific dictatorships in many parts of the world. If you can get people to consent to the state of servitude, then you are likely to have a much more stable, a much more lasting society; much more easily controllable society than you would if you were relying wholly on clubs, and firing squads and concentration camps."

So, there you go—straight from the aristocratic horse's mouth. To this day, Huxley is worshipped as practically a god by social engineers and political strategists.

Medicating and drugging citizens, making them obsessed with the Kardashians and MTV is less messy than genocide and a more scientific solution of controlling the masses for the agenda of the ruling classes than genocide. So remember this the next time you are giving your children their Ritalin: you are in the firing squad, you are their oppressor. They don't need machine gun towers and mass graves any longer—they've got a government tri-fold leaflet and some pharmacological 'miracle drug' to do this instead.

In very rare cases, the psychopath has the ability to make their own discoveries—financed by wealthy benefactors. Coupling this with their psychopathic deviousness, manipulation and desire to play god, the results can often be appalling for the entire planet if this rare creature makes it to the top. Or even, for that matter, sets up an office and starts consulting.

## THE MIND RAPISTS

Experimental psychologist John B. Watson (1878-1958) used his own psychopathology on his eleven-month-old son Albert for his personal experiments on the human mind. Watson is quoted as having said, "Give me the baby, and I'll make it climb and use its hands in constructing a building of stone or wood... I'll make it a thief, a gunman or a dope fiend. The possibilities of shaping it in any direction are almost endless."

In 1957, the American Psychological Association (APA) awarded Watson a gold medal for his work in developing scientific methods of parenting, which included never showing affection to children. Watson stated "... Remember when you are tempted to pet your child, that mother's love is a dangerous instrument. An instrument that may inflict a never-healing wound, a wound which may make infancy unhappy, adolescence a nightmare, an instrument which may wreck your son or daughter's vocational future and their chances for marital happiness." By the time Watson won his medal, his son Albert had committed suicide.

In the past year I have researched how the mental health profession deals with the issue of psychopathology, both from assessing the condition to how those recovering from psychopathic relationships are treated. I was appalled to discover repeated instances of an almost willful ignorance in the profession's attitude regarding the reality of psychopathic emotional and psychological abuse within society.

There also appears to be an over-complication of the pathology with the usual psychiatric labelling porn of overlapping and confusing terms and descriptions for what is perhaps one of the most easily identifiable mental disorders. To my amazement, I recently caught a segment from a US TV programme where a panel of psychiatrists claimed that psychopathology was a product of bad homes and disadvantaged socio-economic conditions. Why this drive towards obfuscation and softening? Precisely who is the mental health profession so terrified of offending? And why?

## MAMA, WE'RE ALL CRAZY NOW

Soon after WWII, there were half a dozen or so officially-designated mental disorders. In the 2010 edition of the *Diagnostic and Statistical Manual of Mental Disorders* (DSM), that number is approaching four hundred. The DSM is the manual used to define mental illness by the American Psychiatric Association (APA). It is also the generally accepted benchmark for determining mental illness worldwide. Each new entry into this manual is by member vote versus research and discovery of known pathology.

The mental illnesses contained within the DSM represent a selection of arbitrary classifications of thoughts, moods and behaviours decided upon by a committee of psychiatrists who are picked by the American Psychiatric Association. Contrary to the objectives of the DSM and APA, we still cannot tell who is and who is not mentally ill by only reading brain scans or taking blood samples. When all is said and done, the present version of the DSM is a work of ad-hoc fiction, with each disorder in the DSM an invention based on a commercially-driven agenda. Psychiatry believes that we were all superstitious neurotics until the arrival of their profession and in the century or so since they have set about to redeem us of these archaic notions. Have they succeeded? Apparently not. According to their ever-expanding bible that is the DSM, we are more insane than ever; cue the launch of the latest designer mood drug. Should we ask for our money back?

I have been contacted by several individuals who turned to various psychiatric therapists once they managed to extricate themselves from a psychopathic relationship. In most cases, their stories were almost identical: the therapist really hadn't a clue as to how to treat them. Worryingly, there appears to be an agenda on the part of the psychiatric profession to convince their patients that they never went through the experience at all but in fact merely imagined the nature of the entire relationship. Each psychiatrist prefers their own favourite technical term including, but not limited to, the usual *DSM* suspects: Borderline Personality Disorder (BPD) to Anti-Social Personality Disorder (ASPD), towards Sociopath or Narcissist or a score of others. The ultimate objective of treatment is to promote more treatment in the form of on-going psychoanalysis and medication. It almost as though the profession aims to convince the patient that they alone are the root cause of the issue, not the psychopath who put them through the love-bombing, silent treatment, projection, gaslighting and mind games.

## PSYCHOTHERAPIST
## PSYCHO·THE·RAPIST

I realise I am going to upset a lot of people when I make the following statement. I do not do this lightly, and some people advised me not to include this section within this book—but as I have gone so far beyond the pale already, I might as well go all the way and say it:

Psychiatry is not a science. It is a religion.

Like all ambitious religions, they seek to acquire as much power, money and devotion from their flock as possible. Keep them brainwashed for life and then prevent them from committing the blasphemy of personal growth and alternative healing. There shall be no God but the *DSM*. Unfortunately, there is little or no organised resistance to this dogma and the horrific history of human misery, and social and psychological destruction it leaves in its wake . Scientology appears to be the only large-scale opposition to psychiatry which, despite their otherwise excellent critique of the psychiatric profession, is sadly dismissed every time Tom Cruise jumps up and down on Oprah Winfrey's couch.

We are left with a situation where we have one religion at war with another religion. What is interesting about both psychiatry and Scientology is that both are an intrinsic part of the fabric of the social-cultural dynamic of Hollywood. There are times I wonder if Scientology's attack on psychiatry is a Machiavellian set-up to make psychoanalysis and psychotherapy appear to be the lesser of two evils. You have to wonder.

When you look at the core agenda of psychiatry, it is a religion based on the belief that everyone should be happy all the time. Apart from the ethical aspects of medicating people to achieve this state, it is not natural for human beings to be constantly happy (or constantly depressed). Recently, a well-known Irish consultant psychiatrist (and former politician) Dr. Moosajee Bhamjee called for Lithium to be added to municipal drinking water supplies in order to lower rates of depression, citing one article in the *British Journal of Psychiatry* referring to the beneficial uses of Lithium when it was added to the water supply in parts of Texas. He then stated that the Irish government should consider a pilot project for a town in Ireland where Lithium salts could be added to the municipal drinking water in very small doses. Dr Bhamjee then went on to state, "There is already a strong precedent for governments intervening in the operation of public water supply for health benefits by adding Fluoride."

Although chronic depression is a real factor in some people's lives, the cause may be any number of complex physiological, economic, social, cultural, emotional and environmental factors. Psychiatry never seeks to address the possible causality in any holistic manner, they just stand back and continue to throw medication at the problem.

Normal depression—in and of itself—is neither a disease, nor necessarily a problem. The flux between the two states of happiness and sadness represents a metaphorical cathode and anode of the consciousness which amplifies our intellect, the richness of our human condition and, thereby, our compassion for others. Most of the great works of art, music and theatre are a by-product of melancholia and strife. Depression and emotional turmoil are often a pit stop on the road to personal enlightenment.

To consider such states to be unnatural is to deny all that makes us human. Our sadness is an engine of our consciousness and integral to the human experience. Something is very wrong when psychiatry is approaching 'the blues' as a problem to be solved—especially by proposing mass-medication as a remedy. Normal states of depression are not a consciousness parasite within our humanity—psychoanalysis and psychotropic drugs are.

While the Catholic mass celebrates the Eucharist with bread and wine, the transubstantiation of the psychiatric mass delivers its host to their high-paying congregation in the form of communion wafers of Prozac, Lithium, Ritalin, Xanax, Zoloft and Lustral. Most of these 'miracle' psychiatric drugs are psychotropics with an 'HCL' suffix. HCL is hydrochloric acid. When these drugs pass through the blood-brain barrier and bind with their intended target area in the brain, they literally eat the brain structure away—ravaging brain cells, destroying neural pathways and dissolving motor neuron functions—leading towards what is essentially a chemical lobotomy.

Patients entering a psychiatrist's office and suffering from the post-traumatic stress after being devalued and discarded by a psychopath will nearly always be given a prescription for Xanax or similar medication which adds to the feelings of torment, confusion, lack of critical thinking, an inability to express their emotions or connect emotions to thoughts, muscle tension, restlessness, insomnia and helplessness—all of which the patient is already suffering from. The victim of psychopathic abuse is having their abuse not so much addressed, explored and treated as continued by the therapist. So if the psychopath hasn't completely destroyed your mental faculties, the psychiatrist will happily finish the job off. It would be interesting to discover how many people who have been traumatised by psychopaths and sought psychiatric help broke NCEA compared to the ones who undertook a self-help or other less official treatment.

Psychiatry is also the first major religion which refuses to accept that there is no such thing as evil—that people can be driven by predatory evil intent. To the average psychiatrist, an evil psychopath is just someone who hasn't been prescribed the right drugs. It is really astonishing that the concept of evil—a central motif within human history and mythology—is dismissed by the psychiatric profession as a form of archaic superstition. I believe this is one of the reasons that psychiatry is so poor at coming to terms with the issue of psychopathology. They do not believe human evil is a reality, ergo, they have essentially reduced psychopaths to the level of fairies, leprechauns and goblins resulting in the individual who has been through a relationship with a psychopath being patronised as though they had walked into the psychiatrist's office and claimed they had seen a ghost or the Loch Ness Monster.

The influential Anglican philosophical theologian John Macquarrie explained his own insight on the fundamental nature of evil: he claimed that all of us at some point run the risk of being 'eaten' by evil. Isn't this what a psychopath does to us as humans? The psychopath's energy vampirism feeds upon us until we are used up and then discarded. Yet when a person who is targeted by a psychopath attempts to explain how they feel 'emptied out' in the wake of psychopathic abuse, they are more likely than not told that they are the problem.

In the Hindu *Vedas* and *Puranas*, psychopathology is conveyed as Brahma being the creator of both good and evil. In the *Mahabharata*, he grew jealous of people and their heavenly destiny and planned to delude them—producing 'creatures in whom darkness and passion predominated'. In the *Markandeya Purana*, it is said that Brahma created both 'cruel creatures and gentle creatures, dharma and adharma, truth and falsehood'. In Hinduism, not only is evil inevitable in creation, but it is said to be a necessary dynamic factor in the universe. For thousands of years, humanity has been grappling with the forces of evil—while recognizing and coming to terms with psychopathic individuals.

Apparently, the entire human race was afflicted by a neurosis until psychiatry came along to set us all straight. It must also be pointed out that most of the quality research into psychopathology has been undertaken by neuroscientists and criminal psychologists. These professionals would be more likely to be empathic and sensitive to the needs of abuse victims than the psychiatrists who are supposed to help victims of psychopathic targeting. Something is very, very wrong here.

Psychiatrists across the entire planet are all indoctrinated with the same dogma by their educational authority figures, working for the same elites who pushed this religion upon humanity: the concept that mental illness is wholly biologically-based as a genetic, chemically-imbalanced brain malfunction. As they see it, the only solution is to correct this imbalance with psychotropic drugs supplied on behalf of the multi-billion dollar pharmaceutical industry with whom they work in tandem.

Psychiatry has become (and probably always was) a consciousness parasite which not only invades the minds of people who are probably more sane than the average psychiatrist treating them, but now encroaches upon all facets of our lives including education, public health policy, child care legislation and even religion. How has this come about? These are serious questions that need to be answered. Why must every aspect of human behaviour be assumed to be a result of a chemical imbalance, when the so-called science to underpin this claim is groundless and flawed? When it comes to psychopaths, the APA does not want to accept their existence, as there is no such thing as good and evil people, yet this insanity continues within 'the madness industry' and those who search for help are routinely dealt with by drugs and the gross interventions of Electro-Convulsive Therapy [ECT] and/or insulin shock treatment.

What is really going on here is a form of psychological collectivism—hardly surprising, as psychiatry was developed from the same aristocratic obsession which gave us 'Survivial of the Fittest' and Karl Marx, the driving forces behind the current Transhumanist movement; the belief that humans are just not good enough to be human, and what is clearly not desirable needs to be either controlled or removed entirely, even at the expense of our humanity.

Psychiatry forces a person to obsess over problems which may be either real or imagined. This obsession leads to a neurosis, trapping the patient in an endless labyrinth of psychoanalysis where patients talk about their past and delve into past 'traumas', ultimately achieving little more than endless rumination. They become trapped in a downward spiral and never improve—until they escape the cult. Psychiatric patients thus become dependent on the 'drug' and mind manipulation of the psychotherapist.

Psychiatric patients always think of themselves as defective and broken—just like a psychopath makes their targets feel with gaslighting and projection. When you alter/destroy the actual chemical functioning of a person's brain with extraneous manipulation of their brain chemistry, they lose any ability to think clearly and normally. It is just the same as when a psychopath uses love bombing and the silent treatment, leading to mental debility. Targets become dependent on the 'drug' and mind manipulation of the psychopath.

Are we beginning to see a picture developing here?

A population is much easier to control to the benefit of the ruling aristocrats when people are moulded into robots all doing the same thing. Such a mindset cannot recognise the psychopath as the parasitic, quasi-humanoid predator for what it is. Accepting this reality would have the effect of undermining the notion that all humans are the same inside, and thus can and should be treated, medicated, programmed and controlled with basic methods of behavioural and pharmaceutical therapy to bring about the desired results needed for a 'sheeple' society.

Individuality is not recognised by the Psychopathic Control Grid. Therefore, the ultimate outsider and individual—the psychopath—is considered a thing of mythology. Hence, why we are encouraged to think of fictional Hannibal Lecter and not the real-life Henry Kissinger when the term 'psychopath' is mentioned.

Another factor at work here is the psychopathology of the ruling elite projecting their own pathology onto the masses. A little known, but remarkable British movie entitled *Demons of the Mind* (Hammer, 1972) explores the incestuous, genetic neurosis at the heart of the aristocratic family structure and is probably the best 'whistle blowing' insight into how the elite of society are obsessed with altering and controlling the classes 'beneath' their own.

The story concerns an aristocrat who believes his family line is infected with 'bad blood'. He had married a peasant woman to offset this, but ended up murdering her during a psychotic episode. He has also imprisoned his son and daughter, and is physically bleeding the bad blood out of them. Probably inspired by the work of Dr. Benjamin Rush (1745-1813), one of the Founding Fathers who signed the American Declaration of Independence. Dr. Rush believed that too much blood in the system caused psychiatric and physiological disorders.

All the while this is going on in the film, peasant women are being raped and murdered on his estate, a known centre of incest, madness, hysteria, paganism and murder. The grand mansion in which the family resides becomes a metaphor of their own pathology and consanguineous fetishes. It is literally a labyrinth, mirroring the maze created by the voluntary and involuntarily-incarcerated occupants. In the script of *Demons of the Mind*, we see the pathology of the aristocratic landscape mirroring the psychological inner landscape of their neurosis. The subtext is a clash between the scientific process and religious superstition with a free-thinking young man who gels both concepts together in order to finally deal with the issue once and for all, as he proves to the local peasants that there are indeed demons inside the mind. In the climax of the movie, he 'heals' the community with a narrative which communicates the message in a way their religion cannot. Yet at the same time, he sees the priest and the scientist as useful allies. Natural Philosophy at its finest.

What makes this dark, surreal and disturbing piece of cinema so interesting is that we see the inbred elite psychopathic mind projecting their shadow upon others, as they ultimately have no spiritual self-awareness. To compensate for this spiritual vacuum, they develop a blood and lineage fetish. These aristocrats are the cause of all the misery in the society around them, yet they continually blame others for not fixing it. Much like the Darwins, Wedgwoods, Huxleys, Russells and Galtons did following the publication of *On the Origin of Species*.

There is also one montage scene in the film in which the elite psychopathic psyche is unravelled during a long close-up shot of the patriarch's eyeball. The film is really telling us about why and how psychiatry developed, and is set in the same historic period when the father of modern psychiatry—Sigmund Freud—projected his own psychopathic tendencies onto the human race.

## THE DRUG OF THE NATION

Mass media, hungry for Big Pharma advertising revenue, are completely bought and owned by the psychiatric church, particularly in the USA. Anyone who expresses even the most tranquil concern about the relationship between mass media, Big Pharma and psychiatry are declared to be insane conspiracy theorists, Scientologists, and kooks who must also still believe the Earth is flat, and conveniently ignoring the truth that there are people with the highest scientific credentials including scientists and some psychologists who advocate against the use of psychiatric drugs. Mass media and journalism tells us that a chemical imbalance theory is fact, when no scientific test has ever been developed to prove this chemical imbalance empirically. Constant guests on TV news programmes, psychiatrists are wheeled out to spew forth this appalling propaganda—but are never called to task for their statements and glibly-issued psychobabble concerning 'cool' new drugs.

Governments also play their part in protecting the psychiatric profession, as the *DSM* can be used to classify just about anyone as insane—most especially, people who question the authority of government. This is very handy during a time when politicians tell their citizens that they have to plough billions into failed banks as if it is some natural law of the universe. The *DSM-IV-TR* now labels free thinkers, non-conformists, civil disobedience advocates and those who question authority as mentally ill with Oppositional Defiant Disorder or ODD. With ODD, psychiatrists and mental health 'professionals' are only upholding a long-held tradition going back to when drapetomania—a mental disorder said to have existed in slaves who ran away to freedom. Hysteria was a very popular diagnosis in the Victorian era as well, used to classify women who rebelled against male domination or who tended to 'cause trouble'. Hysterectomies would be performed on 'hysterical women' who questioned their husband's authority right up until the 1970's in most Western nations.

You would think that bastion of scientific rationality and reason, The Richard Dawkins Foundation, would express concerns about the scientific validity of psychiatry. After all, it is not a science as much as a commercially-driven form of Voodoo. An article was recently posted to their site which endorsed psychiatric methods, including everything from electroshock therapy to dissolving the human brain in order to help cure people of their spiritual beliefs. The article also expressed concern that people who have lost loved ones are more likely to turn to their priest or rabbi than to a trained medical professional such as a psychiatrist.

In answer, the Richard Dawkins Foundation praised psychiatrists for being the least religious field within the medical profession. The article also touched upon several important realisations when its author, Farr Curlin, MD, Assistant Professor of Medicine at the University of Chicago stated, "Something about psychiatry, perhaps its historical ties to psychoanalysis and the anti-religious views of the early analysts such as Sigmund Freud, seems to dissuade religious medical students from choosing to specialize in this field."

It is not just religious medical students who turn their back on psychiatry—I would wager the more ethical ones do, also.

This raises the prospect of some rather disturbing scenarios. Will some radical atheists put their children on Ritalin for believing in Santa Claus and the tooth fairy? Fortunately, this is unlikely; a 2011 survey published in the December issue of the *Journal for the Scientific Study of Religion*, based on in-depth interviews with two hundred and seventy five scientists at twenty one 'elite' research universities in the United States told another story. Sixty-one per-cent of the participants described themselves as atheists, and had attended church more than once in the past year for mainly 'cultural reasons'.

Reading these stats really makes one wonder how many of these 'elite' atheists are sincere in their convictions. Is it simply part of a current trend; an 'academic peer pressure' placed upon them in order to prove that no hint of religious affiliation contaminates their research per the exacting standards of The Richard Dawkins Foundation? I find it ironic that a foundation based on promoting radical atheism approves psychiatry, one of the most fanatical and dangerous religions ever devised.

## FREUDIANITY

Sigmund Freud was not only a charlatan and a cocaine-addicted sex freak, but I strongly suspect he was a high-functioning psycho-path. His work with dream analysis has always struck me as being conducted by someone who never had a dream himself and at-tempted to imagine what dreaming is like. Due to repressed fron-tal brain activity, psychopaths generally stop having dreams after puberty and Freud's dream interpretations are almost farcical. Al-though it has to be said that this is a real science in which he played his part to promote, his own work into this subject is highly suspect and riddled with his own neuroses and pathology clearly projected upon his patients.

Freud's ability to perform highly theatrical fainting fits at mo-ments when others such as Carl Jung questioned Freud's research is another overlooked aspect of his personality. Why would a man of his considerable stature and influence resort to drama queen-style fainting fits in order to avoid debating aspects of his work which his peers found dubious? Even more interesting a question to ask—why did Freud perform these fits when alternative theories to his own 'dogma' were proposed? Freud had such extreme narcissistic traits that he deliberately changed the date of his book, *The Interpretation of Dreams*, so that he could be seen as a visionary for the next century.

Who decided, and why was it decided that for most of the twentieth century, Freud's theories—especially his theories of sexuality—were to become a cornerstone of not only psychiatry and psychoanalysis, but much of the social fabric of Western society?

Jeffrey Moussaieff Masson, an ex-psychoanalyst and former Projects Director of the Sigmund Freud Archives, blew the lid off the Freud godhead status as a man of science and reason in his brilliant exposé, *The Assault on Truth*. His book contained letters and long-held secret documents demonstrating Sigmund Freud's control freak nature and inability to accept any kind of criticism of his work. Yet this is the same individual who set forth from Vienna at the height of the Hapsburg Empire to treat the rest of the world who suffered from 'diseases of the personality'. In 1896, Sigmund Freud's 'Seduction Theory' stated that sexual abuse and violence inflicted on children are the main causes of adult mental illness. Almost a decade later, Freud completely reversed his position, insisting that these sexual memories were actually fantasies that never happened. If this wasn't disturbing enough, the mental health establishment went to extreme lengths to conceal the fact that Freud had about-faced his 'Seduction Theory'. *The Assault on Truth* was met with intense hostility by the Freud family and his followers, ending in Jeffrey Moussaieff Masson becoming an outcast within the psychoanalytic community.

Yet, to this day, Freud's work is still held in high regard and enthusiastically taught in colleges and universities all over the world. Freud is still touted as a valid module in the BSc Psychology degree programme in the UK, even though classical Freudian therapy (couch, free association, therapist as the 'blank slate') over the past twenty years has fallen from favour—mainly due to the fact that it didn't work. Today there are several schools of clinical psychology and although there is still a large representation of Freudian-influenced schools there is also an increase in the number of cognitive behavioural schools. The wane in Freudian therapy—especially in the USA—is a result of insurance companies no longer paying for several years of Freudian therapy when empirically-supported cognitive behavioural treatments have been shown to produce actual behavioural changes.

As a result, Freudian therapy has generally been reserved for private-paying and/or wealthy clients who can afford to pay vast sums out of pocket for several years of a treatment style invented by a raging cocaine addict and narcissist who smoked up to 20 cigars a day. The damage his legacy has left in its wake, a legacy protected by a dwindling army of Freudimentalists, has been staggering. This (probable) psychopathic individual has destroyed the lives of countless millions and—along with his nephew, Edward Bernays, the advertising evil genius—has infected humanity with a consciousness parasite which is still eating away at our souls.

## THE PSYCHOPATHIC FEAR OF INDIVIDUALITY

Anyone in a relationship with a psychopath will remember how the psychopath used everything from the silent treatment to ridicule in order to 'trim' the target's world view down to a limited interest in subjects and hobbies. It's not that you weren't allowed to think outside the box, but that you were never allowed to think outside the psychopath's box. Your intellectual scope had to be narrowed in order for the psychopath to control you. A sudden interest in a new subject, especially a fringe subject which required a whole new learning curve and novel insight, the psychopath would always put an immediate stop to.

What the psychopath feared was you wandering outside the emotional, sexual and psychological perimeter fence they had trapped you within. The greatest enemy of the psychopath is a free mind—the greatest friend of the psychopath is a controlled society filled with fearful, dumbed-down followers who question nothing.

If there is one political philosophy which screams psychopathic, it is Collectivism. Psychopaths are drawn to collectivist ideologies as they can rise to the top as a service to the collective social or political construct. This is straightforward enough. Within a specific collectivised system, the rules are the same for all. There is no need to be dynamic, flexible and original. You just do as you are told and wait for those ahead of you to die so you can move up into their position.

While in big business, the clever and slick psychopath can and often does rise to the top through flattery and plagiarism, the collectivist system allows mediocre and less dynamic psychopaths to do the same. This makes them far more dangerous since once they have achieved a level of power, a reign of terror will be unleashed on all below them in order to maintain their own status.

Collectivism is the political theory that states that the will of the people is omnipotent—that an individual must obey; that society as a whole and not the individual is the unit of moral value. Collectivism states that, in politics, society comes first and the individual must obey. According to Karl Marx, the individual is and should be subordinate to society. Marx was a strict determinist in his view of human nature, holding that social and economic forces 'condition' man, shaping every aspect of his character, personality and life. Since society is his master, it stands to reason that a man should spend his life as society's slave, obeying its every command. Within Collectivism, an individual has no value in himself—he/she is merely a fragment of the group and must serve its needs. Within a collective system, there is no need for original thinking. This is perfect for psychopaths. They just play the game, follow the script and wait to move up the ladder. With each step they ascend on the pyramid, they enjoy a new strata of power above enablers and targets below them. RED FLAGS, anyone?

Karl Marx was the first of the great nineteenth century icons to lose his prestige. While the 'scientific' part of his 'scientific socialism' was always dubious and inhuman to say the least, the appearance of information technology put his world view to rest. Later, Sigmund Freud was likewise shown to be an unscientific charlatan, as patients undergoing therapy have a significantly worse recovery rate than those who rely on their own resources. Both Marx and Freud can be seen as the benchmarks of the Psychopathic Control Grid—the concept that all humans are of the same general baseline of personality and can be treated as worker bees to conform to a certain collectivised 'scientific' system.

As they waged war on Natural Philosophy, Darwin, Marx and Freud portrayed humans not as biological and spiritual beings, but rather, as animals or robots who inhabited a universe ruled by purely impersonal forces and whose thoughts and behaviour were dictated by the unbending forces of biology, chemistry, and environment. This materialistic concept of reality eventually infected every area of our culture from politics and economics to literature and art, and is the underlying ethos of the Psychopathic Control Grid all around us today.

## THE PATHOLOGICAL TRINITY

The Victorian era presented us with the first non-religious attempt to destroy human consciousness. The three great iconic figures of this 'age of reason'—Darwin, Marx and Freud—cast such an intense spell across collective Western consciousness that to this day we are still recovering. Darwin turned science into a religion and all one has to do to see this is to gauge the reaction of his followers: they allow absolutely no room for debate. Marx turned the individual into a unit of measure to be dehumanised and used as a component within the machine community. Freud destroyed human sexuality and took away the confidence of the individual to explore the true meaning of their own life story. Each of these scientific methods had one singular goal—to crush the human spirit and reduce us to the level of soulless automatons with no concept of a more transcendental view of our own humanity. In other words, to make proto-psychopaths of us all.

As with any psychopathic construct there is always a kernel of truth leading to an eventual epiphany buried within the pathology. Darwin did indeed prove that random mutations within organisms do lead to evolutionary changes, though as we have seen with Epigenetics, along with the countless holes which still remain within his Natural Selection philosophy—it is not the full picture. Marx, with his Communist Manifesto, gave us the roots of such ideas as public health services, and the notion of social safety nets for the poorest members of society. Likewise, Freud deserves credit for promoting and popularising dream analysis as a tool for personal understanding, but just as in a psychopathic relationship the target will always find one or two aspects of the psychopath's persona that throws up red flags. In amongst the chaos, torment and misery they left in their wake—be it great sex, excitement or just some funny moments of shared joy—we have to step back from the canvas and look at the larger picture in order to make sense of the individual brush strokes.

*Red Flag*: Darwin's 'survival of the fittest' led directly to the first scientifically-mandated genocide of an indigenous people. The elimination of the Native American population was justified and implemented according to Darwinian philosophy. What began with Darwin's 'Favoured Races' resulted in general stores selling a tobacco pouch made from the dried skin of an Apache female's breast. Darwinists refused to accept this reality in the same way many Catholics refuse to accept the horror of the Inquisition.

*Red Flag*: Marx and his promotion of the individual being sub-servient to the collective dogma resulted in some of the greatest genocides of humans the world has witnessed, from Stalin's purges to Mao's Cultural Revolution and on to the European intellectu-ally-educated Pol Pot wiping out half the population of his home-land, all the while—*Red Flag*—Freud destroyed the mind and self-confidence and perverted and twisted the psychology of countless numbers of people in Western society.

Another interesting aspect surrounding these scientific messiahs of the Victorian age is that they were all products of empires and imperialistic structures which were soon to be victims of their own hubris. The epoch of Jesus of Nazareth is the story of the end of the Roman Empire as much as it is about the birth of a new global re-ligion. Darwin and his obsession with bloodlines was a mirror into the neurosis of the British ruling classes who believed (and still do) that Darwin's 'Favoured Races' granted scientific legitimacy to their historic obsessions with inbreeding and 'pedigree'. As history reveals, the religion of consanguinity promoted by the Darwins, Gallons, Russells, Wedgwoods and Huxleys of the world produced aristocratic psychopaths and deformed monsters hidden away in secret mental hospitals—out of sight and out of mind. Karl Marx was very much a by-product of the Prussian Empire which developed the public education system in order to provide basic training for military service, and absolute conformity with the mandates of authority figures—not to mention the manner in which the public school system is only now coming to terms with the fact that individuality and creativity are noble attributes in young children. Freud, a product of the Austro-Hungarian Empire, based most of his theories surrounding mental dysfunction of the human mind on his wealthy clients, the vast majority of whom were the aristocrats of Viennese society who would have been as inbred and perverted as the upper echelons of any imperialist hierarchy of the day. All three dogmas were to coagulate within the meat grinder of the First World War in which countless millions of 'useful eaters' were to be slaughtered for 'King and Country'. This resulted in the survivors of Flanders, the Somme, Mons, Gallipoli, Verdun, Isonzo and hundreds of other mechanised murder rampages returning home from these scientific bloodbaths looking for a new social order to replace the imperialist systems which led them to the slaughter. What they got was a bait 'n' switch—another version of the Psychopathic Control Grid took over from a previous version.

The Hindu Vedic traditions have a very different notion of how time functions compared to our Western linear concept. The Vedic tradition applies a cyclical nature to time—in that each cycle of time (yugas) eternally repeats itself. In the way that seasonal cycles repeat and planets orbit stars and stars orbit their galaxies, so does human history and personal life stories. This presents us with an ability to not so much predict the future, but to expect similar patterns to come around again. In the case of the Pathological Trinity of Darwin, Marx and Freud—similar to the story of many religious figures from Jesus to Buddha—it resulted in devoted and powerful followers who entrenched their philosophy within the human consciousness.

The same happens in our personal lives. When we reach middle age, we can at times look back and understand with exceptional clarity how we repeated the same mistakes until we finally dealt with the core issue. In this sense, the psychopath is a wake-up call. We have to learn to recognise these patterns—both as individuals and as a society—if we are to move to higher levels of consciousness and on to the next level of evolution. We are not at the mercy of fate as much as we are led to believe.

"Conscience? I see it as a middle-man between you and your goals. From everything I understand about it, not having one makes you see the world more clearly."

*- Dispatches from Psychopaths*

## CHAPTER SIX

# LUCIFER'S PARADOX

**W**hen I was a child, my favourite board game was Snakes and Ladders. I played no other board game—none of the others interested me. I must have played Snakes and Ladders every day of my childhood. When I had no one to play with me, I would play as the two players all by myself and roll the dice twice until one of my buttons reached the magical one hundred score at the top of the board. Then I would begin to play the game all over again.

The game of Snakes and Ladders is based on an ancient Indian board game played between two or more players on a board featuring numbered squares. Depending on the version, there is a random number of 'ladders' and 'snakes' on the board which always connects two specific board squares. If you roll the dice and land at the base of a ladder, you move up the board. If you land on the head of a snake, you move back down the board. Later on in life, I found out that the Indian version of the game is actually a morality play of sorts, representing the players' virtues (ladders) and vices (snakes), and was known as Moksha Patam, emphasising the role of fate or karma in the Hinduism consciousness.

In terms of my personal journey into and out of the labyrinth of the psychopath, it has begun to dawn on me how this game is a pictorial allegory of the long, strange trip I'm on, and how playing this game as a child feels like precognitive insight into the underlying theme of this book.

The snakes represent the hyperactive Reptilian Complex of the consciousness parasites, the psychopaths and the manipulators who hold us back from reaching our full potential. The ladders on the other hand represent the DNA double helix assisting one's individual journey of personal evolution to the next level of human consciousness (number one hundred) which we activate through Epigenetics and creativity intentions. When we land on the head of a snake during our final steps at the end of the game the slide down always becomes a learning experience. The lesson we learn is that we are still very much in a game and we will all eventually win if we keep playing. Matters not who reaches number one hundred first; all human players will arrive there.

When we are targeted and personally damaged by a psychopath and/or oppressed by one of the consciousness parasites manifesting from the Psychopathic Control Grid, we still remain 'on the board'. We are still in the game. Psychopaths can slow our growth in personal consciousness, but they can't stop it completely. One way or another, every player of Snakes and Ladders will reach one hundred. Psychopaths are always trapped at the head of the snake. This prevents them from reaching the end of the game and enjoying the satisfaction of playing to the full experience; the reptile in their brain is always their undoing.

There is meaning to the pain of having been in a psychopathic relationship or situation. The consciousness parasite feeding on your life energy is there to be defeated; the dragon left inside your psyche must be slain. Your post-traumatic stress is real. You have been moved down the board by the snake inside the mind of the psychopath, and you are experiencing changes based on learning from your journey up (and down) the Snakes and Ladders number grid. The solution to this is always the same: to roll the dice and keep playing the game.

Move forward, find meaning and you will eventually land on a ladder to move you up towards consciousness evolution. This is why psychiatry is not your friend in this situation. You are an individual and your psychopathic abuse situations were unique to you alone. You must walk the path to recovery on your own unique journey.

Humans are not meant to be robots all doing the same thing and thinking and living to the same script. We are all different with varied gifts and unique talents. Most of these gifts are ignored as they are outside of the tiny box of mainstream belief. To begin moving up the board again from your fall down the snake, listen to your intuition, pay attention and understand.

Acknowledge, then release emotions instead of disassociating from them and your humanity with psychiatric drugs. Shower kindness to the eternal and all-knowing intuition of your own inner voice. Listen to the signals and follow the path to freedom rather than allowing the consciousness parasites of the psychopath and the DSM to force you back into the mainstream mould again. Find the true meaning of your own personal experience with a psychopath. Settling for dissociation is not moving back up the board. Drugging the pain merely pins you at the same level which the snake landed you on, and since life never holds still, the struggle you feel is your desire to let go and be free and move forward. The longer you postpone moving on, the greater the tug to move forward will be, and the greater the pain you experience. The psychopath/snake landed you where you are; staying where you landed or moving on is entirely up to you. Lose the fear and roll the dice again.

Generally depicted as hiding in seclusion on the ground waiting to strike, serpents were depicted in religion, mythology and folklore as guardians of the underworld. As snakes grow, many of them shed their skin at various times, revealing a shiny new skin underneath. This is an appropriate metaphor for the psychopath when they move from one persona to the next. For this reason, snakes have also become symbols of rebirth and transformation. The Aborigines of Australia considered the snake a symbol of death, evil, or treachery. The Nagas of Hindu and Buddhist mythology show snakes as deceptive shape shifters, including the image of a fully human-looking snake. They often appeared as human heads on serpent bodies, cruel and vengeful. Our ancestors knew about psychopaths, but they also knew that encounters with them could also represent important turning points in life.

## PSYCHOPATHS IN CHILDREN'S FAIRY TALES

Mythology and folklore are an early form of psychology. In a pre-scientific era it was the only means by which people could anchor their frustration and warnings to others regarding consciousness parasites and other pathological predators within the material world without having to rely exclusively on religious concepts such as demons, succubi and so on. This was accomplished by presenting an allegory of monsters, demons, fairies and elves in human form and was probably done to avoid charges of witchcraft and blasphemy when religious sectarian tensions unleashed psychopaths in the guise of Witchfinder Generals and the sadists of the Inquisition.

The majority of European fairy tales from this period are about psychopaths and psychopathic behaviour and serve as an instruction manual on how to recognise the traits and deal with them. A collective folk memory was generated and maintained in these children's stories of wicked stepmothers, deceitful kidnappers or sly wolves disguised as kindly and familiar people ultimately revealed to be killers, cutthroats and cannibals.

This medium of oral tradition was the only option available to educate and warn the mainly illiterate population of the time without risking ridicule or censure; it was linguistic folk art designed to encourage change in the collective consciousness and also served as a collective therapy session to heal past trauma within a community caused by psychopaths in the guise of spies, swindlers, kidnappers and killers. Such tales were—until the era of movies, television, graphic novels and popular fiction—retained within the tribal consciousness through re-telling in order to keep the community's 'spirits up'. The effort of creating a vast and complex canon of fairy tales demonstrates how people of the past must have known what they were dealing with: an alien force within the human community. These 'uneducated,' pre-Freudian folk were acutely aware that the mind contained different levels of awareness. Trauma was not always retained within the ego—but in 'another mind' behind it. In the collective sense, fairytales are linked to the overall emotional health and safety of the community at large.

Anyone who has been damaged by a psychopath will freely admit that there is something unearthly about the experience. I have spoken to hardcore atheists who, when searching for the right term, finally settled on the word 'demonic' to describe the effect it had on them. They had discovered that what they had gone through was both deeply visceral and profoundly primal and possibly the nearest they had ever come to an encounter with a fairytale monster.

The proliferation of references to psychopaths in European fairy tales shows us just how seriously the psychopath was taken by our ancestors. The arrival of Bram Stoker's *Dracula* turned out to be a metaphor that detailed with pinpoint accuracy the relationship between human and psychopath, and the impression left upon the mass consciousness can only be described as cataclysmic as evidenced by the enduring popularity of the vampire mythos in entertainment today. This is how the Psychopathic Control Grid can deny their own existence to the masses: by writing off vampires as 'fiction', whilst simultaneously portraying impossible, doomed and toxic love stories between human and vampire as 'romantic'. As I've mentioned before, Robert Hare came up with the ingenious term, Intra-Species Predator. If that does not conjure up a folklore monster then I don't know what does.

## CRACKING THE CODE

In *Puzzling People*, I stated that the human race was on the threshold of being overrun by psychopaths and that we needed to get wise to this issue fast, then move on from it before we are completely destroyed or relegated to the position of sub-species to *homo psychopathicus*. In the book, I outlined why indulging the genetic predisposition of psychopathology as being somewhat of a sinister cul-de-sac was of no real benefit to anyone except certain scientists' egos and/or research funding, various bigots and racially-minded eugenicists.

I also want to mention briefly the absurd notion that psychopaths, or the *homo psychopathicus* strain as I have come to term

them is somehow the next stage in human evolution to replace
the empathic homo sapiens on this planet. I can best address this
by stating: if the psychopath became the replacement for homo
sapiens, they would eventually all turn on each other until there
was only one specimen left. This is their nature. This last surviving
'victorious' psychopath would have no ability to pass on its DNA.
Therefore, nature would be making a mistake if psychopaths were
the next step in human evolution. Unless nature has a plan to make
humans completely extinct, then the *homo psychopathicus* muta-
tion/sub-species becoming the dominant human would make
sense. This also goes a long way to understanding why the anti-
human, frankly insane and perverted Transhumanist Movement is
a nest of psychopaths who preach that humans are now an obsolete
and defective species that needs to be replaced with machines.

To others who claim that psychopaths are only unfortunate
victims of their own mental illness and that I am being bigoted
against them by embarking on a crusade to oppress them—well
then, guilty as charged. If by 'oppression' this implies cutting off
their main source of sustenance—kind, caring, creative and loving
people—then I must be honest and wear that badge. It is one thing
to embark on a crusade against a specific strain endangering the
human population with misery and eventual extinction, but without finding meaning in this experience, there can be no personal or
social evolution. I am not driven by hate—I am driven by healing
and understanding.

## YOU SURVIVED A WAR, NOW WIN THE PEACE

All relationships—particularly ones with psychopaths—are
ultimately a learning experience about ourselves. We must come
to terms with the fact that even though the psychopath was still
a monster who ravaged our souls and left us broken, it still happened for a reason. There was something in our personalities which
(in most cases) allowed us to open that door when the demon
knocked. It could have been anything from an overwhelming sense
of not wanting to be alone to just being a decent person looking to

be loved, and we placed this desire above everything, even our own common sense and instinct for survival.

Perhaps even a 'karmic debt' of sorts needed to be paid for the possible hurt caused to others in the past—either through an extra-marital affair, pulling out of a wedding at the last moment, or even having damaged someone in your childhood—which you have long forgotten about. Either way, you are being given something which you must self reflect upon in order to move on. The psychopath-target dynamic is highly symbiotic. Be honest with yourself—something about you needs to be worked on so this does not happen again. This does not make the psychopath right and you wrong—not at all. It just means that you need to start building the firewall around your consciousness so these monsters never have the chance to get in there ever again.

I have been fortunate to have experienced only one relationship with an entity I would consider to be a psychopath. This was during a brief period in my early 20's while living in New York. A month-long whirlwind of intense sex and excitement and then it was suddenly and brutally over—and it messed me up for years. She has, from what I gather, spent her entire adult life this way. Typical psychopath. There is a major difference between being a troubled and self-absorbed human being and being a psychopath. Only psychopaths see themselves as perfect, without responsibility to the needs and feelings of others, and they all view humans as energy devices to be used up and discarded.

## REPRESSED MEMORIES

I had no idea what a psychopath was until a young Wall Street investment banker named David presented me with a backstage pass into his world by—completely out of the blue—blurting out that he 'was a psychopath'. It wasn't until later that I developed a sustained interest in the subject, not because of him, but because of my aforementioned relationship with her—the beautiful, young fashion model with whom I was having sex five to seven times a day, and who claimed she loved me forever on a Friday and told me to 'fuck off and stop annoying her' on a Monday when she moved on. I was recently told that she has continued to follow the same pattern and has at least one murder-by-suicide to her credit.

The experience almost killed me, but I did recover and went on to enjoy a good, productive life. I now see that all my work dealing with psychopaths, right up to the publication of *Puzzling People,* was my way of trying to comprehend what really happened during those four weeks when I was just barely out of my teens and why it affected me so profoundly for many, many years afterwards.

Everything odd about this woman and the experiences which I was never able to understand finally made sense. What she really meant when she told me, "I wished I had a dick on top of my cunt so I could fuck myself all day…" Why she suddenly became so intensely sexually excited after visiting the Bronx Zoo that she demanded sex in the bathroom of a Metro North train during which she would emulate a feral animal. Why she always had large amounts of cash and vanished for long periods of time during the day and night—she was working as a prostitute. Why she had a pronounced Adam's Apple and could beat me in arm wrestling and how during sex she would practically pull the hair out of the top of my head by dragging my forehead in towards her with such intensity. In retrospect, I believe she was trying to completely possess my frontal cortex.

As suddenly and explosively as it began, it was all over and I was never the same human ever again. I emerged after one month a completely changed person. A part of me—something vital in the truest sense of the word—had been taken, and I began my quest to understand and to fully share with humans what I have learned about psychopaths.

## WHO IS INSIDE YOUR HEAD AND HOW DID THEY GET THERE?

We have the ability to transcend the Psychopathic Control Grid of government, major corporations and media and liberate our consciousness by learning to look upon the world with new eyes to see and new ears to listen. There is a clandestine radio station which transmits its often perverted and malicious agenda into our psyches 24 hours a day. Due entirely to the ignorance most people have of how this secret channel broadcasts and at what frequencies, we can spend all our lives captive until the moment we realise that we can release ourselves.

There are hidden meanings to art, symbolism, design, language and motif, and in my employment as a graphic designer I was trained in this 'art' of mind control. I learned how corporations play upon people's insecurities in order to manipulate them into purchasing 'dreams' that they do not need and how maintaining the captivity of the consumer is the top priority of all big business, since without it the machinery that drives the Psychopathic Control Grid will grind to a complete halt. So, how to begin to be free? We need to learn to see the big picture and ultimately stop the manipulation...

Our modern Western society and the culture it enforces upon us goes right back to the rich and fertile Mesopotamian plain between the Tigris and Euphrates rivers known as the Babylonian Empire. It is this ancient civilisation that is considered the ground zero reason of how our present world actually works today. From 1894 BC to 320 BC, Babylon was essentially the capital of the known world, and although there is compelling evidence that human civilisation goes back many thousands of years before, Babylon is considered to be the starting point of our present-day civilisation. It is also, in a very real sense, the birthplace of modern politics, social structure, religion and culture which we experience today in the twenty-first century: The Psychopathic Control Grid.

All the trappings of modern Western society, including our concept of social classes, the sciences and technology, specialisation of skills, media, secret societies, banking, even the celebrity worship under which we currently suffocate, have their origins in Babylon. The habit of building monuments, icons and effigies to kings, gods and demons came out of the Babylonian civilisation. Even the concept of journalism and media have their origins there, as the priest class of the time was the middle ground (the medium, the Media) between royalty and the populace, disseminating culture, realities and belief packages from on high to the masses, just as mainstream journalism and 'advertorials' do today.

The concept of celebrity and stardom comes from Babylon; the idea of a supernatural entity which can either be 'the good guy' or 'the bad guy', then encapsulated into a clay, wax or bread effigy until the time comes to release the entity by pouring water on it and dissolving it to make way for the next icon. The star having served its purpose, it is then considered to be 'washed-up'—it all goes back to Babylon.

The name Babylon comes from an adaptation of Akkadian Ba-bili, which translates as the 'Gate of God', as it represented the connection between mankind and the god beings. This is where we get the concept of the gateway between heaven and earth—'The Pearly Gates' and so on. This is also why the concepts of the gate, the door-way, the arch and the portal play such a significant role in the occult and mystery traditions which underlines the Psychopathic Control Grid through modern Freemasonry and organised monotheistic religions. The 'star gate' is where ordinary humans become gods and goddesses as they enter auditoriums, stadiums and palaces to collect their Oscars, gold medals and knighthoods. This is just as it was in Babylon, where statues of deities were marched through the Ishtar Gate and down the Processional Way each year during the New Year's celebration while the on-lookers 'oohed' and 'ahhed' as they cast their gaze upon the parade of elusive 'stars' moving along a red floor and through a gateway flanked on either side by twin towers decorated with golden dragons.

The architecture of the modern world from the concept of high-rise living to designated areas for different classes to occupy in an urban environment, all go back to Babylon. Likewise, the development of agriculture, imperial conquest, dynastic families/blood-lines, the repression of the sacred feminine, concepts of visitation from other planets, and religious and political hierarchies. You can draw a line from the contemporary period all the way back to Ba-bylon that will form the ever-present tether binding us all to the present Psychopathic Control Grid, and from which we must slip the lead and develop our own individual intuition and lifestyles.

Where the legacy of Babylon made the greatest impact upon human history was on the sense of self and individual identity when Babylon became the first society to utilise art and symbolism to manipulate human consciousness to its detriment. This is where the art of social engineering began; the first attempts to use art, language and symbolism—the real meaning of which remained in the hands of the few to control the many—took root. This 'art' was further developed by the Greeks, who set the ball rolling for organised propaganda and public relations to the present day.

Among the early symbols utilised by the Babylonian elite, the most commonly recognised would be the Five-Pointed Star. This is a design that is seen on everything from the corporate logos of many major corporations such as Heineken and Texaco to the flags and military regalia of the United States, the Soviet Union, the European Union, Communist China and many others. This is the shape used to denote a sense of exclusivity, privilege and status, such as the Hollywood Walk of Fame, five-star hotels, Michelin star restaurants and numerous other examples.

The five-pointed star originated with the Babylonian Venusian pentagram seen upon the disc of Shamash, the Babylonian sun deity believed to be the god of truth and justice because he is all-seeing. Shamash also wields a knife with a jagged edge to cut his way through the mountains at dawn. These motifs are extremely significant when applied to the imagery of governments and governmental agencies. This is where the image of the sun rising between two mountains that is seen on everything from national emblems to corporate logos has its origins.

Logos, motifs and symbols that originated in Babylon may seem benign on the surface and some would argue that they have retained their popularity because they are attractive and can be easily stylised no matter how tastes in art and aesthetics change over the centuries, but it goes much deeper than this. These designs and symbols are used because their shapes leave deep psychologi-

cal and emotional impressions upon us. They are burned into the
deepest levels of our psyches because this is where these images
originated—they were painted on cave walls by the earliest humans thousands of years before the first cities were built upon the
fertile plains of Mesopotamia.

It was in Babylon that these archetypal symbols were fully re-
fined and utilised to control and manipulate the human psyche at
individual and collective levels to the agenda of a ruling elite. This
mind control technique continues to control our thoughts, deeds
and actions in the modern world, all the while the majority of the
population remains unaware of it.

Every single exterior control methodology and agenda which
is imposed upon you—either overtly or subliminally—is all designed to achieve one singular aim: to guarantee domination and
gain stewardship over your consciousness. This can come in the
guise of a manipulative person playing on your insecurities with a
combination of flattery and criticism, a product brand being marketed as the panacea of your perceived (indoctrinated) shortcomings and failures—be they personal, social, financial or intellectual,
to the relationship, politician, priest, guru or celebrity who has all
the answers you always wanted.

Your consciousness is being altered by me just reading this book
right now. I am writing these words on purpose in order to create
a shift in your perceptions, and, yes, it is indeed a form of mind
control. My agenda is to help you reclaim your mind from the in-
fluences which do not have your best interests at heart and is bent
towards securing your enslavement by the Babylon Mind. The psychopath in your relationship got to you because the psychopaths
on Madison Avenue, Hollywood and TV got in there first. How do
you know I am telling the truth? Learn to listen to your instincts
and then trust what you hear.

Until now, this capitulation of your consciousness to the Babylon
Mind was done without your awareness. Similar to being worked
by a stage hypnotist, you handed over your freewill to the manipulator and were powerless to do anything about it. In the past, this

would've been done through pageantry and ritual—mainly religious, but often through the theatre, ballads, children's stories and other early forms of entertainment.

These days, the primary weapon of choice implemented to control the human consciousness is television, and to a lesser extent, movies and popular magazines. The Internet remains the last vestige of a media where the mind can still roam freely to exercise one's own discernment and discover one's own truths, which is why politicians are so determined to shut it down as it is—according to them—filled with paedophiles and conspiracy theorists. The vast numbers of newspapers and journalists facing their own imminent extinction are only too happy to sensationalise concerns about the quality of the information on the Internet, while they themselves have always reprinted government, academic and corporate press releases without prior critical examination.

Hence why the Internet has been so powerful in allowing countless millions of people all over the world to finally realise just what a greasy profession mainstream journalism is and always has been while masquerading under the guise of serving the needs of the population at large. They don't serve anything but their own and corporate interests and never have; they have simply been the only source of information from the Psychopathic Control Grid to the great unwashed. A journalist starting out with noble intent quickly finds him or herself hobbled by that purity at a major paper or news corporation and must compromise at some point in order to retain employment. In the past, small local and provincial papers were one of the few places where critical and independent journalism took place and this is why their archives have become a gold mine for alternative information and researchers. Looking for deeply significant stories which never made it to the national news often led to staggering insights in which larger agendas were uncovered. This is identical to when you realised you were dealing with a psychopath and proceeded to piece together their confusing and cryptic life story only to uncover the complete picture of what you were actually dealing with.

What we know about the deadly effects of DDT came from independent investigators who were compiling cuttings and stories from small regional papers and stepping back to see the bigger picture. Meanwhile, the Pulitzer Prize propagandists in the big city and national periodicals were too busy hiding anything which could alarm advertisers or challenge their self-delusion of being the bastions of free speech.

Mainstream journalists are not there by accident, or by some organic process where the cream of the crop rises to the top. Major news services and media outlets carefully select and cultivate the journalists who rise in the ranks. These journalists are very often a specific type of narcissistic, uncritical individual, enlisted to regurgitate corporate and governmental propaganda and to defend these second-hand 'opinions' as though they are inarguable natural laws of the cosmos, when in reality it is just 'spin' in one form or another. The purpose of the mainstream journalist is not to think, or analyse or tell the simple truth; it is to sign up to a delusion and then defend this delusion for a pay cheque. That's it.

Many top flight news readers are often related to people who are already in the media and will have been indoctrinated into a certain program from the time they were young, with no developed capacity to think critically. Others will have worked with government and corporate press offices and can't tell the difference between reality and a press release. This is why they can be knee-deep in snow well into late spring year after year and still be writing articles about it being the warmest year ever. They have a need to believe they are on the side of the noble and the just, and then pontificate as the 'progressive' voice of reason and deep wisdom. They only know a viewpoint is correct because a press release told them it was.

Every single mainstream journalist I have ever known also had addiction issues; mainly—but not limited to—alcoholism. The powers-that-be know that a scared junkie will do anything to keep scoring a fix. This is a huge factor in the mainstream media, especially newspaper journalism. They employ people who will write what they are told to in order not to jeopardize the funding of their habit, be it booze, chain smoking, prescriptions, mood stabilizers, cocaine, or underage Thai rent boys. Think of the traditional image of the surly, unkempt hack bashing their nicotine-encrusted digits on the typewriter in a dank downtown office, a half-empty bottle of bourbon next to them; that stereotype did not come about by accident.

Grumpy, arrogant basket cases driven by a need to control others since they can't control or modify their own pathology and addictions, they mock and ridicule bloggers and 'alternative' journalists. The mainstream hack projects all his miserable frustration and quisling world views onto the people he fears the most: free thinkers. Then there are other journalists who are frustrated STASI/Secret Police types obsessed with authority figures and will do anything asked of them in order to prove their devotion so they can one day become editor.

Mainstream corporate journalism is for the most part a rotten, narcissistic and tunnel-visioned propaganda cesspool of existence which draws in extremely unhealthy individuals and always has. They are not stupid as much as they are deeply detached from reality, all the while being emotionally and psychologically bankrupt. This is why so many of them die in their late forties and fifties; a completely negative and vapid existence devoid of personal creativity and psychological independence comes with a price.

Mainstream media goes so much deeper than creating insecurities and fulfilling social role models—immersion in it literally changes your body, mind and soul.

I intend to help you become aware of just how powerful the art of subliminal mind control and manipulation really is and how it impacts society as a whole. If this book accomplishes nothing else but to de-program a single mind from the Babylonian control construct and show how to recover from and defend against further manipulation, I will count the effort of writing it as well-spent. It is time to burn down Babylon and develop a symbolic and creative lexicon that celebrates humanity rather than enslaving it.

## PATHOLOGICAL FEEDBACK

Imagine your consciousness being a non-local phenomena which creates its own reality through personal intention. When your consciousness gives rise to a thought, this is then manifested from the underlying space-time fabric of the universe into what we have come to know as the material world. Consciousness is the spark, the ignition of this process—but it is also the observer and manipulator of the personal experience which is your life.

The consciousness creates your brain and nervous system, which is a processor and antenna that allows you to tune in to this reality which you are currently experiencing and translate that experience into what it means to you. What you create around you, including your own body self-image, is a product of the consciousness creating it. This is why some people just seem to have everything they want, or have their lives work out for them, while others flounder from one disaster to the next; why children look like their parents (even adopted ones); why couples who have been married for many years begin to look like brother and sister, and even why people's pets begin to resemble their owners. This is all down to the manipulation of the material universe by our consciousness and expressed in terms of Epigenetics.

Stop and think for a moment of how profound this realisation is. There is no reason, in terms of biological science, why a Yorkshire Terrier should look like the middle-aged woman who loves her dog. Nothing in science can explain how homo sapiens with two legs and walking upright can develop the same physical 'life presence' as their beloved pet, except for the bond between the two—the loving exchange of sub-atomic flux between owner and dog that re-forms reality. We have all seen this with people and their pets. The evidence is staggering and yet it is ignored by science because outside the world of Quantum Physics (a fancy way of saying magic) it cannot be explained. This experience was created by the human consciousness who—after a few years of information exchange and what we call love—altered the dog physically to resemble their owner. Reality was changed, and this moulding of the fabric of sub-

atomic space-time happens every moment of your life. The problem is that your consciousness has been hijacked to create a reality
which is not the one you want—but the one IT wants you to have.
The demon-worshipping elite class of Babylon is still hypnotising
us to this day in precisely the same way the psychopath put you
under its spell and took you and made you a doppelgänger in its
image, and why it left you an emotional and psychological wreck
after it 'moved on'. It made you into someone else altogether—and
then said you were worthless and you were a fool.

Mass media and the government are the same symbiotic entity
in every country. Both work for each other to socially engineer the
rest of us towards certain corporate agendas, which never represent our views. But this does not matter—the agenda, even when it
flies in the face of reality, will be the culture which is created from
the pathological coagulation of news editors and politicians for the
benefit of the globalists and no one else.

It has reached the point where I am not bothered any longer
about who is wise to this reality or not. I still meet people who
are stocking up on extra heating fuel for the third summer in a row
and they are also still 'terribly concerned about man-made global
warming'. The more educated they are, the more easily led and controlled by mass media and politics they are. They cannot think—
they assume they are too educated (in reality, indoctrinated) to be
conned and manipulated. Look at all the 'liberals' who refuse to
accept that Obama is as much a war criminal as Bush. Look at all
the 'conservatives' who can't accept that the bankers are the biggest
welfare spongers.

Most people will forever deny the obvious in order to feel that they
are somehow on the side of the most righteous and possess the most
authentic moral conviction—when it is just one side of Tweedle-
Dee-Tweedle-Dum media/political duality which they have aligned
themselves with and is nothing other than a pre-formulated 'opinion'
invented for you to pick a side. Then you are supposed to defend that
side while the puppet masters are all laughing.

Humans will go to incredible lengths to deny the realisation that they have been conned by their leaders and mass media. They want so much to believe their politicians, legal structures and public bodies somehow care about them and will protect them from corporate and globalist interests. If someone starts to question their indoctrination and it starts to hurt too much, they can always bark out *Racists! Anti-Semite! Conspiracy theorist! Climate change denier!* like obedient dogs.

Today, most people have an approach to their own reality which is based completely on Hollywood and the current Psychopathic Control Grid. This is the very essence of 'movie magic'—you can see it all the time if your eyes are opened to the sorcery. Sometimes, they even indirectly let the cat out of the bag, and we may be presented with revelations via allegory under the guise of entertainment. Some of these movies are nothing short of transcendental flashbacks to the Greek Mystery Plays and Babylonian processional rites. Often, they can leave the most profound impacts on people who have watched these films and most will never know why.

One of the most powerful examples of a mystery play is Stanley Kubrick's masterpiece, *2001: A Space Odyssey*. People who had no idea what it was about were profoundly changed by the experience. This is due to the fact that Kubrick was a master manipulator of human consciousness, playing on powerful allegorical and archetypal resonances within the consciousness of the viewer. You didn't even have to follow or understand the story of *2001: A Space Odyssey*—you felt it echo within the inner landscape of your soul and rebound in your subconscious mind as a transformative psychological manifestation. You were being given a peek into how new worlds are manifested, one individual at a time, and for most it was a glorious insight into a state we need to attain if we are to free ourselves from psychopathic and pathological manipulation.

Sadly, the vast majority of Hollywood movies are designed to deaden the soul, and are aimed primarily at men. On the other hand, the vast majority of TV shows, magazines and advertising are aimed at women to reinforce a continual feeling of inadequacy that can only be addressed by spending money. Propaganda is for the boys; advertising for the girls. This is based on a need to target and manipulate the unique consciousness aspect of both genders. Boys are programmed to become warriors who will eventually go to war, while girls are programmed to be the princess who becomes a whore. The psychopaths in charge are gaslighting women through the media—while turning men into adult children. The spiritual vacuum left in many people is filled with a sense of self that has been twisted and distorted by the controllers. If your soul has been made empty, you fill it with nothing of any value regardless of the price tag or whatever pointless social status it furnishes you with. It is within this vacuum created by the corporate psychopath that the relationship psychopath finds an open door to your soul.

"Why do soldiers on the battlefield risk their lives saving comrades they don't even know? It makes no sense to me. I genuinely don't understand what keeps society intact if not the threat of punishment."

- *Dispatches from Psychopaths*

## CHAPTER SEVEN

# A LIFE WORTH LIVING FOR

C an you recall the otherworldly experiences you underwent during your early days being infected by the psychopath who entered into your world? Sometimes you can suppress these experiences for years. They may be left over from childhood abuse and trauma, and your resolve had held this toxic tide back, but regardless of when the psychopathic attack happened—whether it was fifty years or fifty minutes ago—it will catch up with you: the sensation of being pulled into quicksand.

Some former targets speak of what felt like succubi and incubi-style sleep paralysis attacks for months and even years after they had been abused and discarded by the psychopath.

*Emily's Story*

"I loved watching the TV show he starred in during my time at college. It was a welcome distraction from pressures of studying for my finals. Upon graduation, I wanted to do something crazy—something good for me, to reward myself. So I purchased a ticket for a convention for this TV show which had brought me so much enjoyment and escapism during my education. Three of the main actors from the show were supposed to come to this event and I was so excited. Now here is the thing: 'he' wasn't supposed to be one of them.

About a month before the convention, I had a vivid dream about him. How he would be coming to the convention and we both met, and in the dream he took me back to his hotel room. Then we talked, and he was full of compliments about how attractive he found me. In this dream,

I had the sensation that he is not really 'feeling' what he is saying to me. They were just hollow words. Then, as the dream progressed, we started to become physical. As I began to give him oral sex, his penis tasted bitter. Then another sensation came over me—almost like a panic attack and I thought 'oh my god, he has poisoned me', and I ran out of the room.

I woke up immediately after this and thought to myself, 'what the hell was that?'. Until this dream, I wasn't interested in him in a sexual way. I wondered why I even dreamed about HIM. In fact, I had a crush on another actor in the same show who was supposed to come to the convention. I even wrote the dream down, in detail—but I changed the end of the dream, as it gave me such a weird feeling.

The following month, on the day before I was supposed to fly out to the convention, I got a message from a friend, who knew about that dream. She told me that the actor from the show, who was the main reason why I wanted to go to the convention, had cancelled his appearance at the event. Then she said, 'Guess who is going to be there instead!' Yes, that was him. The other actor on the show whom I had the strange and unexpected dream about the previous month. I went to the convention and met him.

Instantly, I knew that this wasn't a coincidence. Yes, everything happened the way I dreamt it. We spent two nights together—a magical weekend. It felt like a dream come true. I had finally met my soul mate, and he had met me. He said the same to me, saying 'Finally, after searching for someone like you for the last thirty years…'. The sex was overwhelming. I never had such an experience in my whole life. We laughed and talked, and he made me feel as if I was a goddess—the answer to all his needs. The woman he had longed to meet. I was led to believe that both our dreams had come true.

However, this was the last time that ever I saw or spoke to that person—this 'version' of him. He wasn't real—he was just a reflection of my highest dreams, and he mirrored it back to me in perfect manner. Well yes, he was an actor—I was just his 'co-star' for that weekend. I had totally ignored the end of the prophetic dream I had before we met. I have to admit, ego got the better of me. My vanity also kicked in. That a famous actor was interested in me! I ignored all warning signs and red flags. He seemed so very open, funny and loving. I realise this now because he expected he was never going to see me ever again.

It was not until much later that I started to remember. How I had been forewarned in the dream in a very symbolic way. I came home, and spent an entire week just lying in bed. I was completely worn out, and it was as if all my beauty stayed with him. I looked like a monster, and as if I had just aged ten, twenty years. As if I had given all that was in me to him. All my beauty, goodness, love and life energy. I had decided to just go back to my life and continue. I didn't expect anything more from him.

Then the lovebombing started and I began to have hope. He spoke of how we would be living together. That I was the one he was waiting for all of his life, and that he didn't want to have sex again with any other woman. Following this, we saw each other again twice more in person. Neither meeting was a pleasant experience. Nevertheless, he had me already manipulated to the point where I was deeply trapped within his spider's web. On the second meeting I accidentally stumbled into him doing the same to me with other women. He seemed to be the master of conning women into believing that they were also 'the only one'. Not just one other woman—but dozens! All at the same time. I went back home, and decided to end the relationship. Looking back, I wished I would have stayed in no contact with him, as I was already deeply damaged. It was to get much, much worse.

What I can only describe as a two year 'mind fuck' then began. Manipulation, abuse, giving me hope, using me, and then sucking the life out of me. Holding me in despair, the silent treatment, gaslighting and constantly playing on my hopes and fears. All this just via text, email, Skype. I allowed him to use me as his cyber sex distraction. I was deeply addicted to the 'drug' this man had polluted me with. I was hooked on—or going cold turkey from—his attention every moment of the day. He used intermittent reinforcement to increase the instability between us, which had a highly powerful effect on me.

I had already lost control over what used to be my real life. I was bonded (enslaved) sexually with him so much that I started to break out in tears—constantly distraught. My own sex drive was never high. I could go on for months without sex, without feeling any need. But now things were different—I was under a spell of his sexuality. My body was suffering from a sexual addiction to him. I wanted to see him again, but he always had other excuses why not to. This increased my pain, the desire, and I lost myself completely. My stomach and digestive system became constantly problematic and my doctor could not explain why.

One time I wrote him, informing him that his mind games were robbing me of my energy. Incredibly he answered, 'I am not a succubus!' I was very surprised that he even mentioned that word. As English is not my first language, I had to Google the term to find out the meaning. I was a little bit shocked to see that it is a demon—the female form— the correct word for a male version is 'incubus'. Even that was interesting, as I have since come to understand that psychopaths are asexual in nature. I also suspected that it was very likely he didn't come up with this term on his own. Some other woman or man must have called him this name before.

This one man had caused me two years of torment and misery. I felt like I was not myself anymore. I became unhealthy, depressed and totally lost track of my own life. Everything went down the hill for me—friendships, money, and I dropped my education. I was a complete stranger to myself. I also suffered from three attacks of sleep paralysis—where the body stays asleep, but your consciousness is awake. You want to move your body, but you cannot. On two occasions, I had strong hallucinations of someone attacking me in my bed. Someone I could not see, but it felt so very real. The same stories you read about people having demonic, succubus, incubus night attacks.

I finally stopped contact with him, and of course he was already in several other relationships. He was just using these other women to let me know that he is capable of love—which I doubted more and more. I realised that he had no empathy at all for the pain he caused me. He enjoyed seeing me suffer. He was excited by my increased sex drive he had left me with. A sexual craving that I only wanted to act out with him. I was masturbating constantly. I felt so helpless and ashamed. This wasn't me.

I went to two healers looking for some kind of relief. One was a Sufi priest who was very psychic. He told me that this actor is a monster, and I must never have contact with him again and how he enjoys having me under his control. He did some rituals with me, but it didn't help very much. I guess I wasn't ready yet to let go. I was still looking for validation and wanted to still justify my investment of my whole life in this 'actor'. The PTSD got worse and worse, as did the constant pain. Feelings of dying inside and even my body began to slowly die. I was starting to look like a freak. Eventually in time, I started to pick myself up— piece by piece. I had help from a support group where I made new, understanding friends who went through a similar experience as I did. Finally, someone understood. That helped me tremendously.

Then I went to a second healer who she said she saw a past life connection, where he had already done the same thing to me—the sex bond and the addiction—how these were memories of this other life. How he is not as powerful as I think he is. How he enjoys having me under his control. However, she told me that the root of it was his fear. He was afraid of me on some level. This healer broke the toxic bond between us and I am no longer under his control. The dreams and fantasies about him—they have stopped completely. I started to get my soul back and my sex drive went back to normal.

Looking back, so many things happened that were so horrible, cruel and abusive to me. I still have difficulty remembering them. I can hardly access these events now. His devaluation of me started very harshly after the second

meeting. Now I can see him clearly. I see evilness, contempt, and hate written all over his face, and I have no idea
how I could ever have not seen it back then.

Although this experience had destroyed my life in every
way possible, it also made me wake up spiritually. I was an
atheist before I met this psychopath. I wanted to find a way
out of the pain, and I began searching for answers. I didn't
do anything any more but this. This 'nightmare' taught me
one thing, and that is that we must listen to our instincts
and pay attention to our dreams. I believe the precognitive
dream I had about him was a warning from my higher self.
Which knew, if I'd choose this path, it would be easy for
me. Every time I wanted to put up my fist and say. 'God, if
you do exist, why are you doing this to me?' Then I remember, 'ah yes', I was warned, and it was my choice.

In my studies and my spiritual awakening, I came to the
conclusion that due to my childhood and other unresolved
parts of my life that I needed this experience. I think before
we come into this life, we have certain contracts and agree-
ments, and I am pretty sure that I had one agreement—that
was about waking me up, to stand alone. To not look for
love and strength outside of myself, but to find it within.
Every time I tried that, looking for it outside, I got a slap
in the face.

The other conclusion is, once you understand what
they are—these psychopaths—is they all seem to behave
the same way. It is understandable to think these people
have been taken over—possessed, by an evil archetype, a
thought form, predator consciousness, vampire consciousness. Now I am free of it, and I am grateful for the experience. I still live with the personal ruin it caused to my life.
I am still trying to clean it all up, and it will probably take
some more years. Sometimes I am depressed about that,
but at least it's MY depression, and at least my mind is free
again, and my soul is back with me."

Like it our not, there is most certainly a 'supernatural' aspect to
the psychopathic experience (from the viewpoint of the target) in
terms of how it affects people who have been impacted by the full

effects of the pathology—up close and personal. Is this seemingly paranormal experience real? I have no idea—but it is a very real and common experience for targets while in the relationship, and then becomes far more intense after they finally come out of the experience.

## THAT CHARMING MAN

Although it has been well acknowledged that psychopaths, for all their faults and other negative attributes, have a gift upon initial contact of appearing to be completely charming, people who have been through this experience constantly make reference to the psychopath's charismatic personality preventing the target from spotting the predator beneath the 'million dollar smile.' In addition, the immediate attention and flattery lavished upon the target can be intoxicating.

Take a look at the preceding paragraph and notice the red flag words...

'Charming'. To charm someone is to put them under a spell used to alter the reality of another person. A 'charmer' in the etymological sense is an individual who has the ability to manipulate reality using 'charms' in order to achieve a desired agenda. This is not to say that psychopaths have any intellectual ability to purposely understand how their personality and mind games affect the target. It is closer to an instinctual knowledge which they have cultivated over time based on them observing the effects of their idealising, gaslighting, bullying and discarding on others. The psychopath knows that if they flatter and lovebomb, the target will acquiesce to the psychopath's wishes. Likewise, when he or she devalues the target they notice that the individual often has major weight loss from the trauma. This makes the psychopath feel powerful and further fuels its ego.

Now consider the words 'charismatic' and 'intoxicating'. Just how clearly is someone able to think who is intoxicated by the spell cast over them in the presence of charisma?

When a psychopath does take an interest in the occult sciences, they are usually drawn to the Babylonian magus tradition of seeking power and influence. Their narcissism goes into overdrive and they end up often destroying themselves as a result since they lack the mental and emotional discipline to tame their own god complex. People today have a very simplistic understanding of the term 'magic'; the term itself simply means to bring a plan or idea into physical manifestation. When one considers that psychopaths are natural 'charmers' coupled with their endless schemes and machinations, the natural consequence is that their targets will be spellbound and gaslighted into an alternative ('alter the native') reality where up is down and black is white.

When a psychopath is changing your reality at home—through gaslighting, crazy making and mind games such as the silent treatment—this can be considered just as much a form of black magic as any stereotypical image of sorcerers inside a circle and wielding a wand. 'The Father of Public Relations', Edward Bernays, had an almost supernatural ability to develop and implement crowd psychology. In conjunction with the psychoanalytical ideas of his uncle Sigmund Freud, he could just as easily be considered a black magician as much as a manipulative, cunning, high-flying psychopath. Bernays promoted war for profit (destroying the USA isolationist culture in WWI), while exploiting women's social freedoms in order to addict them to tobacco and fashion, only to spend his latter years in fabulous wealth and luxury, calling the human race 'idiots' and laughing at them while keeping company with the New York high society elites.

The manipulation of an individual's psychology within a psychopathic relationship works precisely the same way as a slick public relations exercise—albeit without a Powerpoint presentation. Discarded targets' nightmares are more than just nocturnal—the sensations are more than just the result of being a 'nervous wreck.' Something has been done on a very primal and spiritual level and the target will experience things that leaves them very different people afterwards. I have yet to meet a single atheist after having endured a psychopathic relationship—they simply stop being unbelievers. Something about coming face to face with a psychopath placed them into a very different reality construct than anything they had been prepared for in years of intellectualising. Humans are profoundly changed in ways they never expected they would be by an encounter with a puzzling person, such is the intensity of this experience.

I have to stress again that I am not claiming that psychopaths are demons or demonically-possessed human beings. They may very well be in an allegorical or as yet undetermined 'supernatural' sense; I honestly can't say one way or the other. For the sake of this book, when I use terms such as 'demon' or 'demonic', I am using them to convey certain sensations and emotions which science as yet cannot quantify. The term 'demon' is an archetypal motif to pin the experience into the material world and what I believe to be the best conceptual yardstick presently available. Even so, I cannot turn my back on sincere statements made by individuals who have shared the most incredible 'supernatural' effects they experienced during and after an encounter with a psychopath. I would no sooner dismiss this as a psychologist would dismiss dreams and dream symbolism in the quest of restoring mental health in their patient.

This 'demonic' nature of the psychopath goes a long way towards explaining how short of the mark science and psychiatry are when confronting the psychopathic individual and their place in society. Mental health professionals depend upon methodologies which are excellent for detecting and evaluating the psychopath but fail to explain how they arrived amongst us. Much of this is on purpose as there is a vested interest in playing down the issue of psychopathology in order to protect the wealthy psychopaths who are running the show at global, political and corporate levels.

It is much the same when the authorities fail to come to terms with a wealthy and influential psychopath who has committed a crime; historically, people would turn to the church to deal with the issue since this would be the last recourse of the peasantry under the yoke of an aristocratic psychopath and his or her powerful family. Nowadays, many people who have been targeted are adrift with no means of support. Religion today (with the exception of

Sharia Law in Islam) has lost its authority in society, resulting in the contemporary psychopathic elite more or less free to get away with what they want. It is not surprising that people in what we call the 'Truther' movement point out the 'luciferian' and 'satanic' events which the psychopathic elite appear to have a fondness for, such as the bizarre goings-on at the Bohemian (Grove) Club in California, the Skull and Bones Society at Yale University (former US Presidents Bush Sr. and George W. Bush Jr. are both members), and the likes of the aristocratic Hellfire Club of times past.

People will always try to see a 'demonic' or 'satanic' aspect to the psychopath as it not only helps to pin down the sheer evil of these individuals, but also aids in the healing process. On one level, it is most certainly an excuse or 'crazy rationalisation', while on the other hand, it is a useful and meaningful healing tool to help cope with and escape from the experience. It is therefore valid and worthy of inclusion in this book—particularly since no academic will touch it, even though it is very much part and parcel of the psychopathic experience.

## A WAR AGAINST BEAUTY

The psychopath is at war. It is at war with the beauty all around them. It knows it cannot attain the state of grace in which any meaningful sense of appreciation and gratitude live, so it seeks to destroy this beauty. Where humans can experience the beauty of the human soul, the psychopath sees only an energy device to be harvested, minds to be tortured and disturbed and bodies to be perverted and polluted. They create equality by bringing all those around them down to their own level. They impose their hatred of the human spirit on the world around them. They poison everything they touch.

One of the most effective forms of public gaslighting has been modern art. It is as though there exists a secret cabal between public bodies, art colleges, some artists and exhibition spaces and the managers of those spaces to fill them with shock art, or art which is as uninspiring as possible. The vast majority of public and corporate funding goes into promoting these forms of art, while gifted and talented traditional artists have to beg private galleries to stock their work and settle for the gallery's demand of a commission of up to fifty percent on the sale price.

I recently came upon one installation; an old telephone on a table with a present-day directory beside it. From the telephone there was a wire extending up to a glass box on the wall which contained a life-sized sculpture of the human ear made of the artist's own ear wax. I see this kind of thing everywhere in public art spaces now— in fact, I can hardly recall a time when this sort of art did not fill public art spaces. Such 'modern' art, dating from around the time of the Dadaist movement, still continues to win all awards and the perpetrators are proclaimed as geniuses. Here's a clue: no other art movement in history has survived for so long.

The rationale used to defend this degradation of art—this assassination of beauty—is that all expression should be free and unlimited; that art should not be escapist; that it should represent everyday reality. This 'everyday reality' extends to an installation composed of flies feeding on the decomposing head of an animal; the artist's own excrement in a can, as well as signed urinals as a 'thing of beauty'. Such expression is not an insight of my everyday reality. What we are witnessing is the Psychopathic Control Grid transferring their own inner mindscape onto the rest of us while claiming that this 'is how we all feel'. We don't. They feel this way.

With this form of art, the underlying concept behind the work is more important than the artwork itself. Highly-paid members of art councils, college professors and media darlings will invoke 'freedom of expression' and pontificate about the Nazis and the concepts of degenerate arts and 'what it led to...' and that dismembered human corpses are 'beautiful'. Public arts and regional administrations will go to incredible lengths to use taxpayers' money to impose this 'beauty' on the general public. Apart from a psychopath, I can't imagine how any sane person could think that beholding a display of human beings dissected and opened up in a case of formaldehyde is an expression of freedom of speech—the irony being that the greatest censorship in the art world today is by these same individuals against more traditional artistic expressions in terms of painting, drawing and sculpture. The reality is that it is not about freedom of expression; it is about psychopaths justifying their dead inner being as if the human spirit and the personality of the person once inside these artistic corpses never mattered to begin with.

As with everything on the face of this planet that makes no sense to most humans, there is always an underlying psychopathic agenda. In this case, it is the degradation of emotional resonance when viewing artwork. They are compelled by their hatred of beauty, denial of the existence of a higher self, and hatred of our common human desire to cherish the cosmos.

I suspect they are also gaslighting the rest of us by changing our perceptions so that corporate advertising looks more beautiful and uplifting than the art inside the galleries. When people visit spaces such as the Tate Modern in London only to result in having their consciousness perverted, twisted and distorted into a mundane cul-de-sac of spiritually and emotionally vapid installations, they will come outside and see colourful advertisements. The psychological impact of the advertisement is then far more powerful on the viewer. Charles Saatchi, co-founder of the global advertising agency Saatchi & Saatchi, is also an art collector and owner of the Saatchi Gallery, recognised in particular for his sponsorship of Young British Artists (YBAs) including Damien Hirst and Tracey Emin. Just business.

## INTO TOMORROW

The medical profession, psychiatry, and the courts are at a loss when it comes to dealing with the needs of those who have been targeted by psychopaths. They can't comprehend how psychopaths can implement actual physiological changes in their target's body chemistry resulting in Post Traumatic Stress Disorder (PTSD). It is reasonable to speculate that many of the death certificates issued since medical records began could be redrafted with cause of death attributed to: 'Destroyed by Psychopathic Mind Control'.

Among the dangerous side effects of psychopathic mind control due to manipulation of a target's oxytocin and dopamine levels are:

- Afibrinogenonemia, which can lead to hemorrhage and death
- Anaphylaxis
- Nausea and vomiting
- Subarachnoid hemorrhage
- Increased heart rate
- Decreased blood pressure
- Cardiac arrhythmia
- Premature ventricular contraction
- Impaired uterine blood flow
- Pelvic hematoma
- Brain damage
- Seizures
- Gall bladder problems
- Uterine fibroids
- Death.

Thankfully, the age of the free-range psychopath is coming to an end resulting in a huge upswing in the general physical and psychological health of the overall population. There will be enormous social consequences from decreased pressures on public health infrastructure, increased longevity, drastically reduced suicide rates, less dependency upon toxic (and ultimately useless) psychotropic pharmaceuticals. Not to mention a massively reduced impact upon the court system, corporate fraud, workplace bullying, child welfare agencies, addiction treatment centres and most mental health services.

## RECOVERY AND RESTORATION

First, forgive yourself for being human. Doing this brings you more than halfway to being restored. You must avoid people who call you 'over-dramatic' and 'only having yourself to blame'—a true friend will not do this. Making mistakes is human—falling into the trap laid for you by a psychopath happened, first and foremost, as a result of your human decency. Any other aspects of your personality which may have made it easier for the psychopath to target you more effectively can and will be corrected over the course of recovery as you develop a greater sense of inner wisdom, personal insight and self-trust.

## JOURNALING

Write down everything about the experience; how it made you feel. How much you loathe and want the psychopath to suffer. No matter how lewd, intense or filled with hatred. Get it out of your system. If you wish to see them eaten alive by rats, then write that down. This is not a sign of your lack of humanity at all. You are cutting into the psychopath's teeth marks in your soul and squeezing out the poison. Hatred always burns into apathy in time, and once you allow this hatred to exit your soul, the 'love' one had for the psychopath will finally be acknowledged as nothing more than a chemically-induced delusion—the hate you have for them is your real emotional response.

Along with exploring and exorcising the toxic and emotionally-convulsive effects of the psychopath, you must write down the following statements/affirmations in large letters as many times as it takes for these messages to sink into your subconscious. Doing this is vital to recovery:

> I am Being Reborn
> This is a Learning Experience
> I Have Survived
> My Soul is Free Again
> I am Being Improved as a Human Being
> This is My Time to Shine
> No Limits
> I am Strong and Getting Stronger

Better still, develop an original mantra of your own to underpin your personal recovery story and write it out again and again. Never stop writing and drawing little pictures to convey how the experience felt for you, and how you are going to move on from it. In the early days, you will find yourself constantly writing in your journals to the point where you can fill up dozens of them in a single year. As the experience begins to find balance within you—both in a neuro-chemical and psychological sense—you will find yourself writing about the experience less and less. Within two years, you'll find yourself hardly journaling any more. You are out of the labyrinth.

## DREAM JOURNALS

In the early days of recovery, you will have the most vivid and significant dreams. Write them all down and—this is very important—do not exert yourself to apply specific meanings to them. The full meaning may not be revealed until months and years down the road, but record what unfolds. Drawing small pictures of the event is important, as it helps to conceptualise and process the experience across both the left and right hemispheres of your brain. Dreams are your subconscious attempting to help you. But the imagery seen in your dreams is not to be taken literally upon waking. Each individual dream and nightmare are brush strokes which will reveal a landscape of recovery and renewal in time.

## POST TRAUMATIC STRESS DISORDER

Following the brutal devaluing and discarding of you by the psychopath, be aware that you have been infected and your sense of self will be distorted. You will, for several months, be frightened, sad, anxious and disconnected, so avoid making major life decisions during this time. The post-psychopathic abuse trauma can be overwhelmingly intense to the point that it may seem next to impossible to escape rumination and anger. Discarded targets feel stuck with a constant sense of danger and painful memories which play over and over again, like an endless tape loop, but this will not last forever.

You will move on; via a combination of time passing, personal growth and observation, and reaching out for support you will overcome the dark days.

PTSD develops differently in each person depending on a number of psychological and biochemical aspects as well as how deeply they were caught in the psychopath's web of deception and gaslighting. While the symptoms of PTSD most commonly develop in the hours or days following the psychopathic devalue and discard phases, they are identical to symptoms displayed by people suffering the loss of a loved one. Except it is much worse—the corpse has risen from the grave.

The mind and the body of the target are in shock. That is, until you eventually make sense of what happened—a psychopath has passed through your life. From this realisation, you then begin to process your emotions, armed with the knowledge that what had been done to you was not the result of a relationship which went bad. It is at that point that you are moving towards recovery. If you develop a cognitive dissonance towards the experience—refusing to accept that you dealt with someone or something that wasn't fully human—you will remain in psychological shock. In order to move on, it's important to face and fully acknowledge your memories and emotions for what they are and understand why this happened. IT WAS NOT YOUR FAULT.

Until the target comes to accept the true nature of the psychopathic experience inflicted upon them, a continued sense of hopelessness can take root, causing them to experience:

- Reminders of the Psychopath
- Avoidance of Social Interaction
- Difficulty Concentrating
- Feelings of Intense Distress
- Guilt, Shame or Self-loathing
- Hypervigilance
- Increased Anxiety
- Intense Loneliness
- Irritability/Anger Outbursts
- Loss of Memory
- Periods of Muscle Tension

- Nausea
- Nightmares
- Pounding Heartbeat
- Rapid Breathing
- Sensation of Blood Pumping Hard at Top of Neck
- Sensation of Dying Suddenly
- Sense of a Bleak Future
- Sleeping Disorders
- Social and Personal Detachment
- Stomach Pains
- Self-medication/Substance Abuse
- Suicidal Feelings
- Sudden Sweating
- Triggers/Flashbacks
- Waking Up in Terror.

It's only natural to want to avoid painful memories and feelings and push your memories away, but in doing so, the trauma will only get worse. You can't escape your emotions completely—they re-emerge under stress. Dealing with them now might help stop them from becoming worse in the future. You may find that you pull away from friends and loved ones and that you are not able to get along with people as well or as easily as you once did. Failing to deal with the post-psychopathic experience can make physical health problems worse. Studies have also shown a relationship between PTSD and heart problems. Rather than avoiding the trauma and any reminder of it, confronting the reality of the psychopathic experience will begin opening an outlet for emotions you've been bottling up. It will also help restore your sense of control and reduce the powerful hold the memory of the psychopath has imposed upon you.

## THE JOURNEY BACK TO THE REAL YOU

Recovery from a relationship with a psychopath is an on-going process. Healing doesn't happen overnight, nor do the memories of the abuse ever disappear completely. Nor should they, as they will help you to reinforce NO CONTACT EVER AGAIN. Even so, psychopaths are so disruptive to every aspect of our humanity—from our sense of self, to our body, mind and soul—it can make life seem impossible and pointless for a long time afterwards. You may be tempted to withdraw from social activities and from your friends and loved ones—and also from the full experience of life and living.

Support from other people who have gone through the same experience is vital to your recovery. We live in an age where the Internet can provide this and we are a most fortunate generation in this regard. Not only do we know what was really done to us, but we can easily discover a world of resources for recovery as well as online friendship and support. Support groups for post-psychopathic abuse survivors will help you feel less isolated and alone. They also provide invaluable information on how to cope with the overall experience and how to work towards your eventual recovery.

Helping others who have been targeted and discarded by a psychopath is not only positive, but will do wonders for your own recovery. You will find an almost cathartic sensation in being there for others. Support groups can also be very healthy for realising that not all men are abusers and not all women are predators. This will also go a long way to restoring your faith in humanity as a whole, which the consciousness parasite almost took from you.

## TOWARD A NEW SELF AWARENESS

Your thoughts are an inner dialogue—not only the ones about yourself, but the ones you allow exterior forces to place inside your mind. Think back to how the psychopath constantly tried to alter and correct your world view. A person has, on average, about sixty thousand thoughts crossing his/her mind per day, most of which are habitually repeated—over and over again. The psychopath and the Psychopathic Control Grid is banking on you doing this with the thoughts they put into you.

These thoughts are what cause emotions—via complex brain chemistry and neurology. But they are not the same as your real feelings. You alone experience these intuitive insights and real heartfelt love—they can't be made to happen inside of you—only faked. Faked with everything from superficial love songs and romantic movies and other ephemeral gestures which all psychopaths excel at during the early stages of targeting. While certain events in the aftermath of devalue and discard may trigger painful emotions, they never cause them. The real cause of your emotions is what you tell yourself.

The psychopath harvested the energy they wanted from the target within the required time frame of the relationship and/or until they got bored, which could have been anything from weeks to decades and then casually discarded the now-devalued target with no more importance than if they were returning a DVD to the rental store. The predator has instantly found the new 'love of their life' to begin harvesting their energy. The psychopathic cycle has predictably started once again and discarded targets and former enablers are left in a state of shock and confusion.

What then? You win the psychopath back? This would be like surviving cancer and then missing it. The predator's persona wasn't real to begin with, and this, along with the wild chemical fluctuations ravaging throughout your body is the reason you are undergoing PTSD. Having implemented NO CONTACT EVER AGAIN, there are now only two choices left to a discarded target of a psychopath: Death or glory.

I am not talking about any form of superficial bravado when I use the term 'glory'. This experience will confront you with one of the most startling—if not the most profoundly traumatic—experiences of your life, and one which has essentially killed the person you once were—more specifically, the person you assumed yourself to be. When I talk about death I am not talking about literal, physical death. Killing yourself would please the psychopath no end—I am talking about the death of the simulacra of the person the psychopath made you believe that you were.

The person you were before you encountered the psychopath is caught in a type of hibernation and trying desperately to wake up from it. The part of you which enabled the psychopath is not only dead, but completely annihilated. The psychopath—during their persona switch to the new version of itself—also killed this previous person you believe you once were. It was a two-for-one deal. You are now confronted with the absolute reality of the situation. You must embark on what has to be your own hero's journey to slay the dragon left within your psyche by the psychopathic experience.

## SHADOWLAND

The psychopath is a virus, and a virus attacks us when our immune system is compromised. We may not be looking after our health or we may be eating poorly, or drinking too much and so on, and this makes our bodies run down and vulnerable. Your psyche works in exactly the same way. You may have become too dependent upon your own ego and that of an overall ego consciousness which allowed the psychopathic predator an opportunity to enter, pounce and attack you.

Think back carefully—on some level there is always a symbiotic relationship between the adult psychopath and the target, but allow me to be very clear: it is not the target's fault they were targeted and infected by a psychopath. These days, we all have essentially damaged psyches thanks to mainstream media, but it is the target's responsibility now to deal with the dark side we all possess. This does not suddenly make the target wrong and the psychopath right. The psychopath is still a predator, a rapist of the soul, but it was aspects of our shadow which brought us over the threshold and into the labyrinth of the psychopath. It we fail to recognise this then we are doomed to never transcend the psychopaths on Main Street and on Wall Street.

When one confronts their shadow then the rest of the work is in finding a balance. Jung termed this 'centering', and this leads to what he also termed 'individuation': becoming your true self and not the bundled ego which the psychopath used to ensnare you. We are all mixtures of dark and light, masculine and feminine and at the same time we have a centre, a higher purpose to ourselves which is—and don't say it too loudly—very much spiritual, and this is expressed through creativity and compassion. Knowing who you really are through self-awareness and self-realisation is where you put on your armour, mount your horse and ride out to slay the dragon. Playing the blame game for all eternity is the coward's folly and there is no evolution in this.

## THE SPIRITUAL PATH

I do not care how much this flies in the face of Reductionist Science; it remains a fact and every single person who has ever been affected by a psychopath will say the same thing: it needed to happen to them, and over the course of time they came to understand that there was a spiritual purpose to the experience. They needed to be shaken out of their childlike view of the world, and more importantly, their over-dependency upon their own egos and find a greater meaning to their own existence.

In the vast majority of recovery cases I have dealt with, there is more often than not a spiritual (not a religious) transformation—or a shift in the individual's consciousness which will allow them to slay the dragon. As I have already stated, I have yet to meet a single person who has come out of a psychopathic encounter who remained an atheist. All targets are so profoundly changed by the experience, that they begin seeking answers among the previously ignored recesses of their psyche. If still in denial, they tragically give themselves over to the world of psychiatry and end up being drugged and psychoanalysed by this psychopathic institution until they are zombified, broken automatons who never get over the trauma while the psychiatrists move up into the next tax bracket.

You are much more than the lifelong amalgamation of neuroses, complexes and sexual dysfunction that psychiatry would have you believe. When psychiatry enforces this notion upon you they are doing to you precisely what the psychopath did to you: projecting and gaslighting. There are insights to be gained by implementing dream analysis and word association testing—as long as you undertake them by yourself or with a friend or family member you trust. Otherwise, these are just tools of manipulation for the psychiatrist, and the main reason why the damaged target on the shrink's couch will never transcend the experience. They are still making the same mistake of externalising their own potential onto a third party. They are not making their own hero's journey that they must undertake if they are to survive the labyrinth of the psychopath and this deeply buried inner world of their psyche has been brought to the surface by the psychopath who entered their life.

As Carl Jung correctly pointed out, we as human beings do not only carry trauma from our past experiences in the tangible world, but also from within us. We likewise carry a collective unconscious throughout our entire species. There are also conflicts which we carry through our entire culture which recycle themselves over and over again. If we do not deal with these issues on a personal level we will either have a nervous breakdown, develop addictions to drugs, sex, alcohol, celebrity culture and—very commonly—we will attract a psychopath into our lives to 'shake it all up' so that we are forced to confront our shadow.

## BABYLON IS BURNING

The invasion of Iraq was bound to happen. It was the Psychopathic Control Grid attempting to devalue and discard the human race as a whole. On the eve of the second Gulf War, two million people marched against it in London, with millions more marching in cities all over the world. They were all ignored. The behaviour of the psychopaths in charge had the same effect on the collective human consciousness as any individual in a relationship with a psychopath as they begin to see beyond the crazy making. I am not surprised that this mass awakening of humans happened in tandem with the gaslighting surrounding the WMDs.

Gulf War Two affected us all deeply—we realised our leaders were not what they claimed to be. This became a catalyst to make us look at every aspect of our own lives, from diet to relationships and—lo and behold—the psychopath seemed to be everywhere— the ultimate solvent. We began to realise we were caged animals in a zoo created by the psychopathic priest class of Babylon, and the elite of today used the mythology of the WMDs as a ritualistically-driven mandate for spellbinding the entire planet and in this sense, the Iraq War could be viewed as the psychopath's return to their own spawning ground many centuries later. The Psychopathic Control Grid marched out through the Ishtar Gate to pollute humanity and we have been trying to get them to go back and leave us alone ever since.

Governments putting Sodium Fluoride into drinking water is the same thing as a psychopath putting mercury into their partner's drinks in order to get them to sign over their home and belongings to the psychopath. Our governments do not care about us—they tolerate us. A psychopath in a relationship with another human being does not love them—they tolerate the other person until they become bored with them, or consider them not worth the effort any longer.

When one gazes upon the image of the dying Christ on the cross, theology leads to faith, rationalism forces us to ask why and compassion places us in the position of his mother Mary, and how she must have felt watching her son die. Psychopaths have never attempted to mimic empathy—they have sought to take revenge upon it.

## THE HERO'S JOURNEY

Carl Jung, and later the American mythologist Joseph Campbell, and to a lesser extent James Joyce in his novel *Ulysses*, have each elaborated that persons of developed consciousness and sensitive/artistic nature will be called upon to slay the dragon in their own lives—in the case of this book, the dragon is a metaphor for psychopaths.

This motif of the hero has lived all throughout human history and mythology, and is the story of the battle between the forces of darkness and light. To defeat the forces of darkness is the supreme test that informs the hero's journey to full potential and by extension, further the destiny of the human experience on this planet. Often in mythology, the hero is slain, but then is reborn.

This will manifest in two ways in our lives: the battle within the inner world of the psyche and the outer world of the manifested. The exterior world we experience is a product of our conscious inner world. In our daily lives, the need to survive and grow—in a material and physical sense—requires us to battle forces to achieve the tangible goals we desire. Then, when we are established as adults, we must then begin to do battle with the dragons of the inner world. In the West, this would be more commonly known as the 'midlife crisis'. This is also the stage where humans are most likely to find themselves targeted by a psychopath, and also the stage in their lives where the traumatic impact is more profound. Rarely is someone under the age of thirty-five as badly affected by a psychopathic infection than someone above this age is and this is because the psychopath and the midlife crisis are essentially one and the same thing—a dragon which has entered our psyche from the material world and profoundly affects and disrupts our inner dimensions.

The only remedy is to defeat the dragon and take the fight against the psychopath into the field where they cannot fight us—our creativity and spiritual development. When we resolve to fight the battle on these terms, the psychopath has already been defeated and targets can then begin their complete recovery and transition to glory in their own lives.

## LABYRINTH OF THE EMPATH

Following a psychopathic infection, the target will be forced to look confront their inner nature, including—and this is extremely important—all the dark realities within us. Did you find the psychopath attractive because you were easily wooed by their superficiality, their sexual perversion, infantile notions of romantic love, their flattery of you or even their alleged financial opportunities? If so, how culpable were you in abandoning your freewill to this individual? Did you ignore the Red Flags one too many times? Suppress your intuition? If you did not seek sexual perversions, would the psychopath have even appealed to you in the first place? This is now the hero's journey into the inner darkness.

Myths such as *Dante's Inferno* have endured throughout human history and in all cultures for a very good reason. We need them. If all the energy in your outer life has been sucked dry by the psychopath, you will not recover from the experience unless you go back into yourself and begin again. If you fail to undertake this, you die and the psychopath wins. End of story.

The misery caused by emotional and psychological trauma

placed within you by a psychopath is not a sickness that has to be medicated and treated. It is an opportunity to perform a deep inner meditation upon your own life and discover how your ego and unconscious mind are interacting with one another. You will emerge from the other side with a new understanding of yourself and previous untapped potentials you were unaware of will suddenly shine forth. Unlike the superficial self-delusions of some born-again seeker of saviours, you have been truly saved by saving yourself. This is the ultimate lesson of the psychopathic encounter: to become your own hero.

Without a psychopath coming into our lives, only a small handful of humans would ever make this inner journey. These would be the artists, the poets and the folk heroes. The people who transform our culture. The dreamers and non-pathological mavericks. The rest of us would be on the sidelines waiting for them to do the job for us.

However, when a psychopath comes into our lives (and boy, are they attacking us in spades now) and we find ourselves under the yoke of the Psychopathic Control Grid, we are forced to go inside. This, for me, beyond a shadow of a doubt, proves that this mutation on the planet known as psychopaths serve a very real social and personal evolutionary function, particularly at this point in history. If you have been a victim of a psychopath in the early twenty-first century, you are being called upon; you have been chosen as one of the pathfinders of the new human destiny.

Sounds very grandiose, for sure. Nonetheless, it is real and I am confronted daily by this realisation. Once over their trauma, people write telling me that they are now dedicated to the mission of making as many people as possible aware of the problem. Ordinary people who were targeted by psychopaths are now discovering that they are not so ordinary after all. They are all on the hero's journey. The psychopaths are in full feeding frenzy right now—likewise, the targets are like the rooks in a tree warning the others of the imminent danger of a predator amongst us, warning all the other birds to flap their wings and fly to safety.

It is the psychopath's impulsive need to exploit the rest of us which is forcing more and more people to sit up and do something about it. This is the next stage of human development and it is not by accident. Nature has presented us with a pressure point; a blockage in our collective unconscious which must be resolved for humans to move to the next level in personal and collective evolution.

As individuals, and collectively as a society, we all have to confront our shadow. We have to meet this very primitive part of ourselves and then we have to shake hands with it. Making this connection is a necessary step towards drawing the road map to where we are going—the ideal destination being a post-psychopathic society. As a bonus, we will transcend personal pain.

Jung tells us that evolution does not happen by indulging stagnation and denial. We can try and remain mindless sheep, defending the authority structures which enslave us, but we won't be happy— the tug towards freedom is too strong and the longer it's ignored, the harder we feel it.

The insane Transhumanist desire to 'improve' humanity is throwing everything they have into the mix to keep us distracted and angry and fearful, fighting amongst ourselves and continually entranced so that we don't stop spending money. We don't have to fall for this anymore and more humans every day are refusing to be taken in by the ruse. The psychopaths know this; look at the endless doom constantly drummed into us by talking-head politicians, TV presenters and journalists. The psychopaths and the Psychopathic Control Grid are running scared and desperate and are frantically throwing their last roll of the dice in an attempt to prevent the human race from dealing with them once and for all. But never be dismayed, for remember:

WE ARE THE HOUSE,
AND THE HOUSE
ALWAYS WINS.

"Other people's inconvenience, their pain, it isn't real to me. It doesn't exist. It's an incorporeal notion that I don't understand. Whereas the aggravation I'd feel having to drive someone to the airport affects me on a comprehensible level."

*- Dispatches from Psychopaths*

# INTERVIEW WITH AN ENERGY VAMPIRE

In early October 2011, I received a phone call from a male living in Dublin who had watched my videos on YouTube. He claimed to be a psychopath and wanted to tell me my analysis was spot-on. I have to say that initially I considered 'Larry' to be pulling my leg—he had a spontaneity in his speaking voice at odds with what I had considered to be a hallmark of psychopaths: calculated behaviour. The way Larry spoke never came across as sounding 'planned'. We began talking over Skype soon afterwards and on webcam I noticed he always had a light source behind him.

As our conversations developed, I began to realise that he was indeed a socialised psychopath. For starters, he kept trying to imply that he should be writing books and be famous since he was the real psychopath and not me. His arrogance was both astounding and hilarious; *'What the fuck do you know, really?'* was a continual theme of his. There was a growing sense of his grandiosity as the conversations developed and he always appeared over-dressed on camera. During one memorable Skype session he was wearing a silk smoking jacket and cravat. Another time, a t-shirt which read, EVERYONE DESERVES A HAPPY CHILDHOOD.

During our chats, Larry boasted about his endless achievements, showbiz and political connections, and his man-about-town status—all this despite him still living in his elderly parents' home and working as a security guard at a city centre convenience store. Amazingly, one of his achievements did in fact turn out to be true; I was able to confirm that he did indeed work as a roadie with a famous British heavy metal band during the late 70's/early 80's and had toured the world with them.

Throughout every conversation he would directly and indirectly insult me, one time calling my artwork 'complete shit'.

He kept asking me to interview him for this book and I responded that I wouldn't do it over Skype—only in person. The reason for this is I wanted to hit him with questions that he would have no time to prepare an answer for. I also wanted to ask questions that—as far as I am aware—no one had ever asked a psychopath in a one-on-one interview.

We arranged to meet in a town in the Irish midlands. I prepaid his train ticket and I would pay for his lunch and drinks during the interview as I wanted no cash to exchange hands on the day. I picked a well known gastro pub with an award-winning chef since I knew this would appeal to his sense of status and he would be more likely to show up. I also made it very clear to him that I had informed others where I was going, what time I would be there and who I was meeting.

The day came in late November 2011. I arrived at the pub and was preparing for Larry's arrival when my phone rang. It was Larry refusing to do the interview unless I gave him five hundred euros in cash, rationalising his demand by pointing out that I shouldn't be the only one making money from the interview. I reminded him of the terms we agreed on and hung up the phone. A minute later, he called back and stated he will do the interview for no money, but that he would take legal action if I tried to be a 'smart alec cunt' and reveal his identity.

When Larry arrived, I called him over. He swaggered towards me in his Leinster Rugby track suit top and sat down. He was smirking. We did not shake hands. I was pleasant and he played along. Larry appeared to be around 60 years old, short and stocky with a very pale complexion. He told me he was 38. He was completely bald and had a large red porous nose indicating years of alcohol abuse. His eyes were exceptionally dead. What made this even more startling was that he wore large, strong prescription glasses that magnified them.

Larry ordered the most expensive item on the menu—a filet steak sandwich on home-baked garlic bread with lobster meat deep fried in tempura batter. He drank three pints of Guinness without needing to go to the men's room once, and we made small talk about this and that.

I began to feel my energy draining away and in the hope of making it through the next half hour, I took out my notebook and began the interview in earnest. Larry spoke in a thick Dublinese accent and his speech was liberally sprinkled with Dublin slang terms. For the sake of this interview, I have altered this slang to make this transcript more clear.

*What is your earliest memory?*

"I can't remember much before puberty. I would say I was about ten when I first had sex. It was with a neighbour's daughter who was a bit simple. She was retarded, spastic or something. No wait, meningitis. We had sex in the coal shed at the end of her parents' backyard. She was in there sitting on a bag of coal and I went over and I showed her my penis and she laughed as it got hard. Then I pulled down her knickers and gave her one."

*During childhood and growing up, what was your relationship with your parents like?*

"Dad was a night watchman on building sites. He never said much to me or anyone else. He still does not. My mother is my best friend. She always stood up for me. Covered for me when I was in trouble. She once bought medicine from the chemist when I had crabs which you put in the bath and sit in. She lied to the police when I was arrested. Bought me clothes. Always food on the table and my clothes washed to this day. I guess you would call it a typical mother and son relationship. I would kill anyone who tried to harm her."

*How was school for you?*
"Crap. Couldn't wait to get out. Left at 13."

*How did you earn your living?*
"My uncle drove a delivery truck for a building supply company. One day when I was about 16 he was visiting my mother and I took the keys of the truck when he wasn't looking and I drove the truck up and down the street. I had no problem with the gears. I had watched my uncle driving and reversing—so I just did what he did. So I got my first job with him doing deliveries up and down the country."

*Do you believe in God or have a spiritual aspect to your existence?*
"I believe in God alright. I do not go to mass or anything like religious stuff. [Larry paused for a long time] There has to be a God—otherwise there would be no laws against murder and killing."

*Do you have a powerful imagination?*
"You mean like making plans? Yes. I spend a lot of time at work thinking about moving to Spain. I would like to move to Australia. A fella like me could be a millionaire in no time in a place like that."

*Have you ever killed an animal?*
"No. Oh wait. I did once. It was an accident. I had a pet hamster which escaped from a cage and this woman I was with at the time annoyed me and I slammed a door shut. The hamster was on the gap between the door and the frame, where the hinges are and was crushed. My girlfriend went crazy when she saw this and started screaming. Real fucking nutcase she was."

*Do you get frightened?*
"I get worried only when something bad is happening to me, or going to happen to me. But I just deal with it. Not scared, I feel more confused for a second. Then I forget about it a minute later."\

*Do you have friends?*

"Hundreds. Hundreds of people love me."

*Have you ever had sex with another man?*

"Not really. A mate of mine when I was living in London, we both got really drunk and he went down on me and sucked me off. I was curious to see if a blow job from a man was different from a woman. It was the same. But that is not the same as fucking him in the arsehole. So the answer to the question is, 'no'."

*How many sexual partners have you had?*

"Just over three hundred, with the whores. When I drove trucks on a regular run between Dublin and Aberdeen. Loads of whores back then."

*Have you ever had sex with an animal?*

"No." [something told me Larry was lying]

*What was the most successful lie you ever told?*

"When I was in England, me and a mate were coming back drunk from a pub. We were well out of it and I was driving. I crashed into the back of a minibus on a country road somewhere in Essex. The car we were in rolled down an embankment and ended up wrapped around a tree. I was still in the car and wasn't even hurt. My mate had fallen out and was on the top of the embankment. When I got there he was fucked. The top of his head was scraped off by the road. I could hear the driver of the minibus calling out. It was pitch black. So I dragged me mate's body down the embankment and put him in the driver's seat. I fucked off into the woods and vanished. I don't know what happened after that."

*Do you feel any responsibility for the death of your friend?*

"Could've easily been me. If he was driving I would be dead now. Just the way things happen. Not like I killed him on purpose. He was just some bloke I knew from the pub. He wasn't anyone famous and he lived alone. No family or anything. It wasn't a big deal that he died."

*How do I know you are not lying?*
"Fuck off."

*Are you a racist?*
"No. Don't care."

*Do you have any hobbies?*
"I used to collect Chinese vases—I was given one as a tip by a customer on a delivery run who had no cash. I liked the way they looked and the shapes. So I went to antique places and bought more—as I knew they would be a good investment. My mother loved having them around the house too."

*Have you ever been married?*
"No, but engaged a few times."

*Can you tell if someone is a psychopath just by looking at them?*
"All the time. They have a certain glow about them."

*Can you name a famous dead person who you believe was a psychopath?*
"Johnny Carson—the American TV fella." [this answer took me by surprise]

*How do you feel when you pull off a scam?*
"I fucking love it. It is the best feeling in the world. The part where you know it is about to deliver the results is like fucking magic. I am like a little kid on Christmas morning. Love it."

*Do you have any children?*
"Not that I know of. But I want to have them. A daughter to look after me in my old age."

*How do you wish people to remember you when you die?*

"Don't give a fuck. Well, I would like a big monument at my grave. I like walking around the old graveyards. Especially the ones with the big monuments with angels, Mary and Our Lord on them. Some of them are class."

*Are you afraid of death?*

"Well I do not want to die and I will live to be one hundred and twenty. I watched a documentary on the BBC and some scientist said that there is no reason why humans can't live that long. I am going to be one of them."

*Do you have a girlfriend currently?*

"Some woman in Kildare I met on Facebook and another one in Sydney for when I move there. She is married right now, but not happy. I would be well set if I got in with her. It would mean I would land on my feet in Australia. Place to stay, no worries. Depends on if I can get her to throw the husband out. Which she wants to anyway. He is a drunk and just uses her."

*Do you have dreams?*

"I think I had them when I was a kid. Not now."

*When you worked as a rock'n'roll roadie, what was that like?*

"It was very good. I got paid to see the world. The tour manager was my cousin and they needed someone who could drive big trucks and set the lighting up. My mother asked him to give me a job and that's how I got that. I went everywhere. America, Japan, Germany, all over. I had to stop after a year when I hurt my neck when I fell off a loading dock in Holland."

*How were you impacted by the experience of different cultures and countries?*

"The first time we went to Japan it was fucking amazing. The Japs have a completely different way of living.

Everything looks and works differently. I fucked so many women there. It was so strange and amazing. The second time we went I was bored with it. Novelty wore off."

*Can I ask if anything you do disturbs you or gives you the creeps?*
"When I am drunk I hate looking at myself in a mirror. If I finish up a pub crawl and I want something to eat I will avoid places with mirrors on the wall. Fucking hate looking at myself drunk."

*When you see two people in love, how do you feel?*
"I see a man who is a fucking idiot. All the cunt in the world and here is some young guy in the prime of his life devoted to the same woman. Makes no sense at all. Why is he doing this? To prove he is a good man to some bitch who needs him to prove this or he gets no sex off her? Stupid."

*What is your favourite colour?*
"Red."

I thanked Larry for the interview and handed him a signed copy of my book. I got up and went to pay for the meal and drinks, then left without saying another word. I felt rattled by the experience and for days afterwards I felt tired and depressed.

To encounter a psychopath without any persona being utilised to work you is a disturbing experience. You feel like you are stuck in a muddy watering hole and bleeding while this crocodile is circling you. The complete lack of consideration for anything beyond Larry's most basic needs was what affected me most. Psychopaths are like no-name brand supermarket items with a stolen label from a popular brand wrapped around them.

## ACKNOWLEDGEMENTS

I would like to thank the following people for their help, support and friendship during the last year: Holly Ollivander, Bernadette Robinson, Diane Schwartz, Gerry Coogan and all the guys in Man at the Window, Ghost1, Deborah Harvey, Huw Thomas, Jackson MacKenzie, Jen Nagy, Fintan Dunne, Karen Sawyer, Lourdes Rivera, ICAN Planet, Raam Baros, Jo Michele Robbins, Lydia Robinson, Pete Kerr, Shawna Nansel, Isabella Ioannina, Maria Noonan-McDermott, 'Viva', Tubbercurry, Lisa E. Scott and the many, many people who have contacted me, met with me and shared their stories over the past year.

Born in Dublin, Thomas Sheridan is an internationally renowned artist, author, musician, public speaker and independent researcher currently based in the west of Ireland. His illustrations have appeared on the covers of newsstand magazines, books and websites worldwide. He is best known for being the author of the book *Puzzling People: the Labyrinth of the Psychopath*. The book was well-received, becoming an underground success and has allowed Thomas' entire body of work to reach a much larger audience.

Driven by his passion for Natural Philosophy, Thomas continues working towards a synchronistic cohesion of the modern human, in terms of positive transcendence from trauma and psychological damage and on towards personal and social renewal.

www.thomassheridanarts.com

## RESOURCES

*Puzzling People/Defeated Demons* Official Message Board
www.psychopathfree.com

Psychopathic Targeting (Toxic Relationship Poisoning)
Support Group on Facebook.
www.facebook.com/groups/NSSSG/

Lisa E. Scott's *The Path Forward Forum*
www.lisaescott.com/vain-forum

Website Dealing with the Psychopathic Control Grid
Signs of the Times
www.sott.net

Portrait of a Psychopath TV Show (channelAustin)
www.publicawarenessmedia.info/performance/tv/pofas/index.htm

www.facebook.com/PortraitofaPsychopath

I am Fishhead
www.fisheadmovie.com/

Lightning Source UK Ltd.
Milton Keynes UK
UKOW01f1504061016

284632UK00002B/27/P